nakaba suzuki presents

12

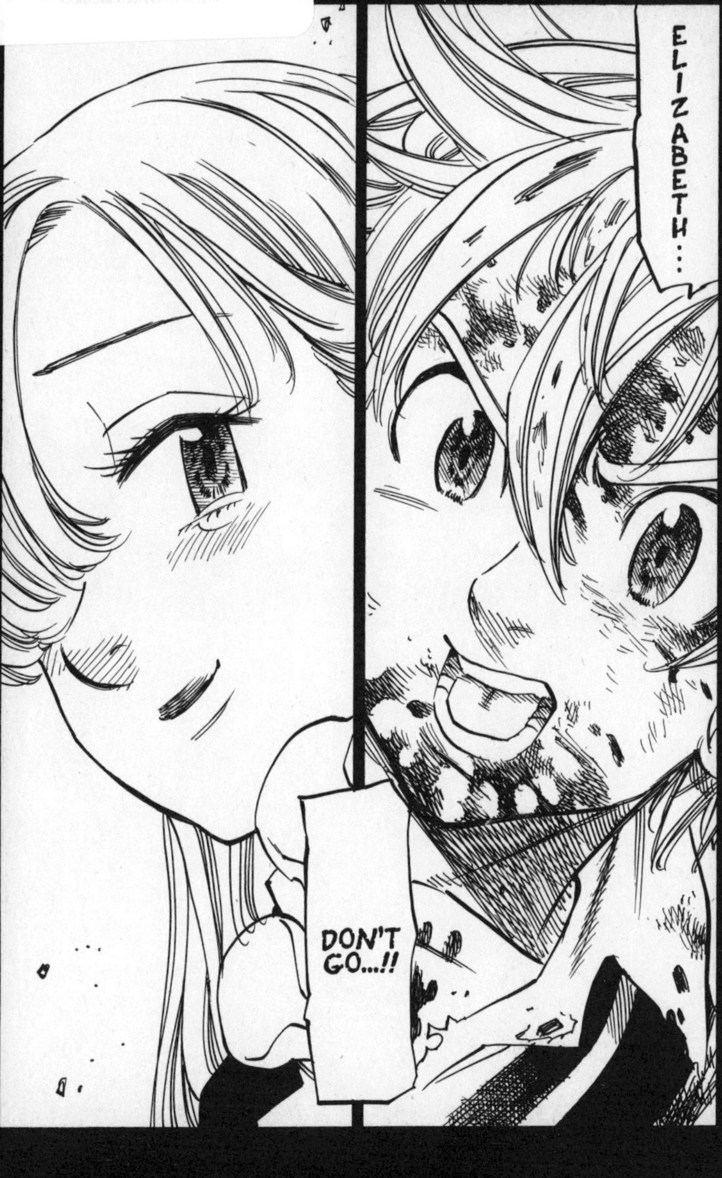
ELIZABETH...
DON'T GO...!!

CONTENTS

BOAR HAT
The Seven Deadly Sins

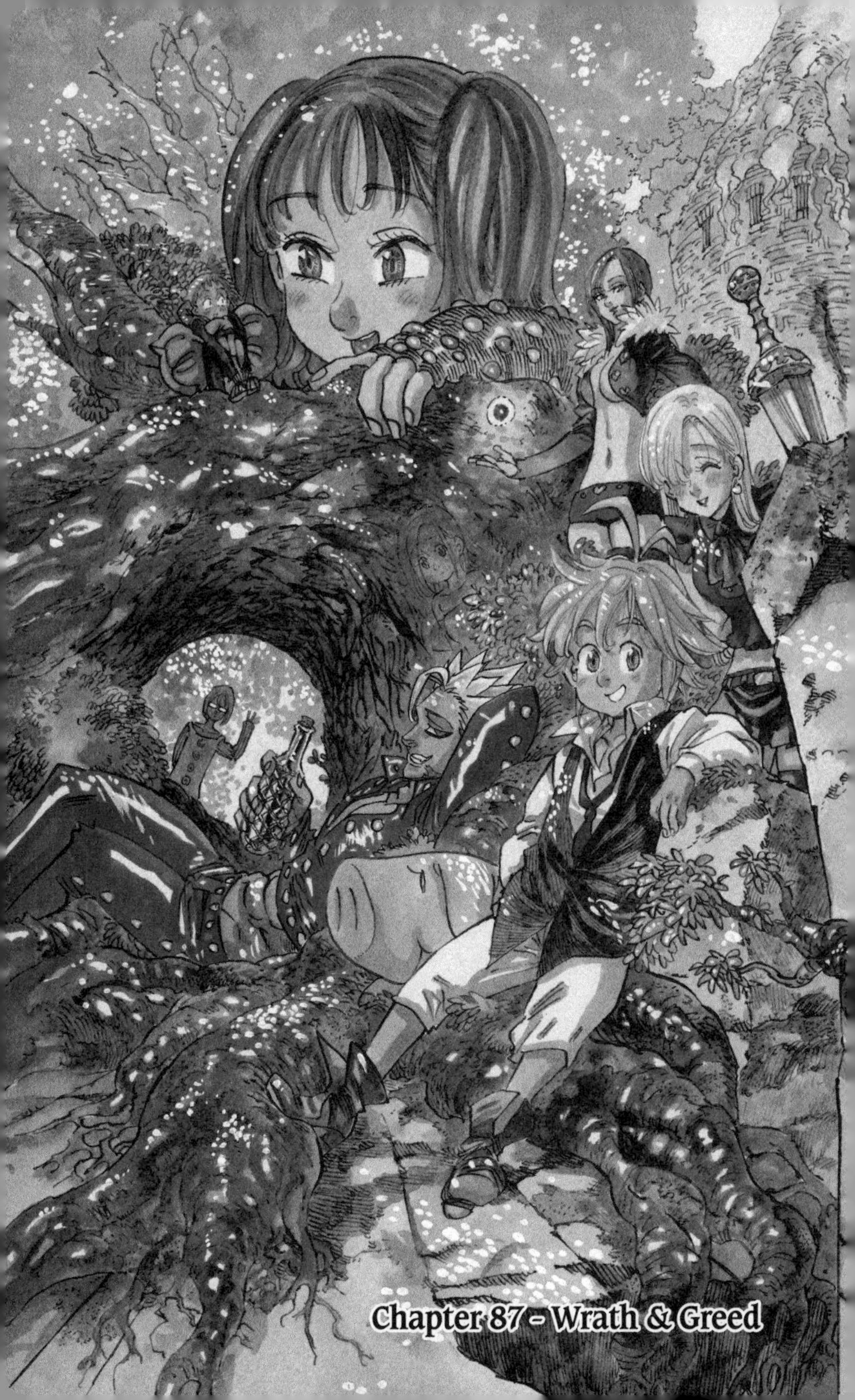

Chapter 87 - Wrath & Greed

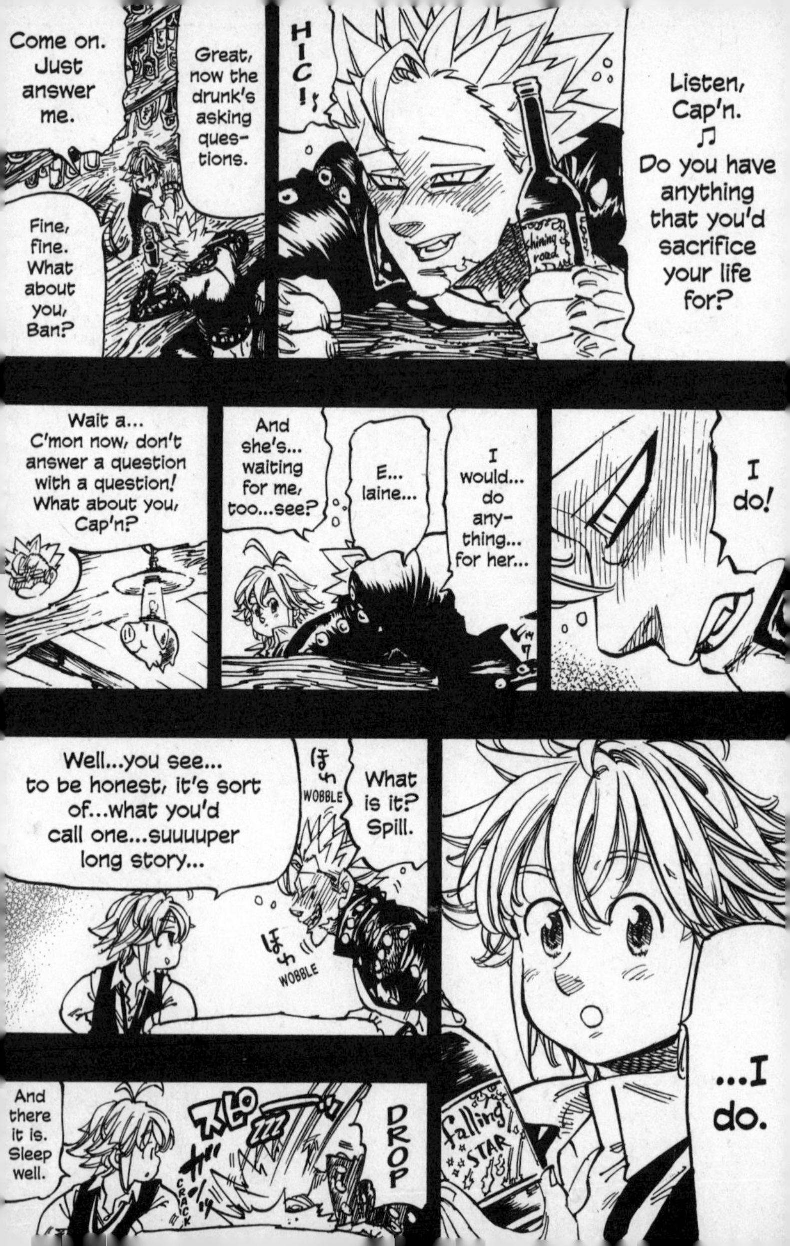
HIC!
Listen, Cap'n. ♫ Do you have anything that you'd sacrifice your life for?
shining road
Great, now the drunk's asking questions.
Come on. Just answer me.
Fine, fine. What about you, Ban?
I do!
I would... do anything... for her...
E... laine...
And she's... waiting for me, too...see?
Wait a... C'mon now, don't answer a question with a question! What about you, Cap'n?
...I do.
falling STAR
What is it? Spill.
WOBBLE
Well...you see... to be honest, it's sort of...what you'd call one...suuuuper long story...
WOBBLE
DROP
CRACK
And there it is. Sleep well.

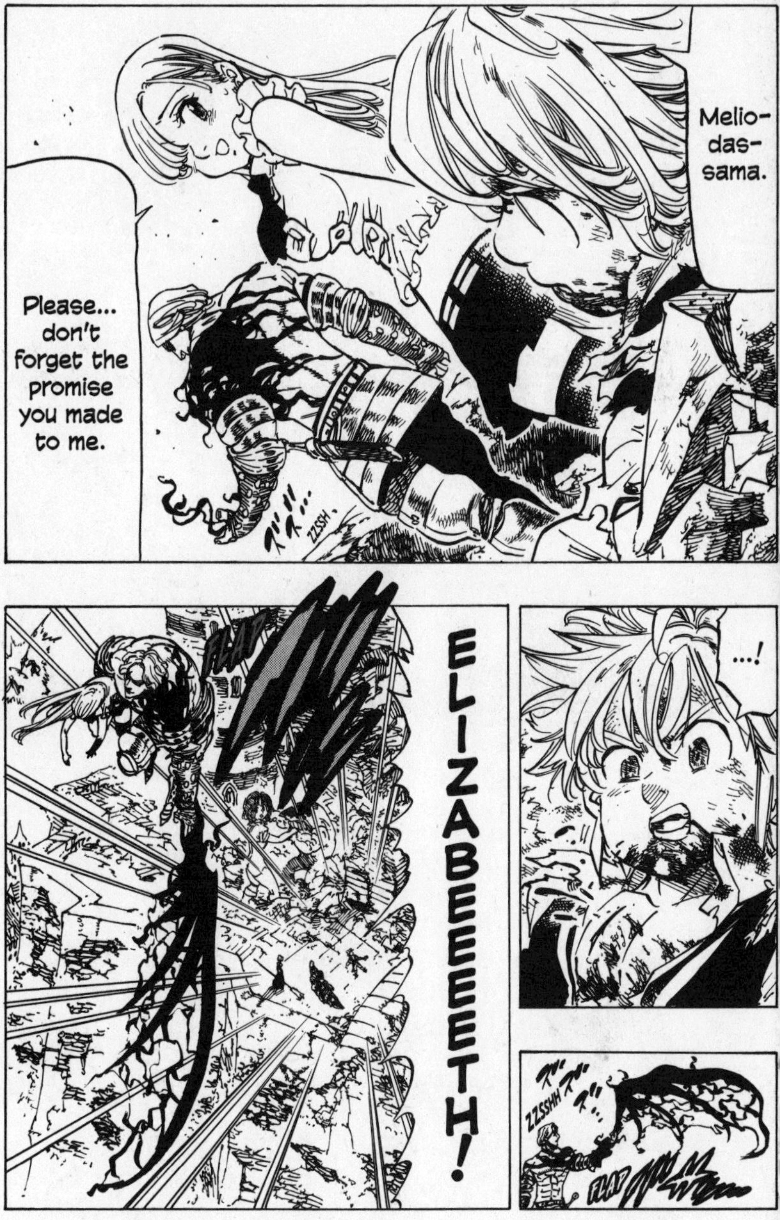
Melio-das-sama.
Please... don't forget the promise you made to me.
ZZSSH
...!
ZZSSHH
FLAP
FLAP
ELIZABEEEETH!

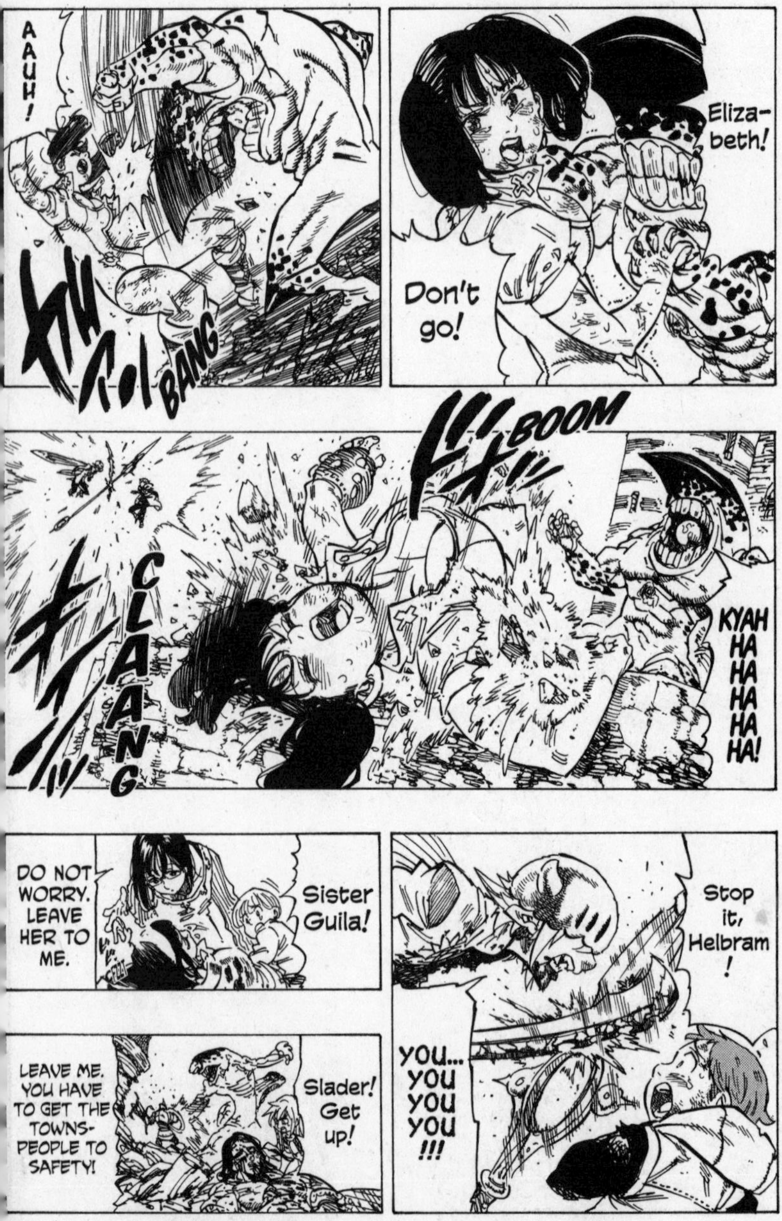
Eliza-beth!
Don't go!
AAUH!
BANG
BOOM
KYAH HA HA HA HA HA HA!
CLAAANG
Stop it, Helbram!
YOU... YOU YOU YOU!!!
Sister Guila!
DO NOT WORRY. LEAVE HER TO ME.
Slader! Get up!
LEAVE ME. YOU HAVE TO GET THE TOWNS-PEOPLE TO SAFETY!

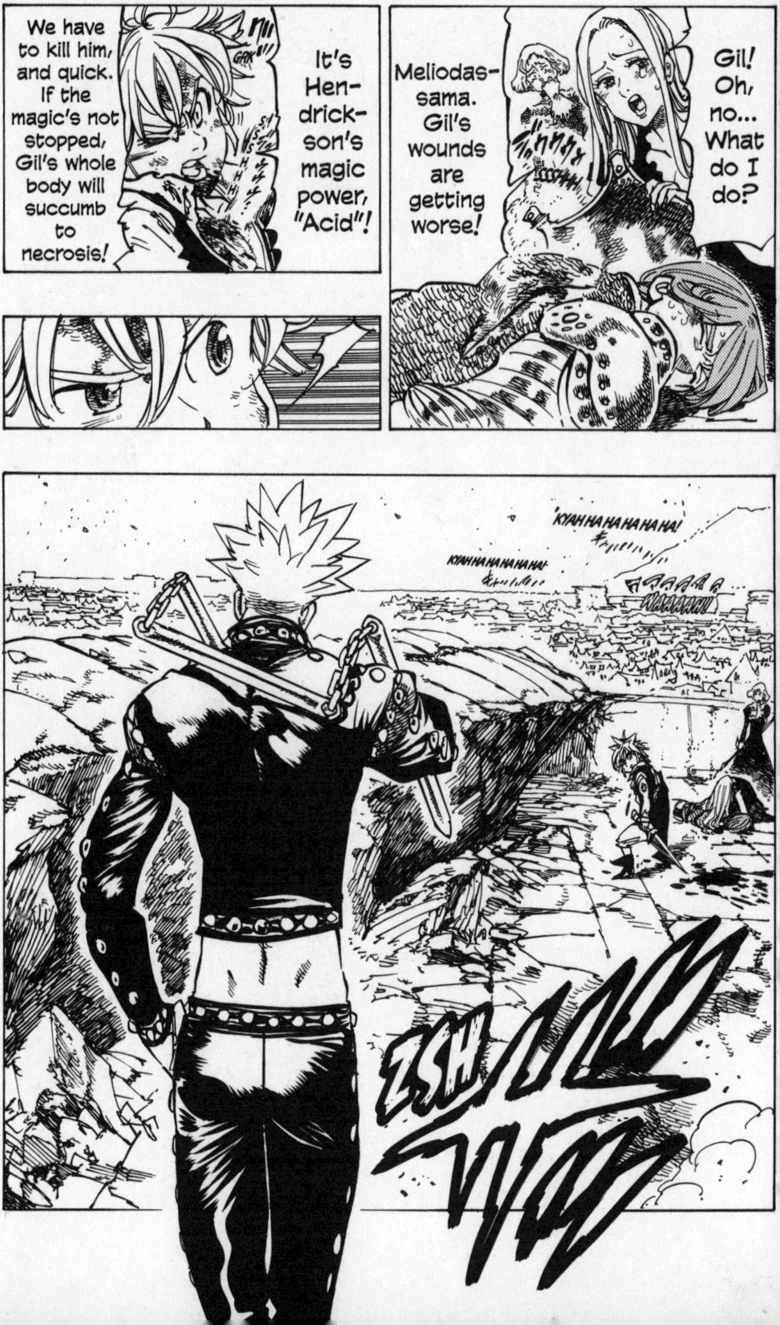
Gil! Oh, no... What do I do?
Meliodas-sama. Gil's wounds are getting worse!
It's Hendrickson's magic power, "Acid"!
GRK
We have to kill him, and quick. If the magic's not stopped, Gil's whole body will succumb to necrosis!
KYAHHAHAHAHAHA!
KYAHHAHAHAHAHA!
ZSH

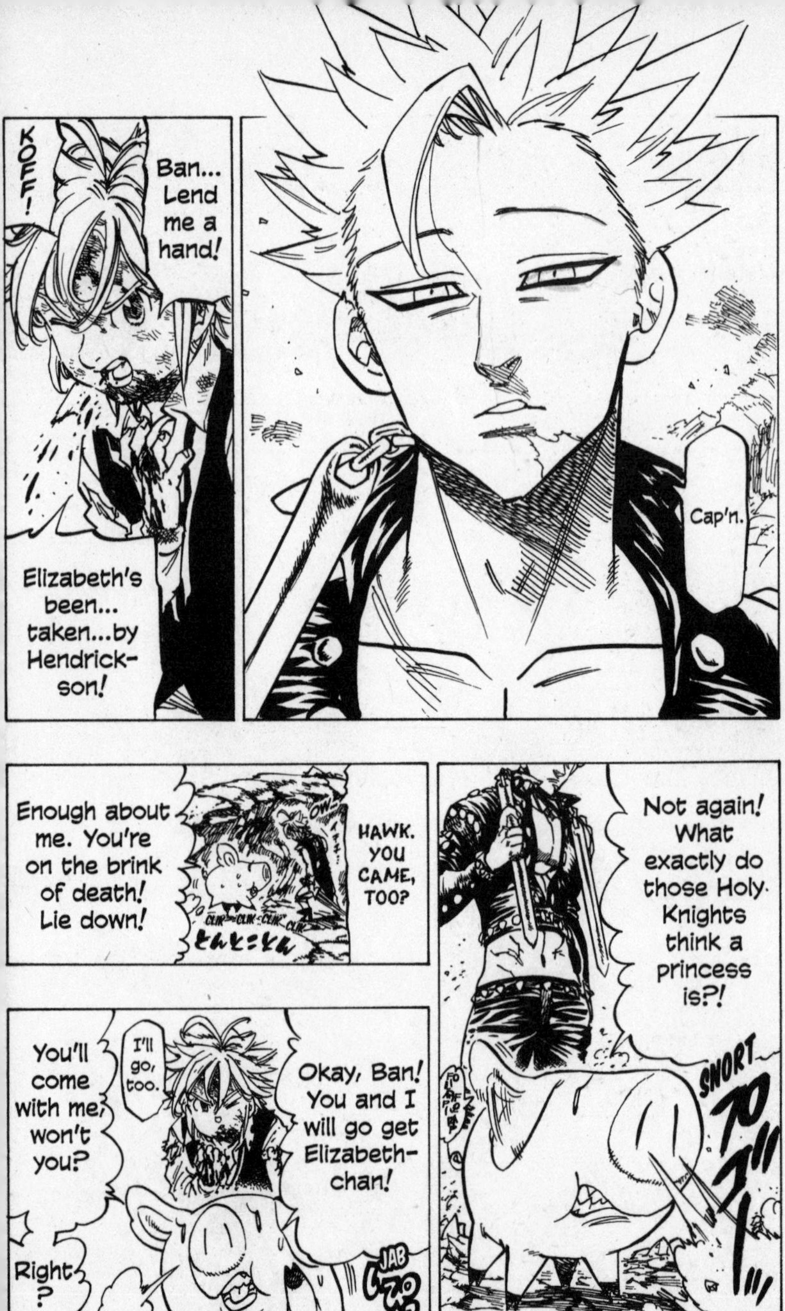

Cap'n.
KOFF!
Ban... Lend me a hand!
Elizabeth's been... taken...by Hendrickson!
Not again! What exactly do those Holy Knights think a princess is?!
SNORT
HAWK. YOU CAME, TOO?
OW...
CLIK CLIK CLIK CLIK
Enough about me. You're on the brink of death! Lie down!
Okay, Ban! You and I will go get Elizabeth-chan!
I'll go, too.
You'll come with me, won't you?
Right?
JAB

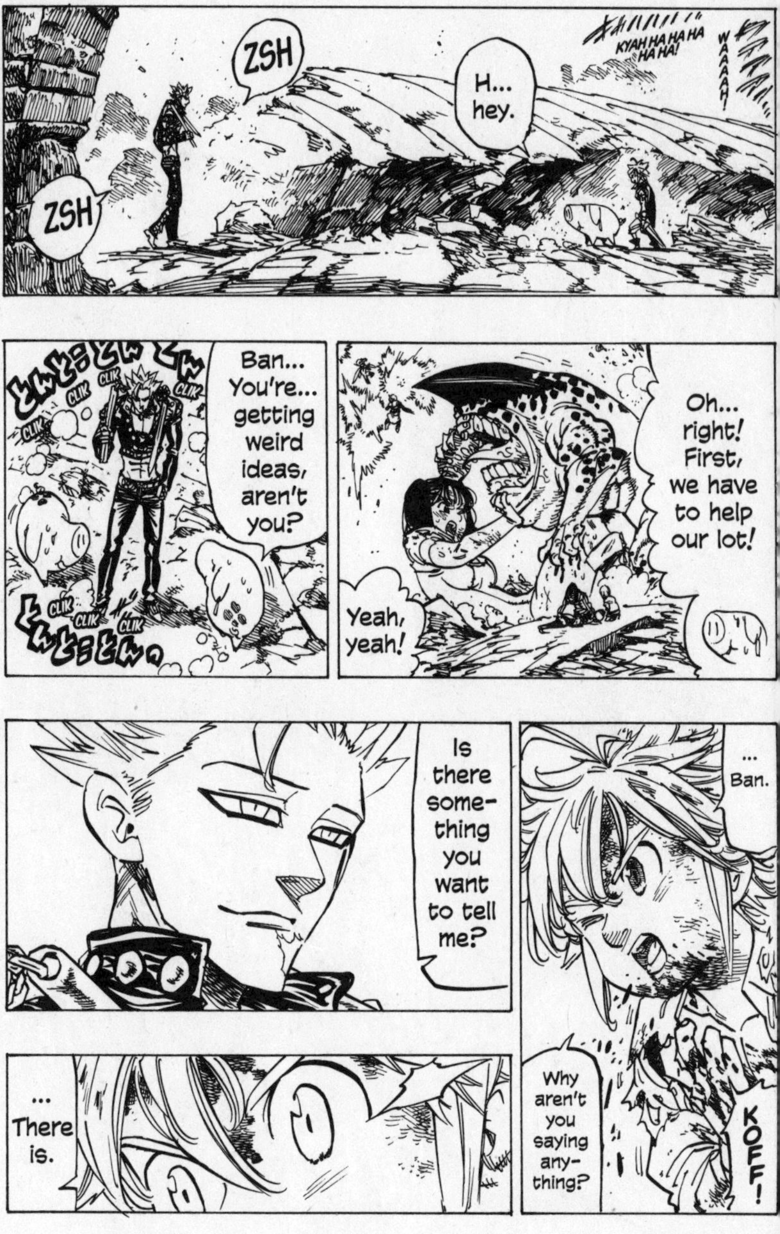

WAAAAH!
KYAH HA HA HA HA HA!
H... hey.
ZSH
ZSH
Oh... right! First, we have to help our lot!
Yeah, yeah!
Ban... You're... getting weird ideas, aren't you?
CLIK CLIK CLIK CLIK
CLIK CLIK CLIK
... Ban.
Why aren't you saying anything?
KOFF!
Is there something you want to tell me?
... There is.

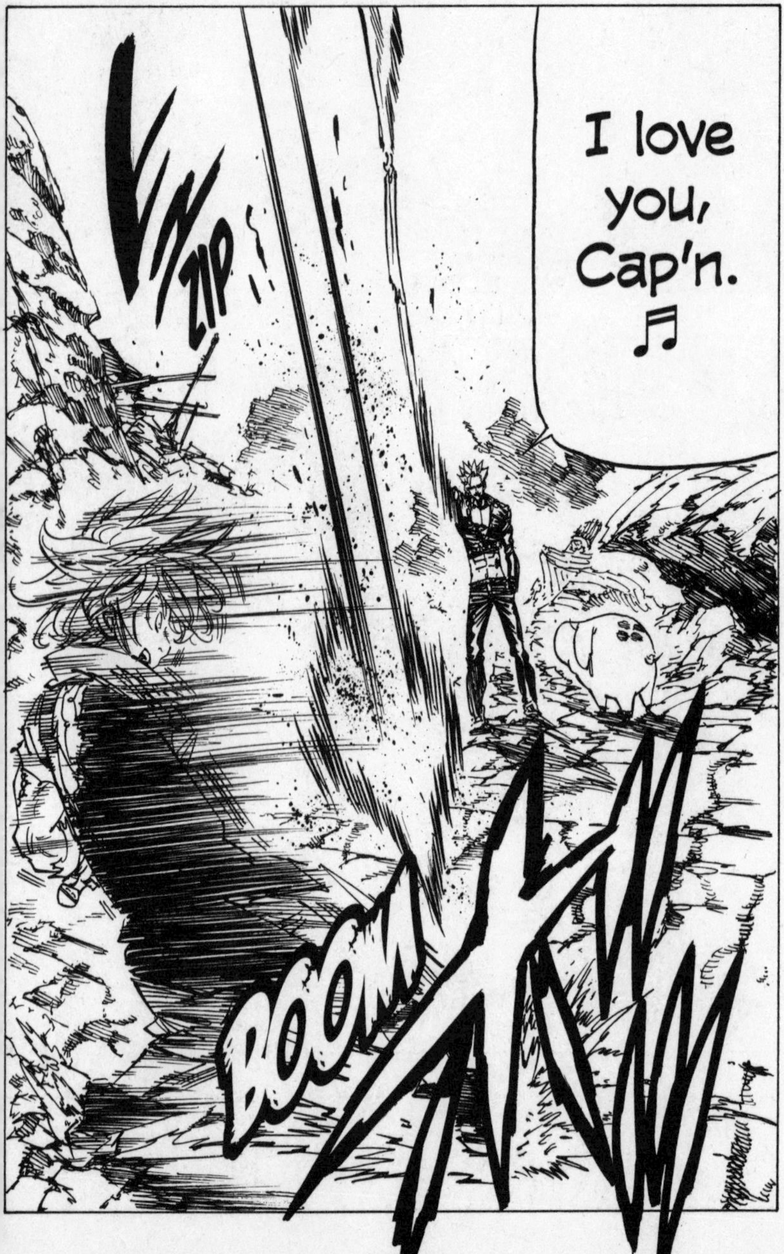
I love you, Cap'n. ♫
ZIP
BOOM

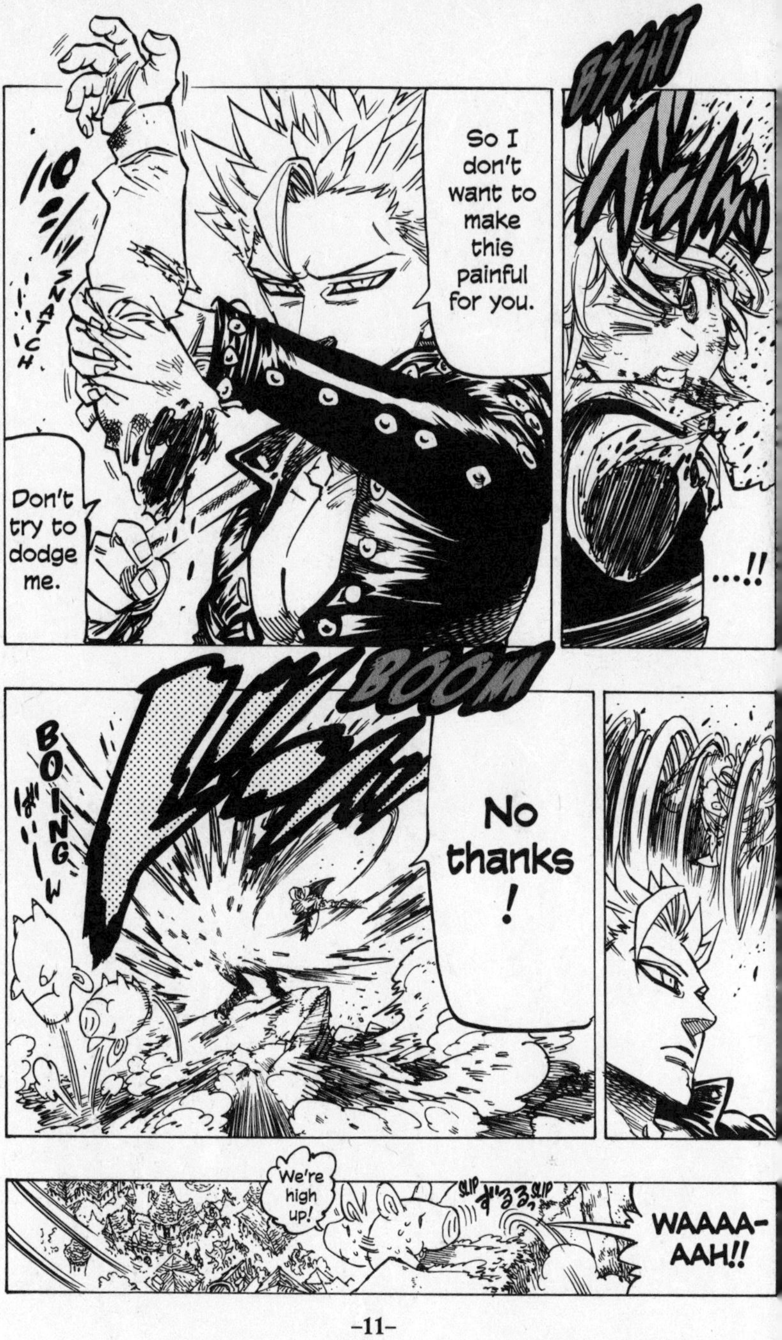
BSSHT
...!!
So I don't want to make this painful for you.
Don't try to dodge me.
SNATCH
BOOM
No thanks!
BOING
WAAAA-AAH!!
SLIP
SLIP
We're high up!

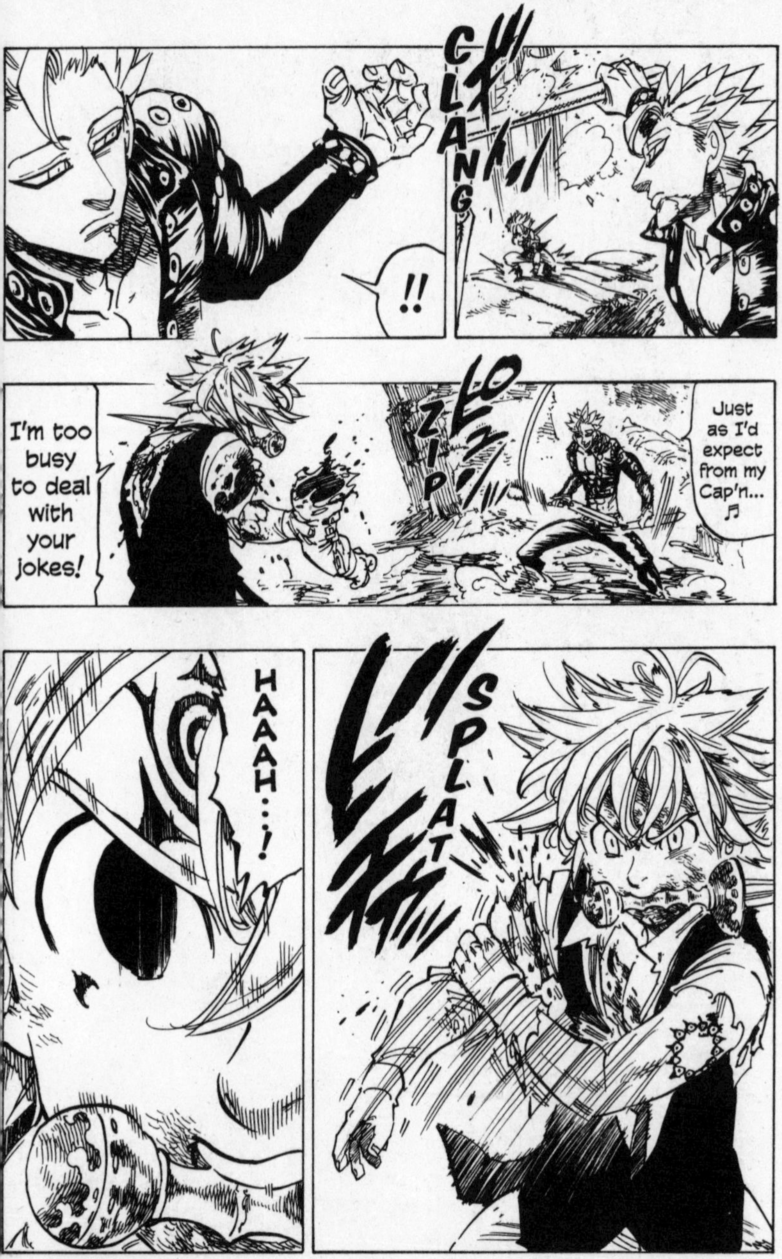
CLANG
!!
Just as I'd expect from my Cap'n... ♫
ZIP
I'm too busy to deal with your jokes!
SPLAT
HAAAH...!

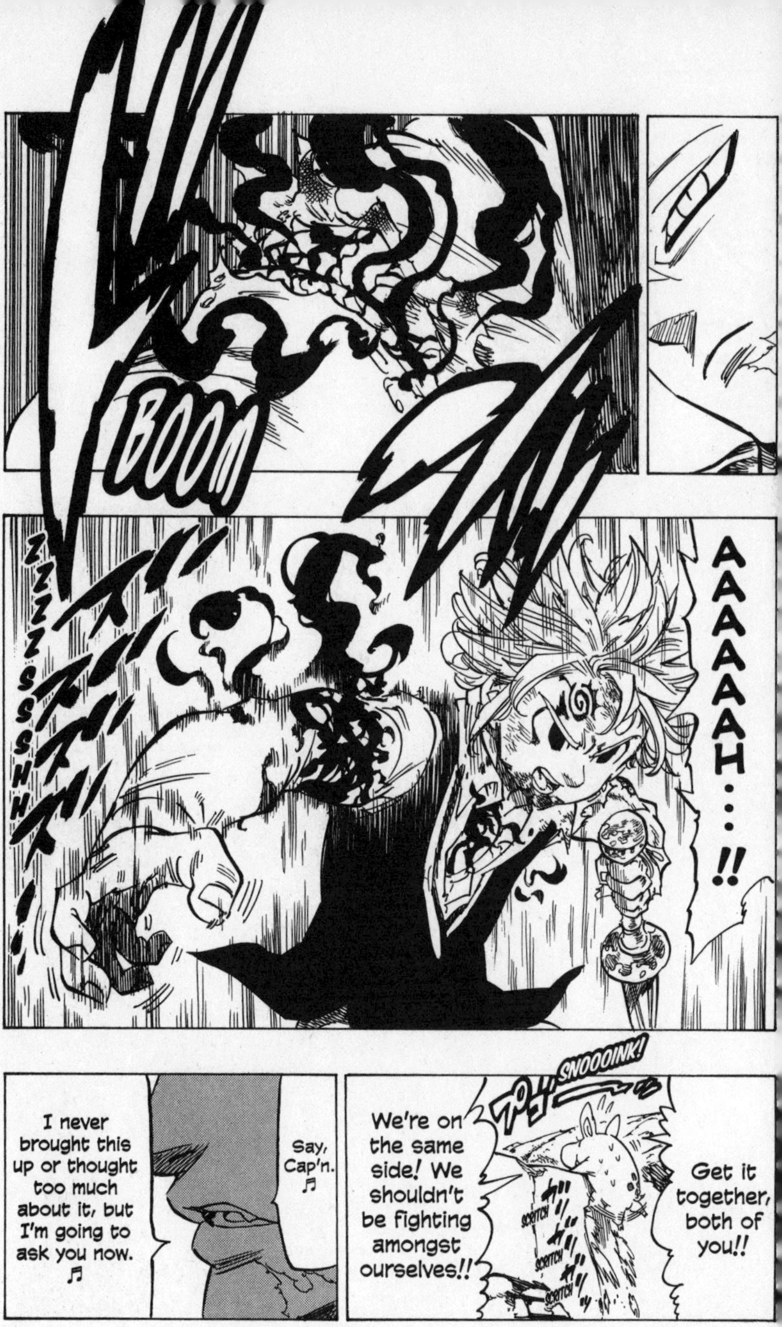
BOOM
AAAAAH...!!
ZZZZSSSHH...
SNOOOINK!
Get it together, both of you!!
We're on the same side! We shouldn't be fighting amongst ourselves!!
SCRITCH
SCRITCH
SCRITCH
Say, Cap'n. ♬
I never brought this up or thought too much about it, but I'm going to ask you now. ♬

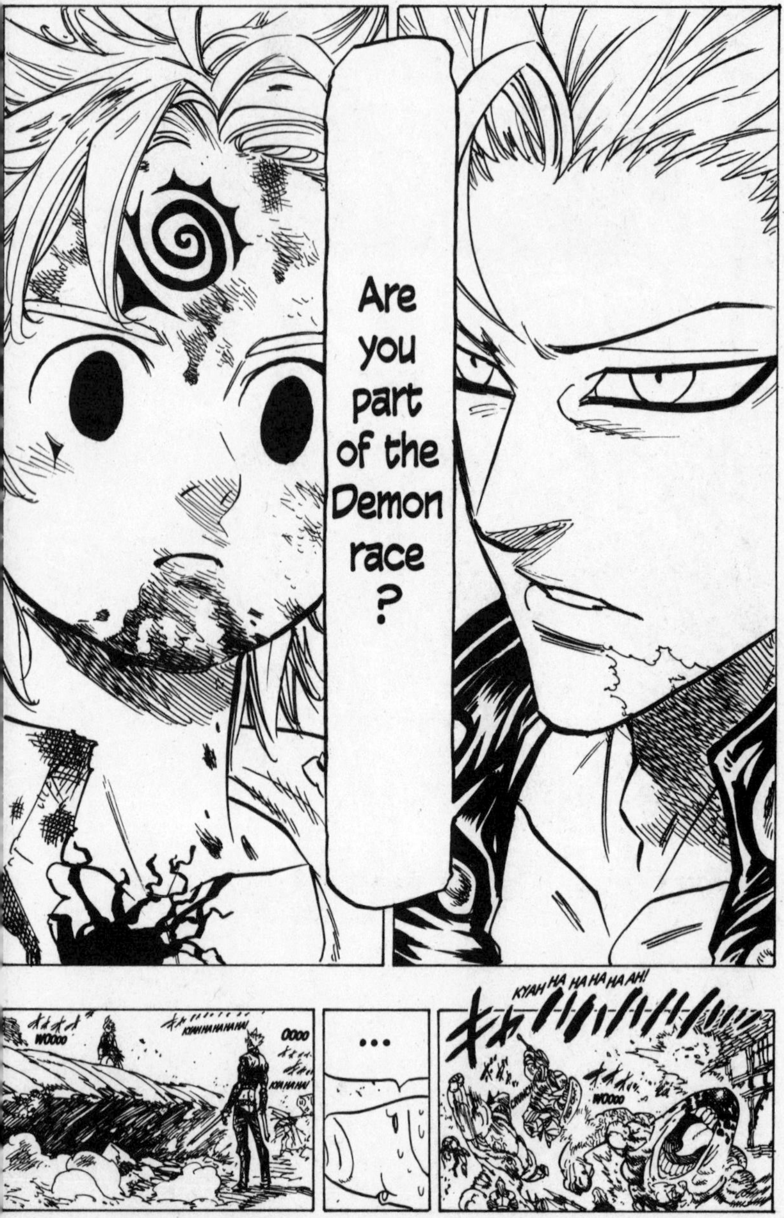
Are you part of the Demon race?
KYAH HA HA HA HA AH!
CRUNCH
WOOOO
...
OOOO
KYAH HA HA!
KYAH HA HA HA HA!
WOOOO

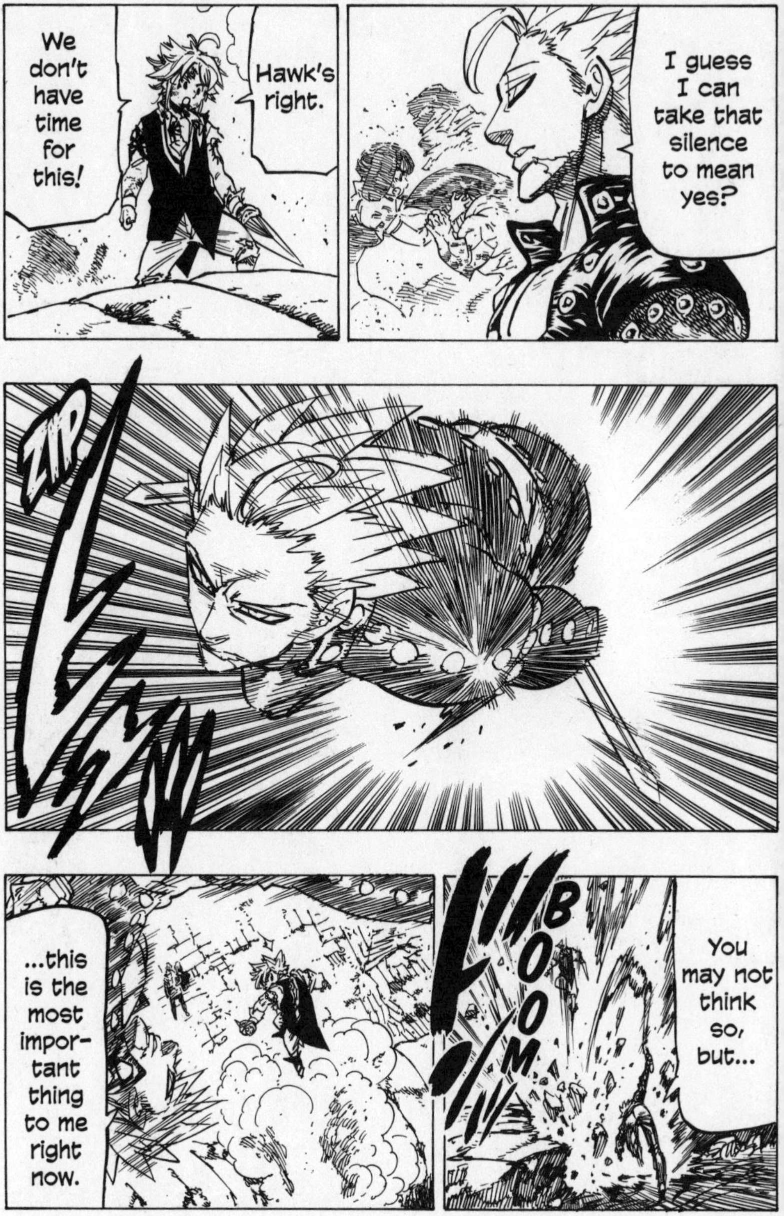
I guess I can take that silence to mean yes?
Hawk's right.
We don't have time for this!
ZIP
BOOM
You may not think so, but...
...this is the most impor-tant thing to me right now.

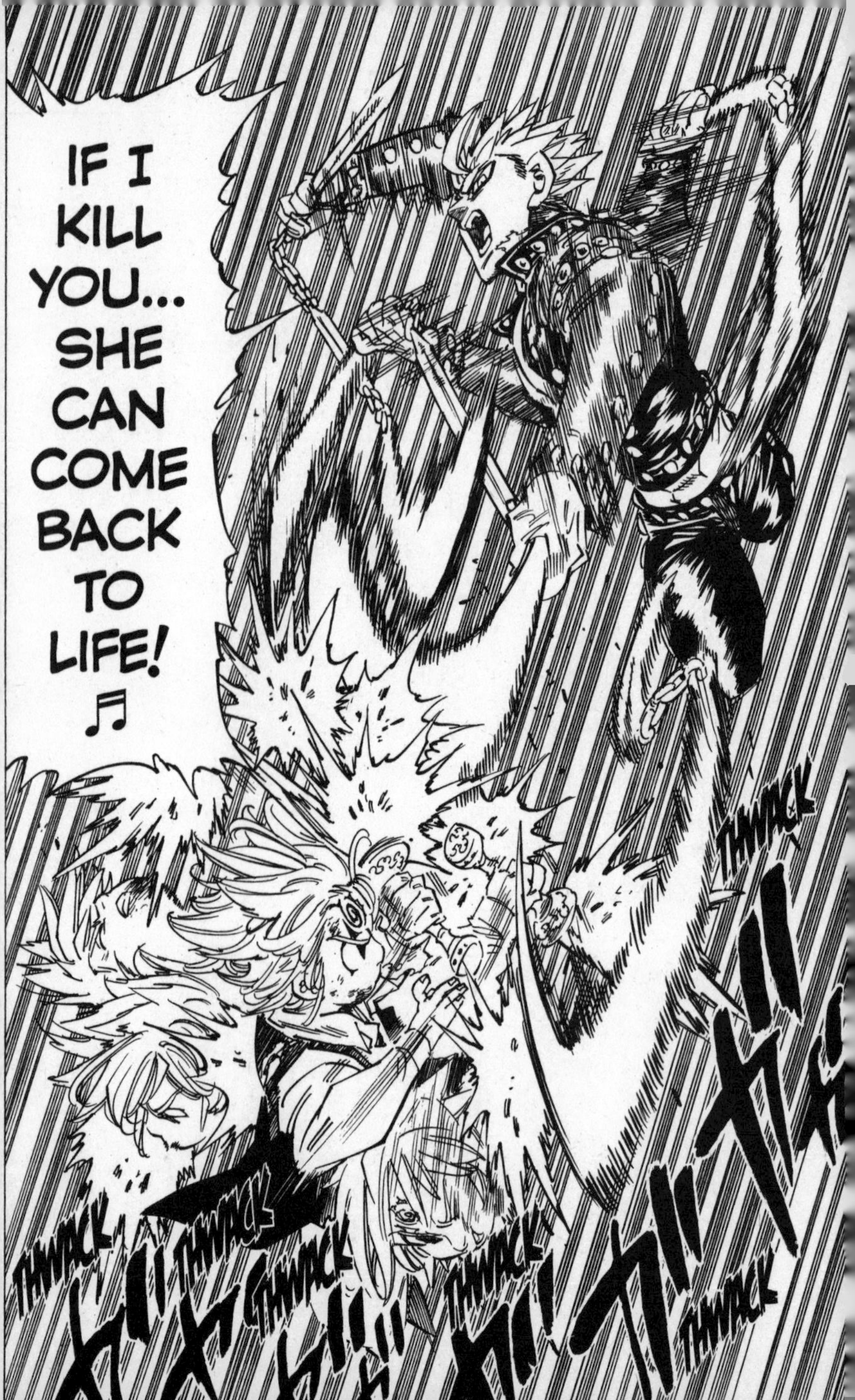
IF I KILL YOU... SHE CAN COME BACK TO LIFE! ♫
THWACK
THWACK
THWACK
CTHWACK
THWACK
THWACK

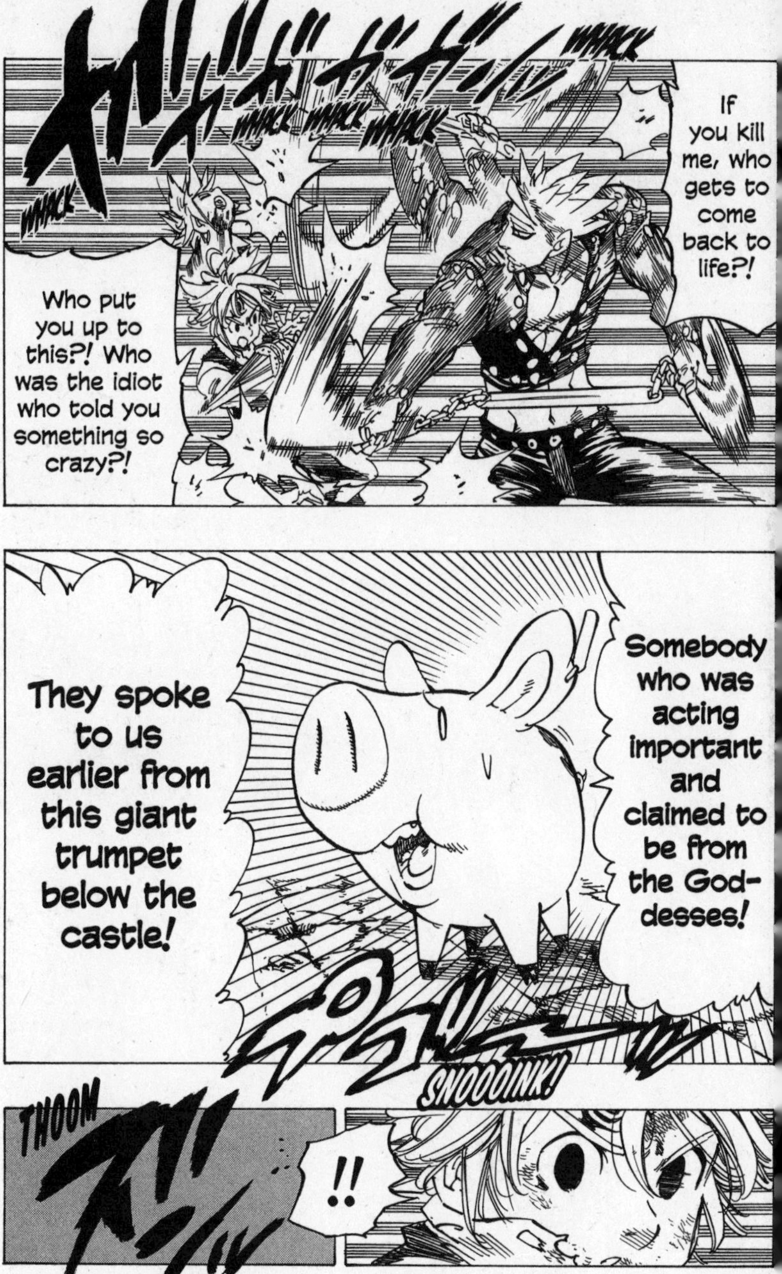
WHACK
WHACK WHACK WHACK
WHACK
If you kill me, who gets to come back to life?!
Who put you up to this?! Who was the idiot who told you something so crazy?!
Somebody who was acting important and claimed to be from the God-desses!
They spoke to us earlier from this giant trumpet below the castle!
SNOOOINK!
!!
THOOM

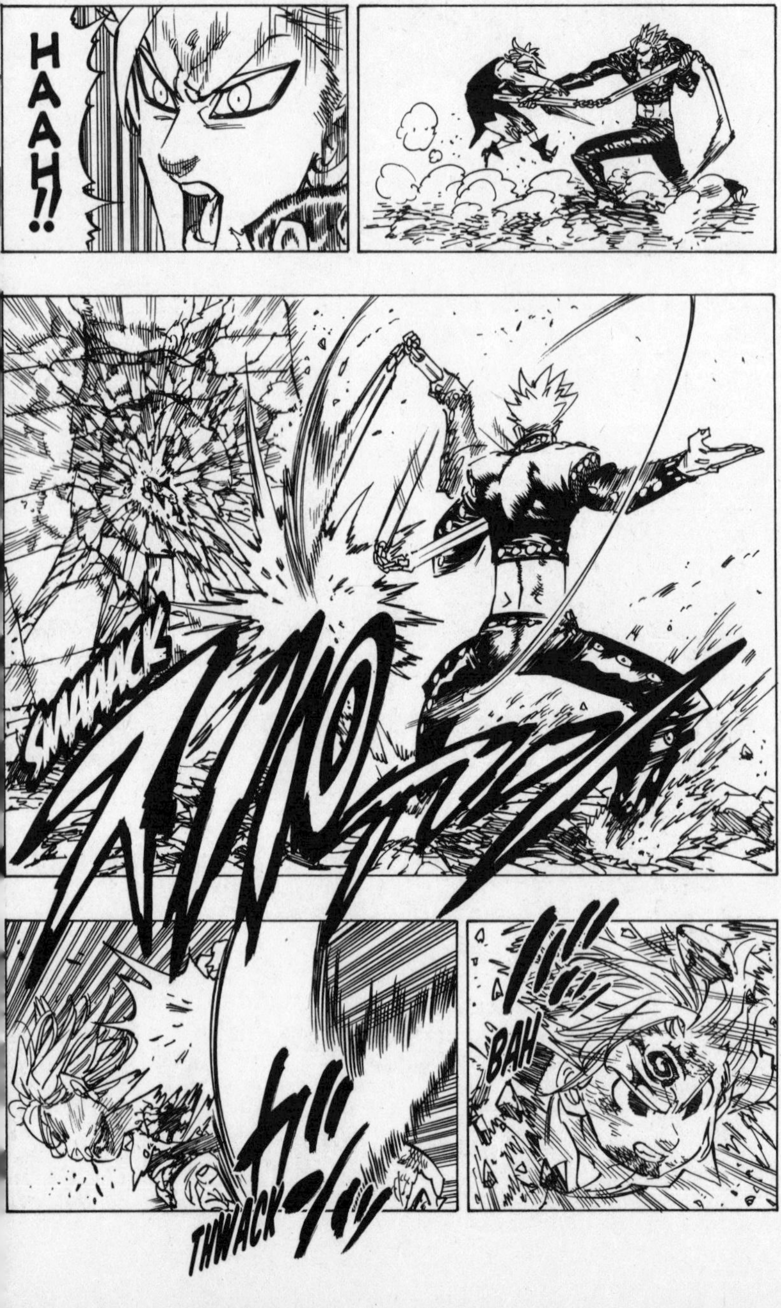
HAAH!!
SMAAACK
BAH
THWACK

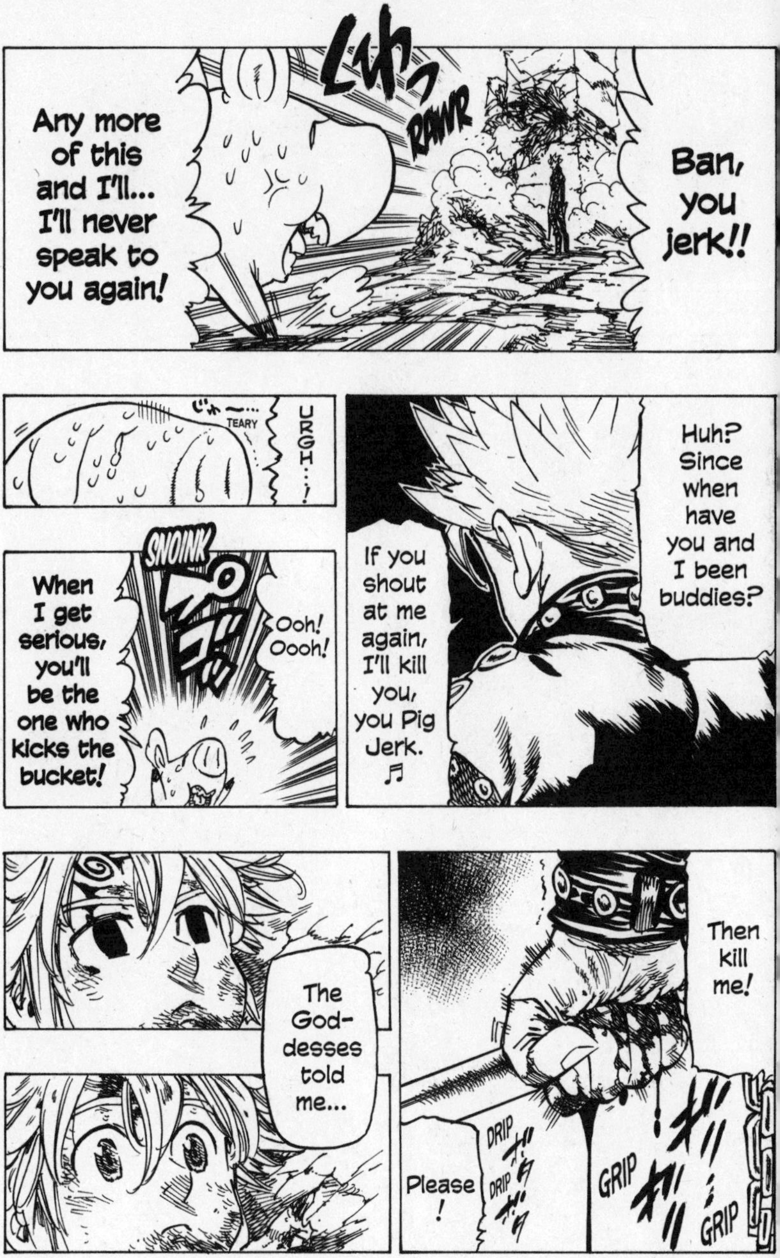
Ban, you jerk!!
RAWR
Any more of this and I'll... I'll never speak to you again!
Huh? Since when have you and I been buddies?
If you shout at me again, I'll kill you, you Pig Jerk. ♬
URGH...!
じゅ～... TEARY
Ooh! Oooh!
SNOINK
When I get serious, you'll be the one who kicks the bucket!
Then kill me!
GRIP
GRIP
DRIP
DRIP
Please!
The God-desses told me...

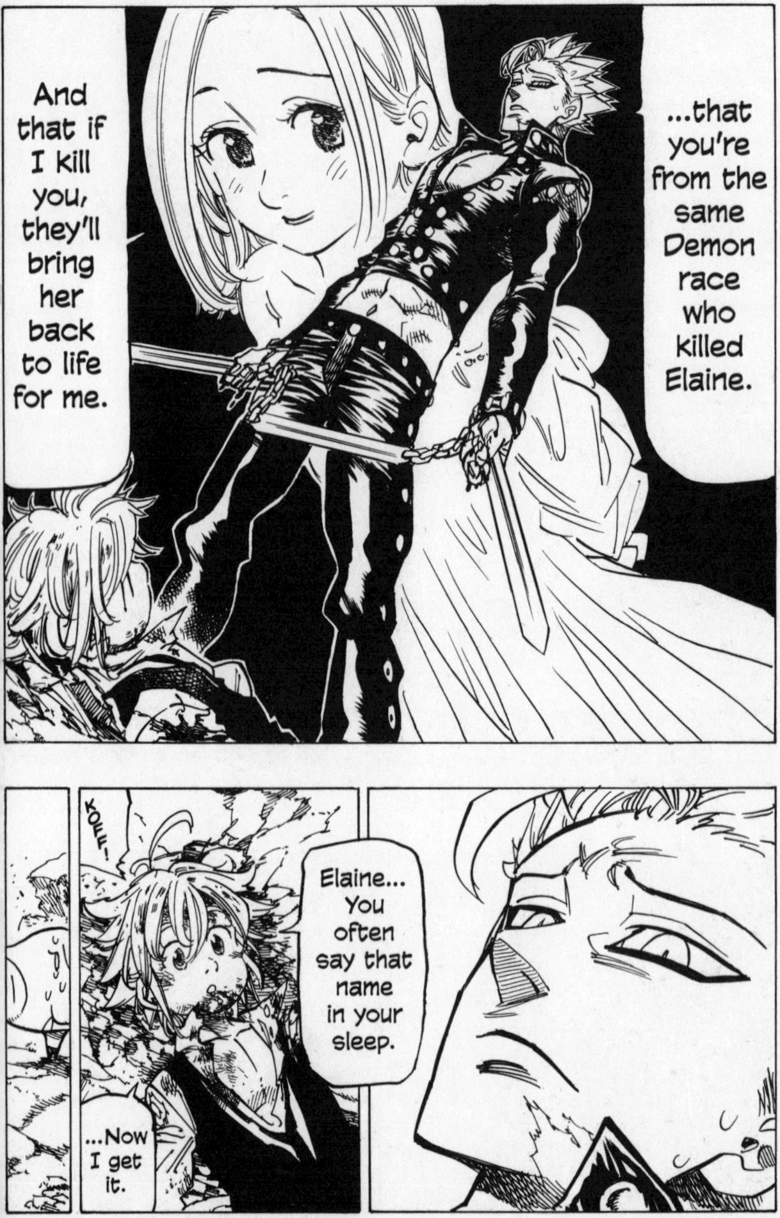
...that you're from the same Demon race who killed Elaine.
And that if I kill you, they'll bring her back to life for me.
Elaine... You often say that name in your sleep.
KOFF!
...Now I get it.

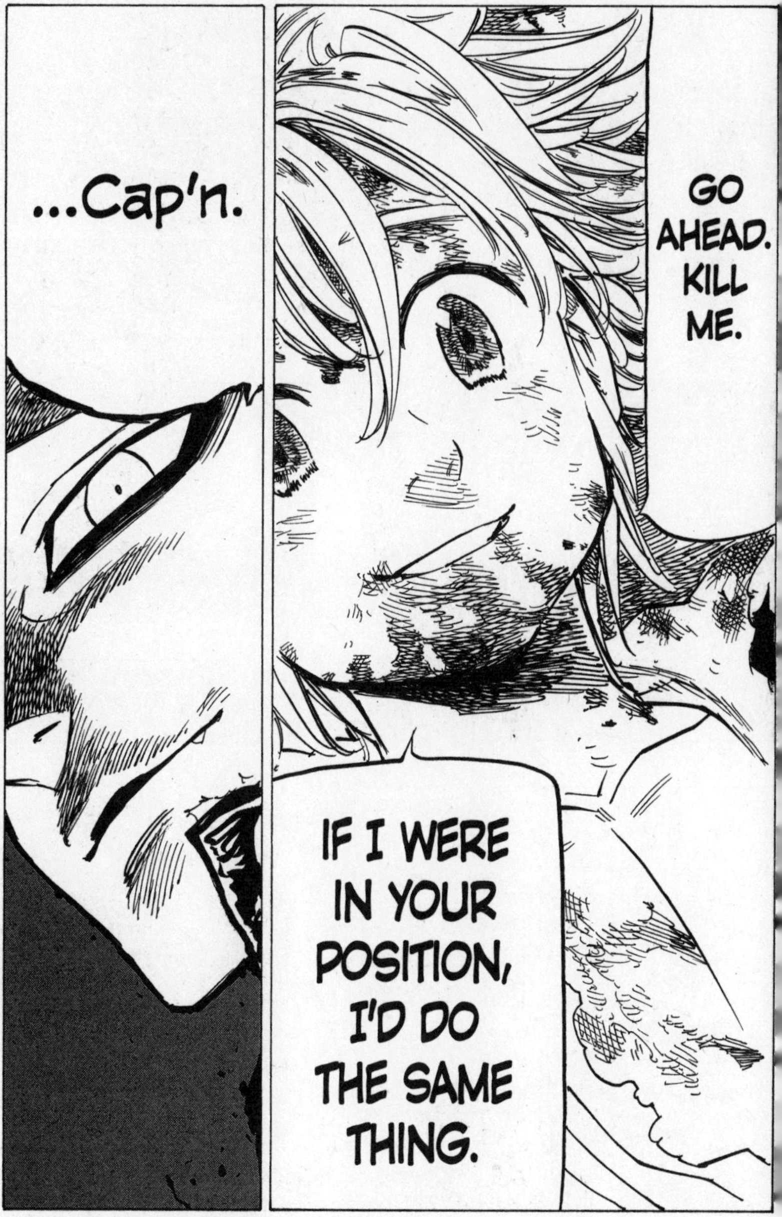
GO AHEAD. KILL ME.
IF I WERE IN YOUR POSITION, I'D DO THE SAME THING.
...Cap'n.

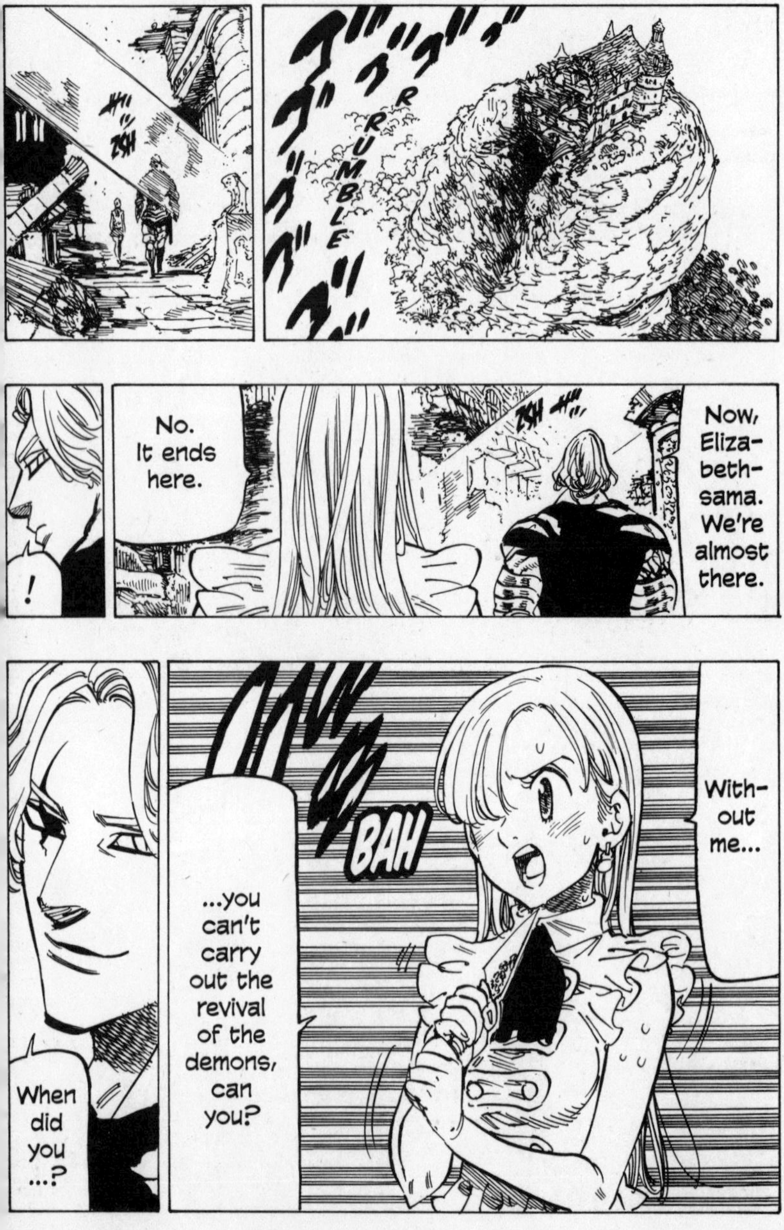
RUMBLE
ZSH
ZSH
Now, Eliza-beth-sama. We're almost there.
No. It ends here.
!
Without me...
BAH
...you can't carry out the revival of the demons, can you?
When did you ...?

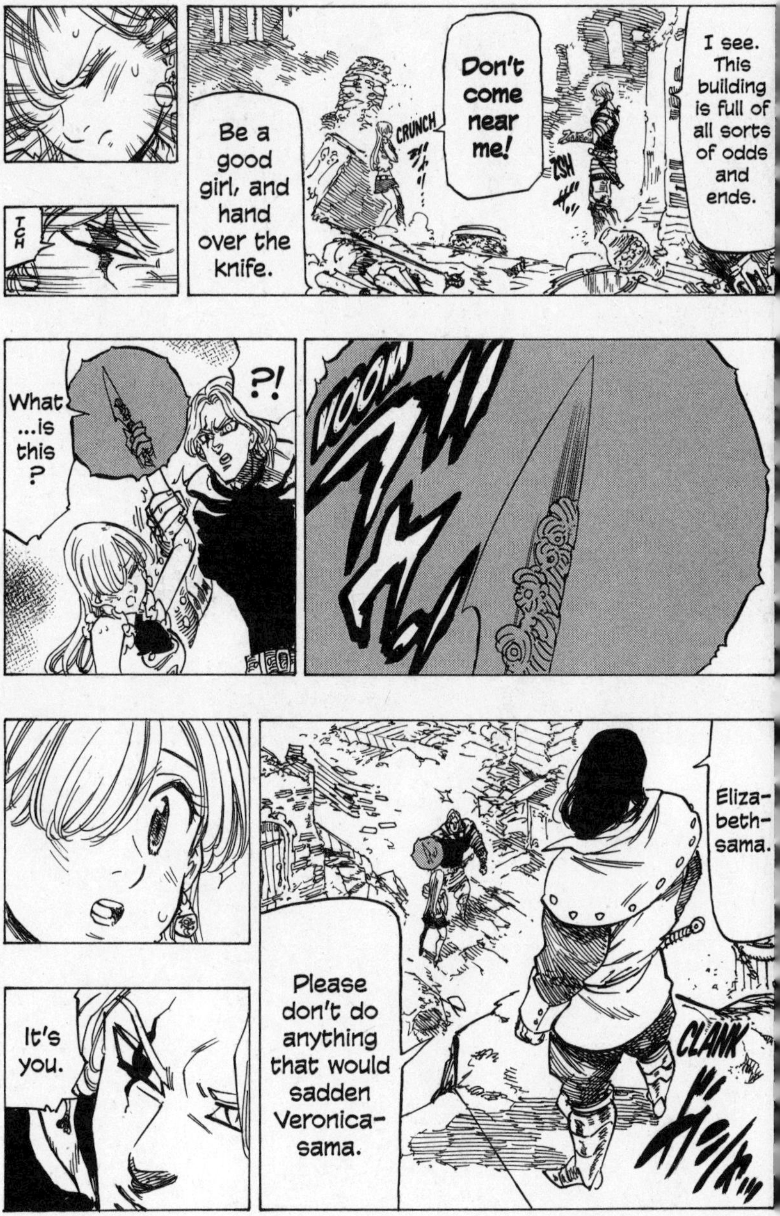
I see. This building is full of all sorts of odds and ends.
ZSH
Don't come near me!
CRUNCH
Be a good girl, and hand over the knife.
TCH
VOOM
?!
What ...is this?
Eliza-beth-sama.
CLANK
Please don't do anything that would sadden Veronica-sama.
It's you.

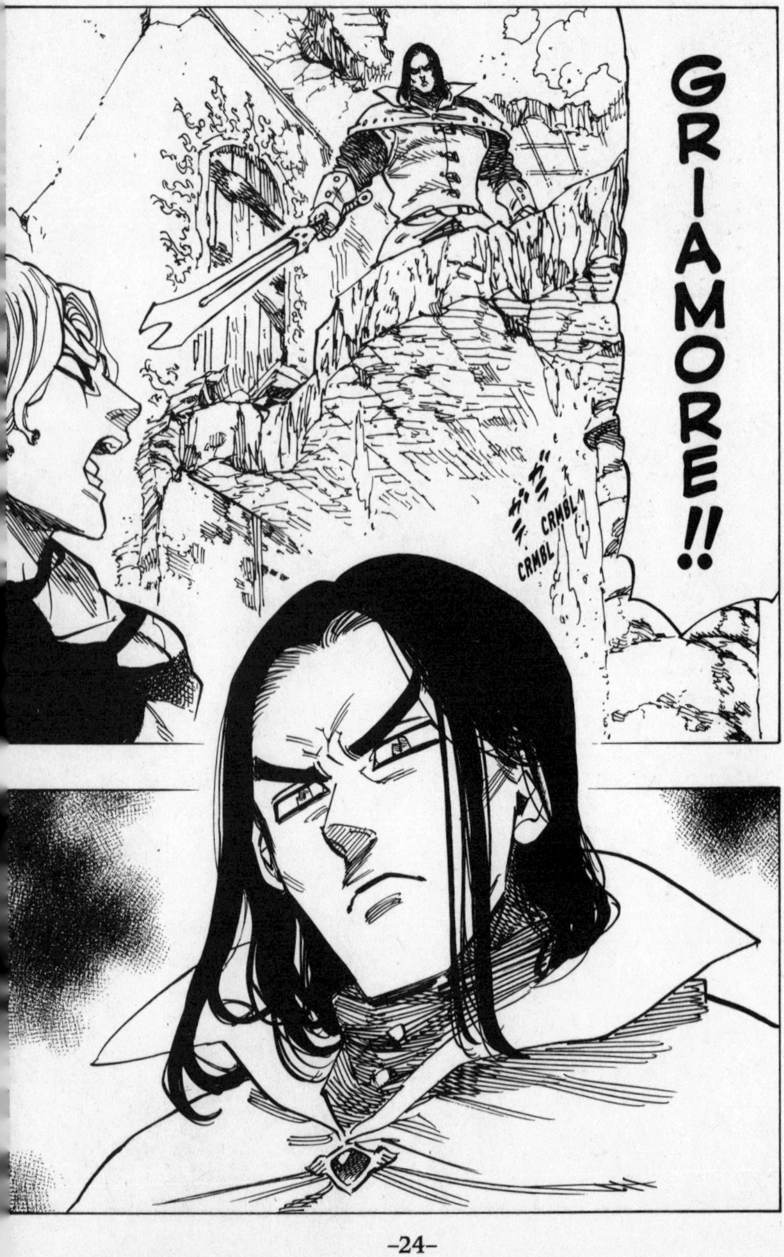
GRIAMORE!!
CRMBL
CRMBL

Chapter 88 - Hell on Earth

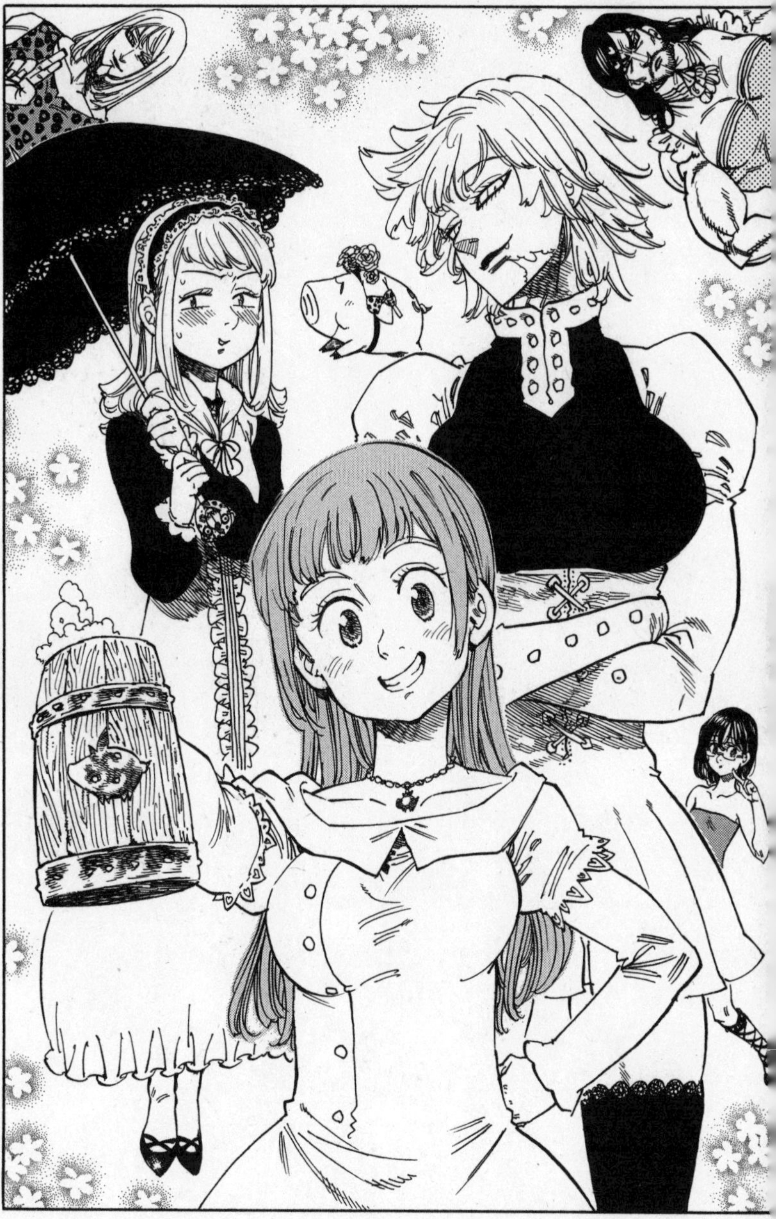

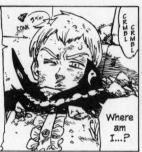

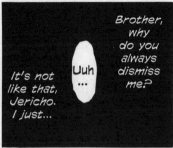

Brother, why do you always dismiss me?
Uuh...
It's not like that, Jericho. I just...
CRMBL CRMBL
CONK
Where am I...?
Oh, yeah... I was under Sir Helbram's mind control "Link" when...
?!!
UUH...
H... hey! Wake up!
The castle's col-lapsed!
What a wretch-ed state...
What on earth has befallen the kingdom?

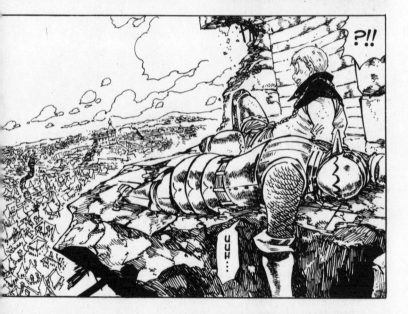

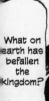

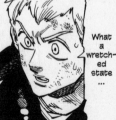

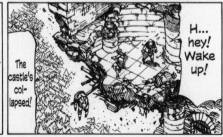

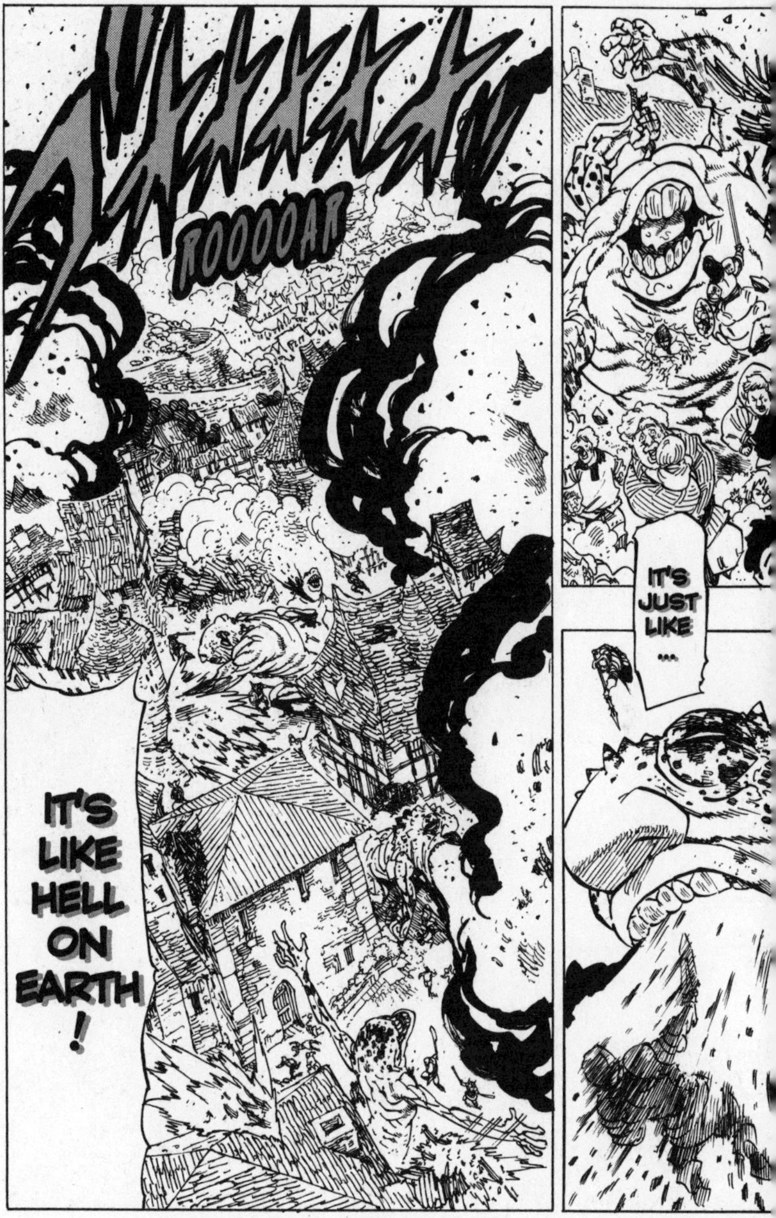
IT'S JUST LIKE ...
ROOOOAR
IT'S LIKE HELL ON EARTH !

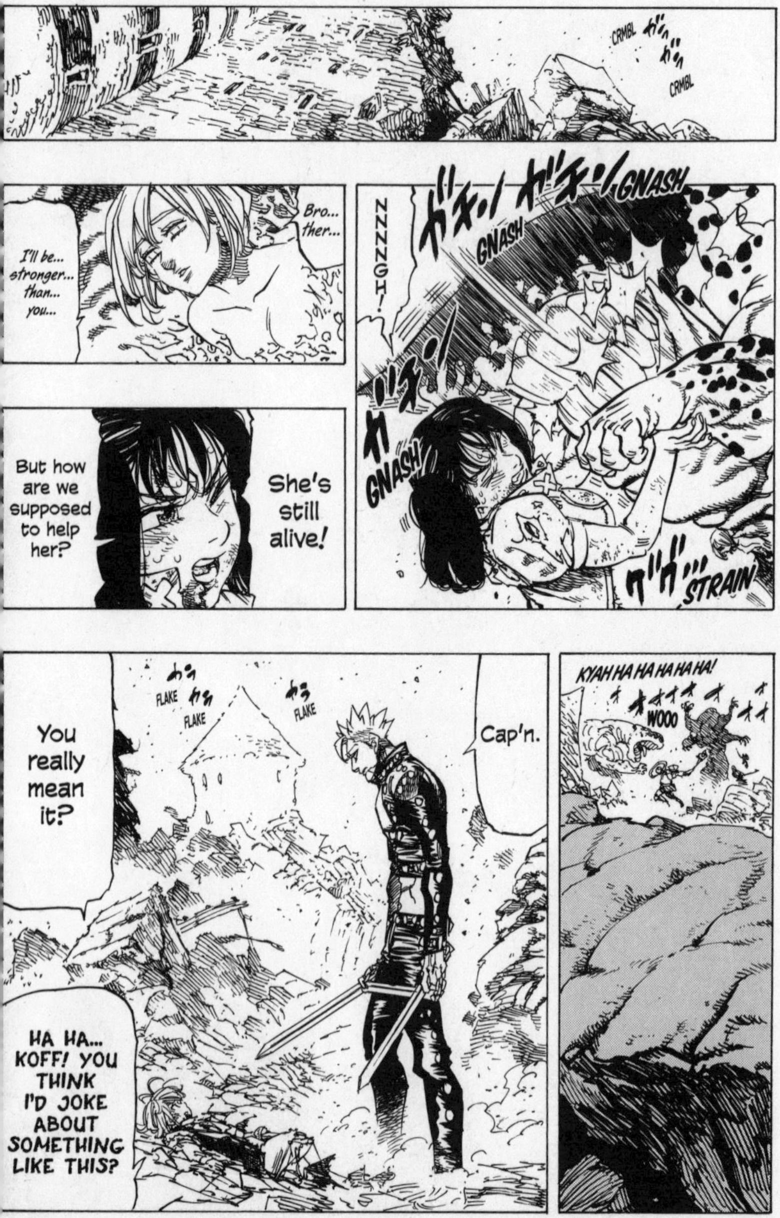
CRMBL
CRMBL
NNNNGH!
GNASH
GNASH
GNASH
STRAIN
Bro... ther...
I'll be... stronger... than... you...
She's still alive!
But how are we supposed to help her?
KYAH HA HA HA HA HA!
WOOO
Cap'n.
FLAKE
FLAKE
FLAKE
You really mean it?
HA HA... KOFF! YOU THINK I'D JOKE ABOUT SOMETHING LIKE THIS?

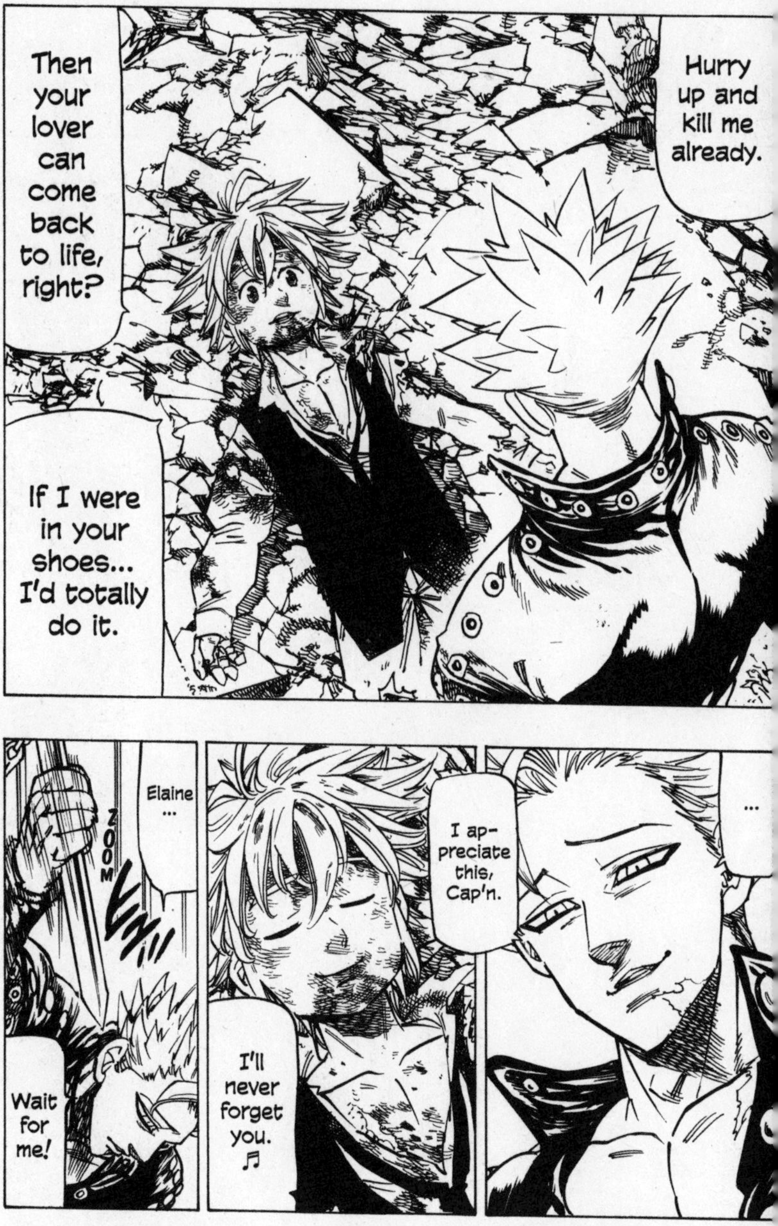
Hurry up and kill me already.
Then your lover can come back to life, right?
If I were in your shoes... I'd totally do it.
...
I appreciate this, Cap'n.
I'll never forget you. ♫
Elaine...
ZOOM
Wait for me!

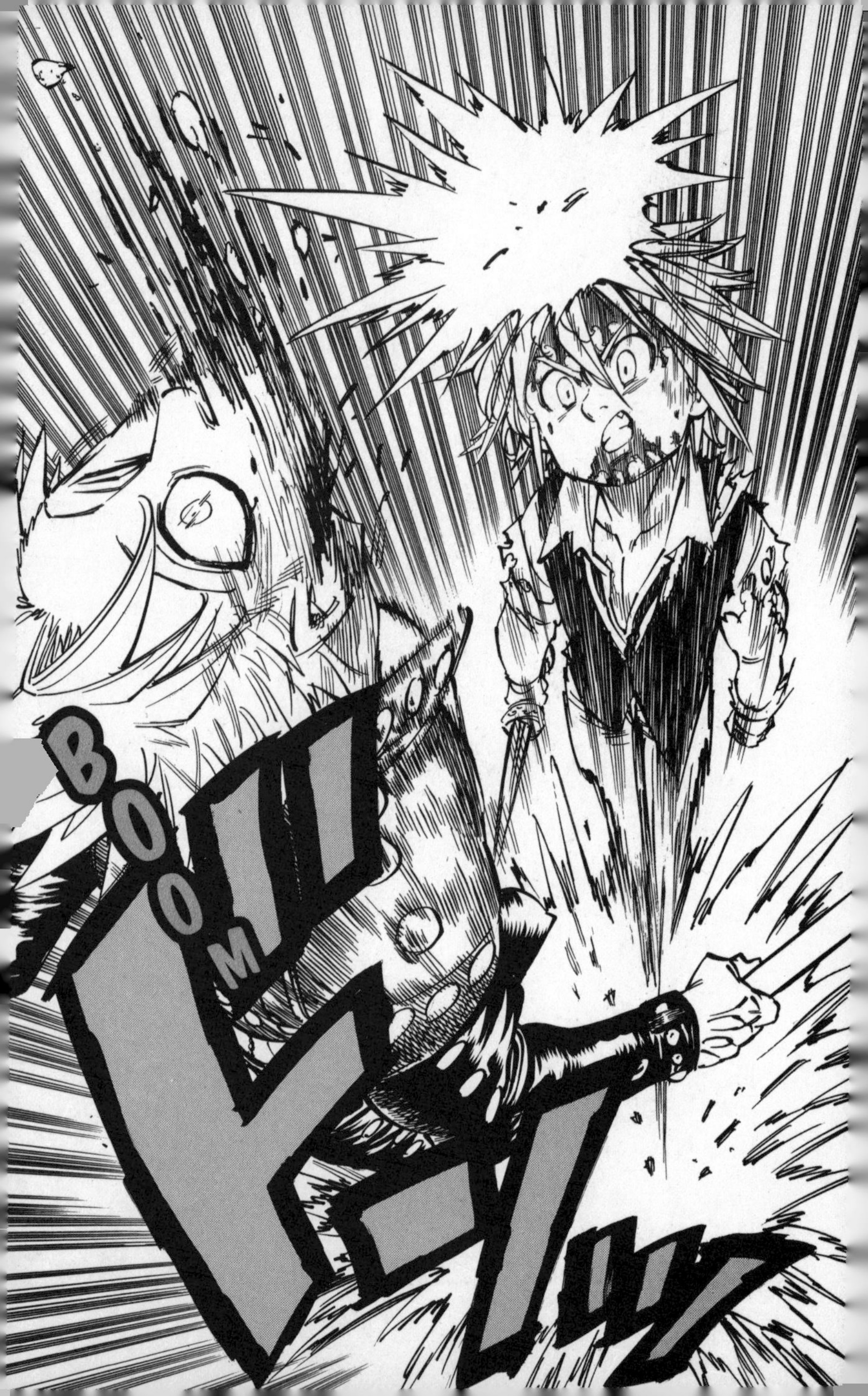
BOOM

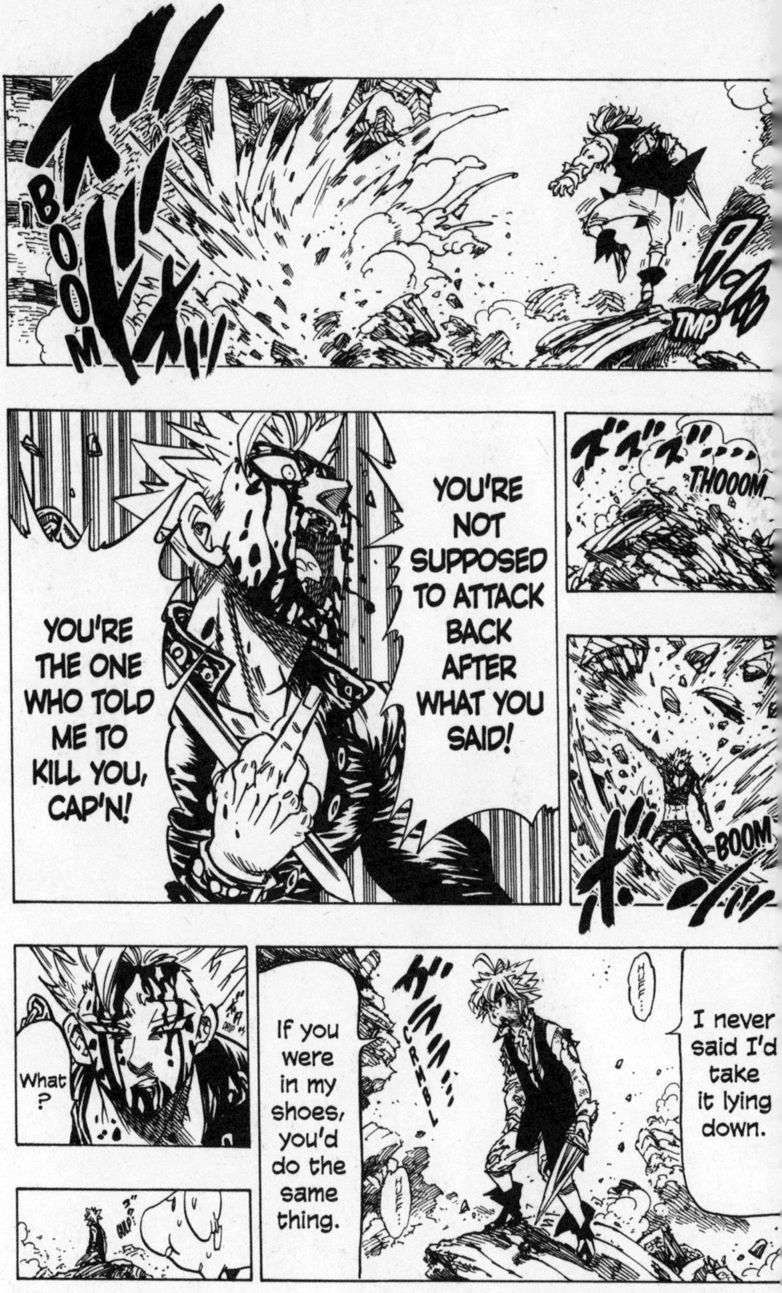
TMP
BOOM
THOOOM
BOOM
YOU'RE NOT SUPPOSED TO ATTACK BACK AFTER WHAT YOU SAID!
YOU'RE THE ONE WHO TOLD ME TO KILL YOU, CAP'N!
I never said I'd take it lying down.
HUF...
CRMBL
If you were in my shoes, you'd do the same thing.
HUF...
What?
DRIP
GULP

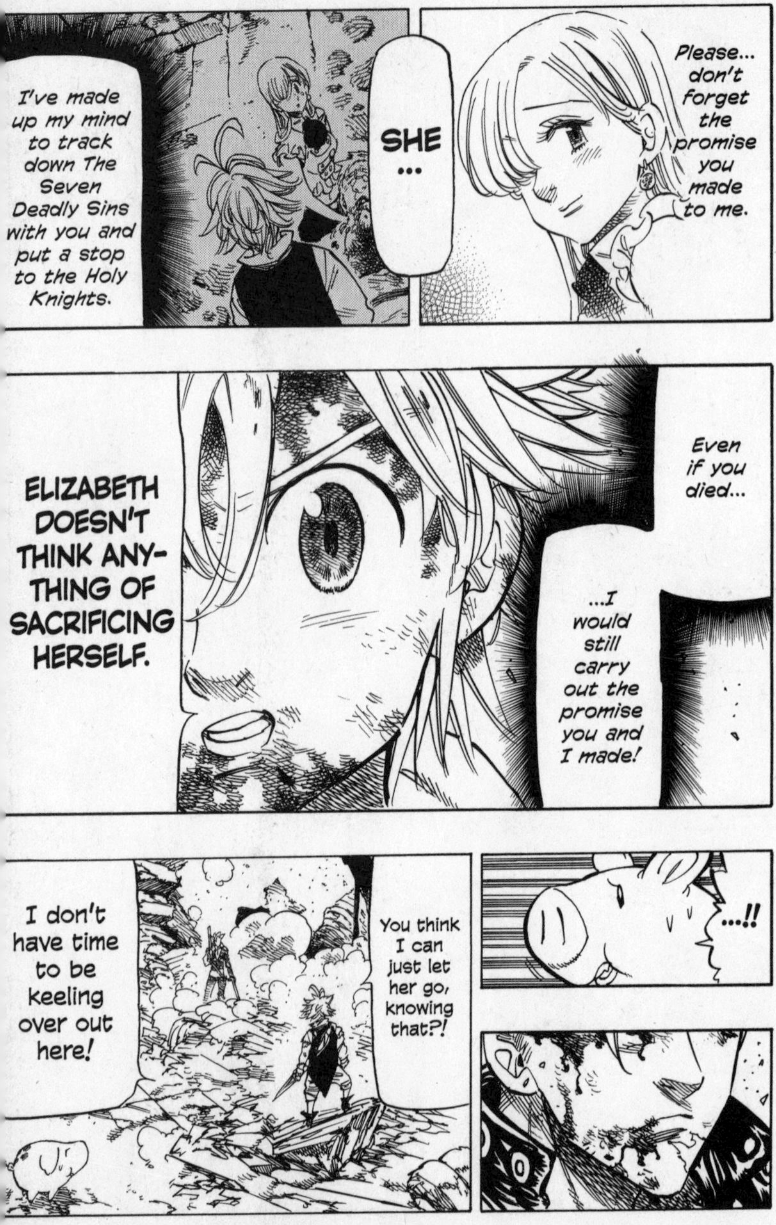
Please... don't forget the promise you made to me.
SHE ...
I've made up my mind to track down The Seven Deadly Sins with you and put a stop to the Holy Knights.
Even if you died...
...I would still carry out the promise you and I made!
ELIZABETH DOESN'T THINK ANY-THING OF SACRIFICING HERSELF.
...!!
You think I can just let her go, knowing that?!
I don't have time to be keeling over out here!

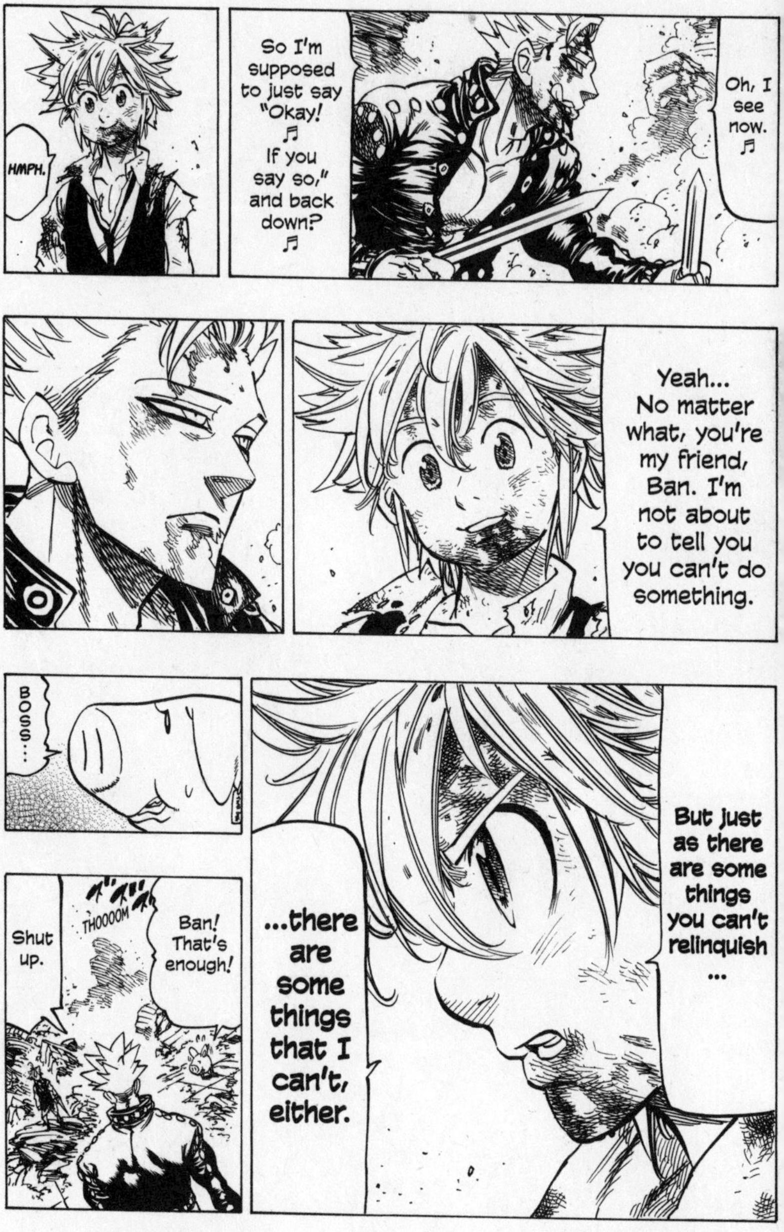
Oh, I see now. ♬
So I'm supposed to just say "Okay! ♬ If you say so," and back down? ♬
HMPH.
Yeah... No matter what, you're my friend, Ban. I'm not about to tell you you can't do something.
But just as there are some things you can't relinquish...
...there are some things that I can't, either.
BOSS...
Ban! That's enough!
THOOOOM
Shut up.

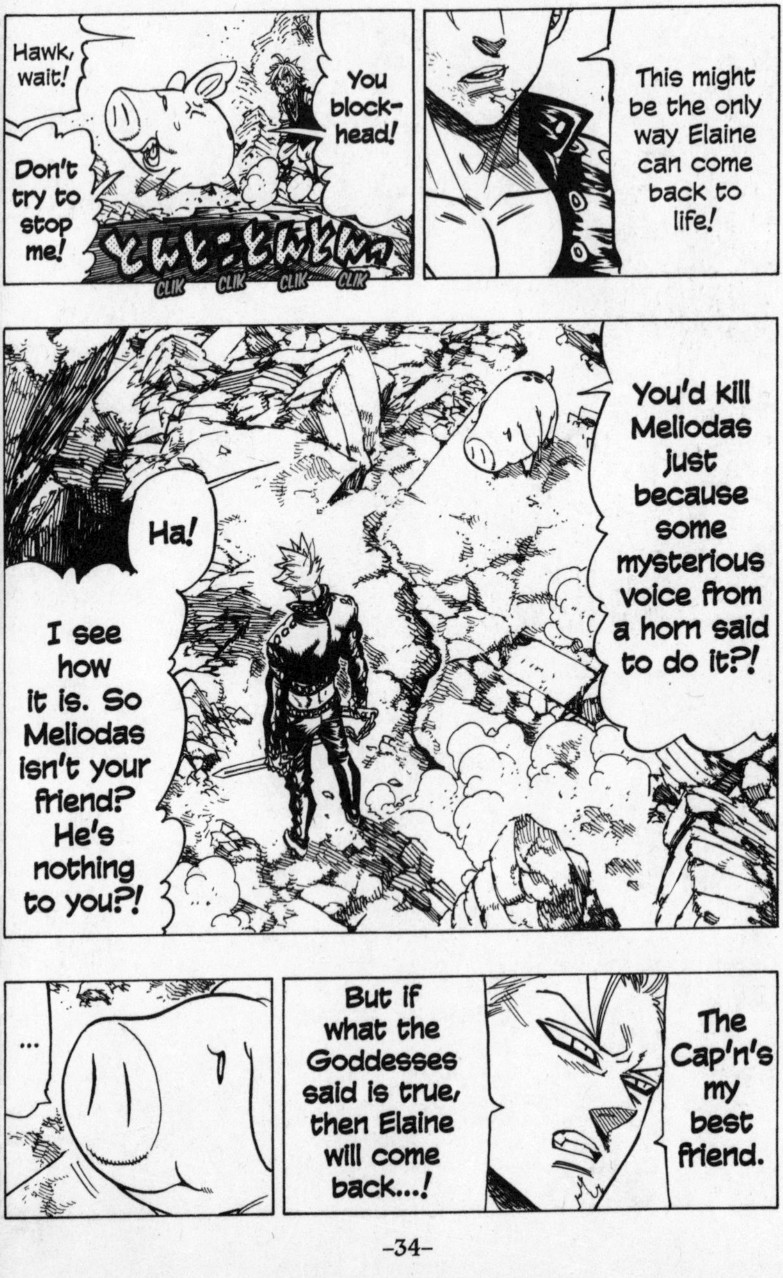
This might be the only way Elaine can come back to life!
You blockhead!
Hawk, wait!
Don't try to stop me!
CLIK CLIK CLIK CLIK
You'd kill Meliodas just because some mysterious voice from a horn said to do it?!
Ha!
I see how it is. So Meliodas isn't your friend? He's nothing to you?!
The Cap'n's my best friend.
But if what the Goddesses said is true, then Elaine will come back...!
...

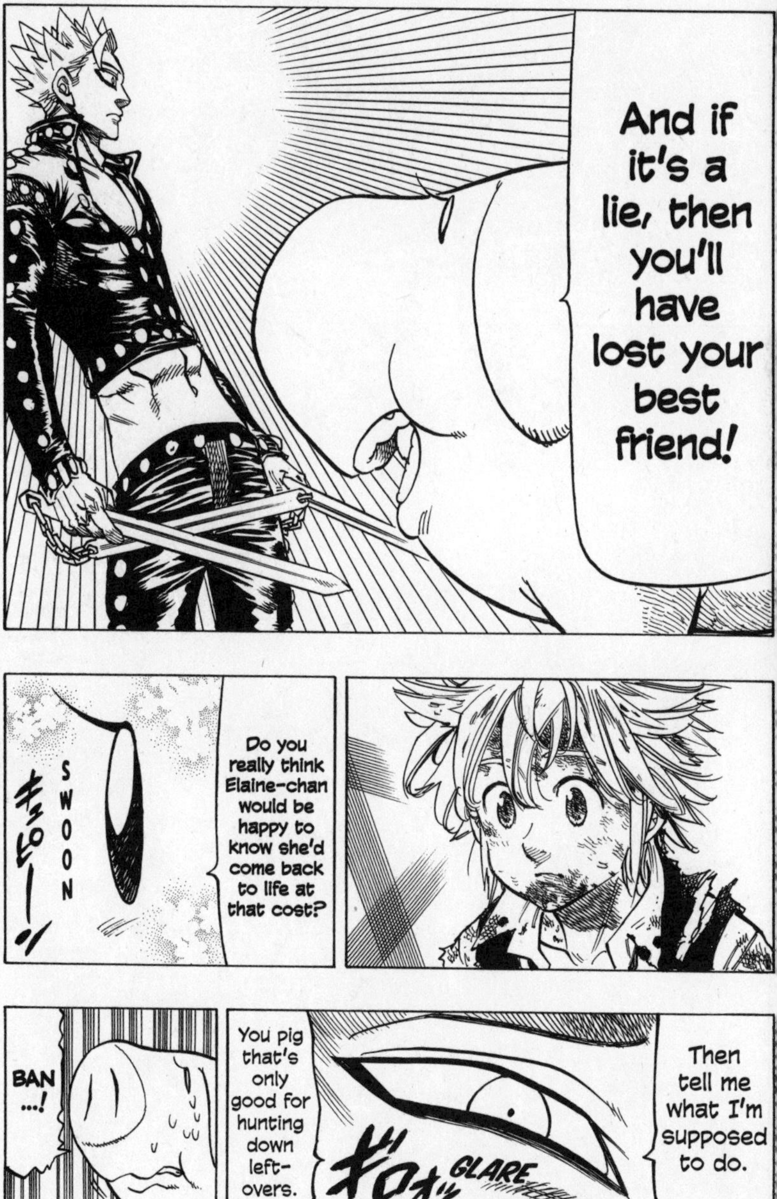
And if it's a lie, then you'll have lost your best friend!
Do you really think Elaine-chan would be happy to know she'd come back to life at that cost?
SWOON
Then tell me what I'm supposed to do.
You pig that's only good for hunting down left-overs.
GLARE
BAN ...!

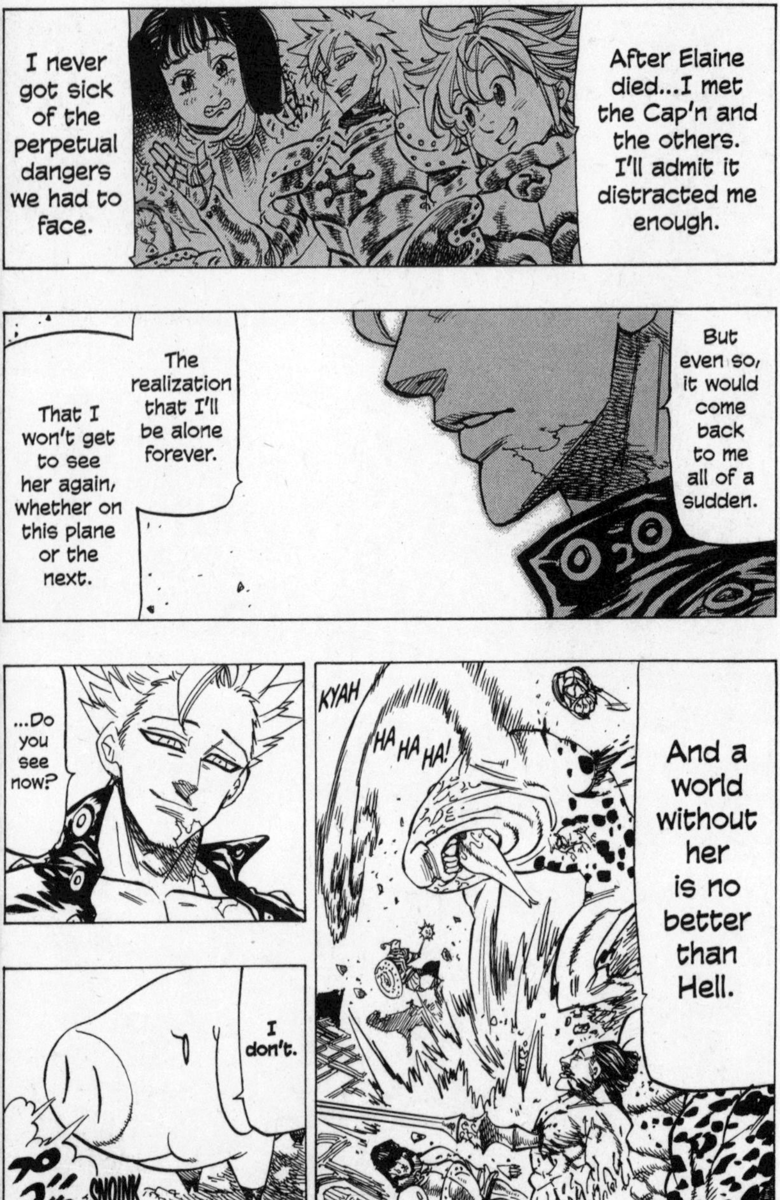
After Elaine died...I met the Cap'n and the others. I'll admit it distracted me enough.
I never got sick of the perpetual dangers we had to face.
But even so, it would come back to me all of a sudden.
The realization that I'll be alone forever.
That I won't get to see her again, whether on this plane or the next.
And a world without her is no better than Hell.
KYAH HA HA HA!
...Do you see now?
I don't.
SNOINK

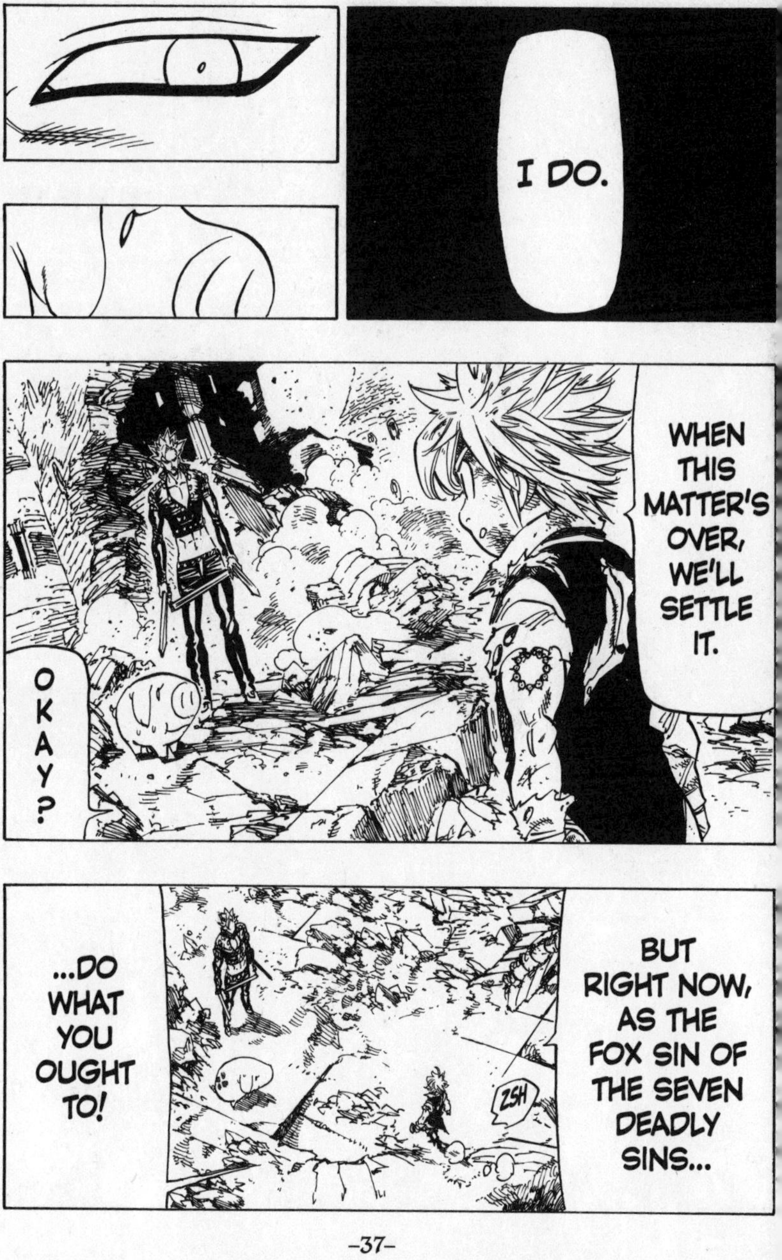
I DO.
WHEN THIS MATTER'S OVER, WE'LL SETTLE IT.
OKAY?
BUT RIGHT NOW, AS THE FOX SIN OF THE SEVEN DEADLY SINS...
ZSH
...DO WHAT YOU OUGHT TO!

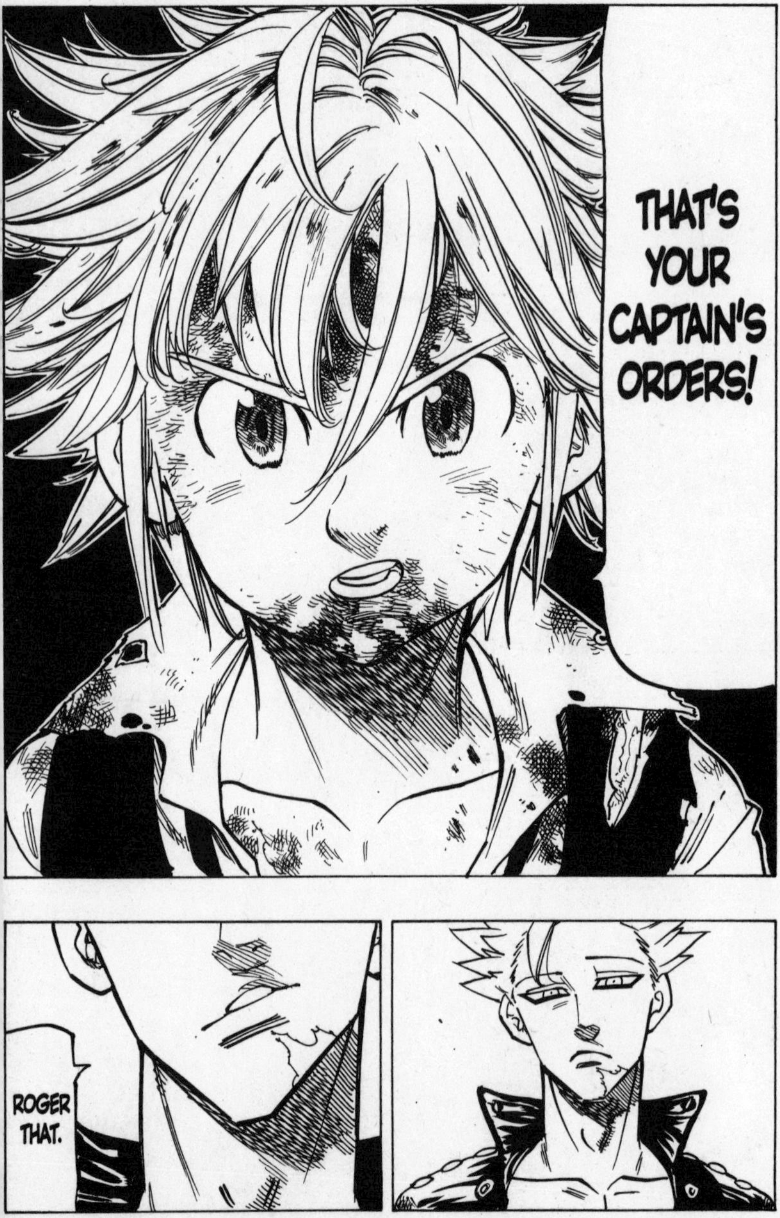
THAT'S YOUR CAPTAIN'S ORDERS!
ROGER THAT.

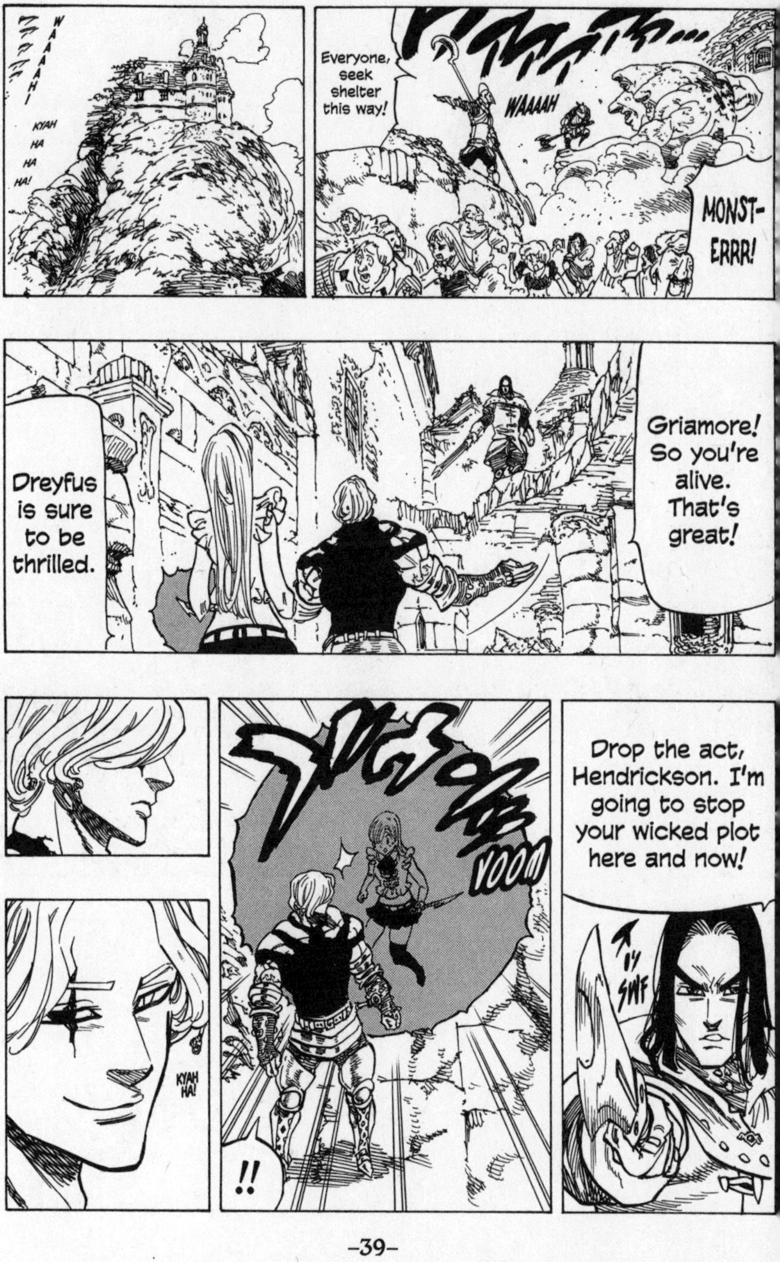
Everyone, seek shelter this way!
WAAAAH
MONST-ERRR!
WAAAAAH!
KYAH HA HA HA!
Griamore! So you're alive. That's great!
Dreyfus is sure to be thrilled.
Drop the act, Hendrickson. I'm going to stop your wicked plot here and now!
SWF
VOOM
!!
KYAH HA!

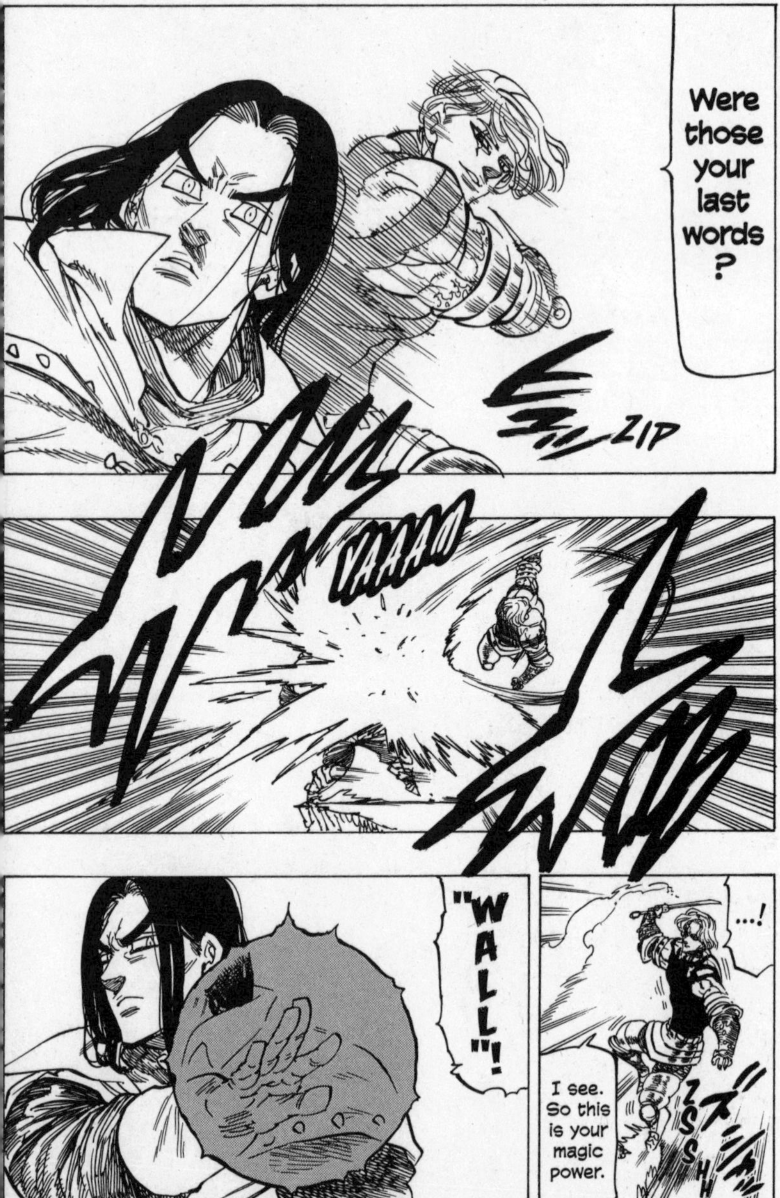
Were those your last words?
ZIP
...!
I see. So this is your magic power.
ZSSH
"WALL"!

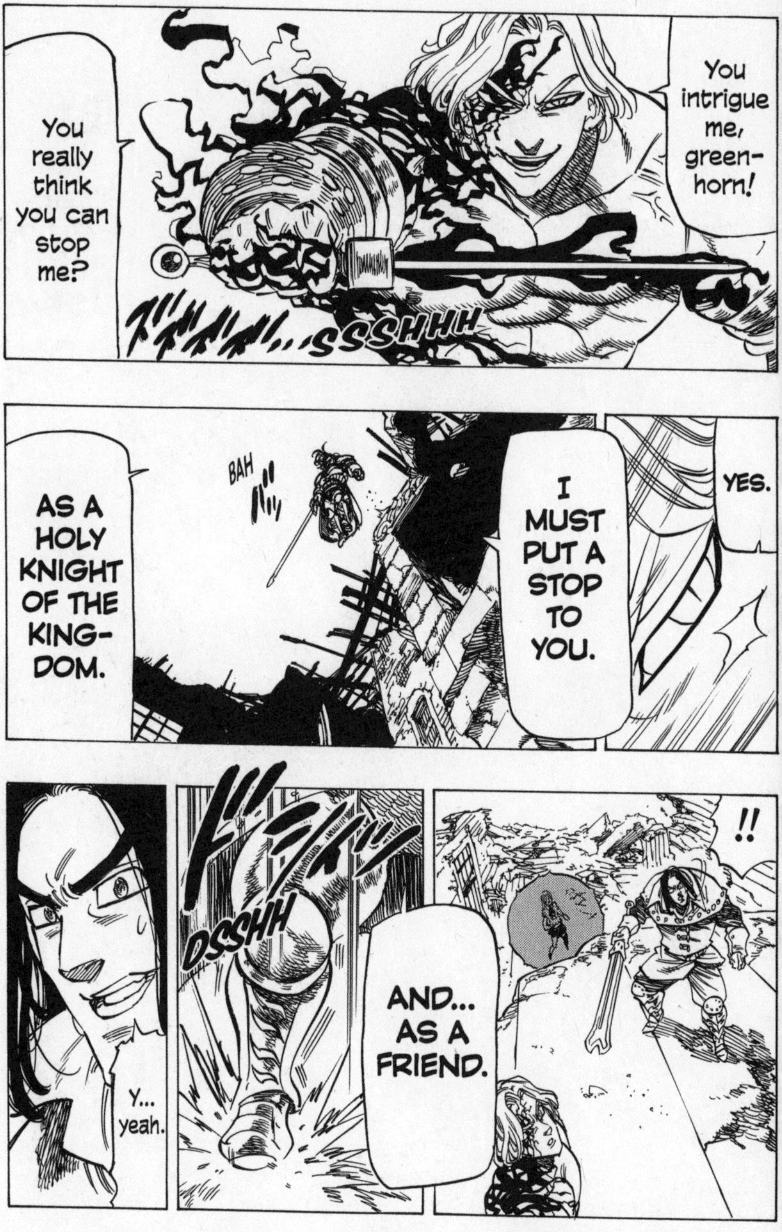
You intrigue me, greenhorn!
You really think you can stop me?
SSSHHH
YES.
I MUST PUT A STOP TO YOU.
BAH
AS A HOLY KNIGHT OF THE KINGDOM.
!!
AND... AS A FRIEND.
DSSHH
Y... yeah.

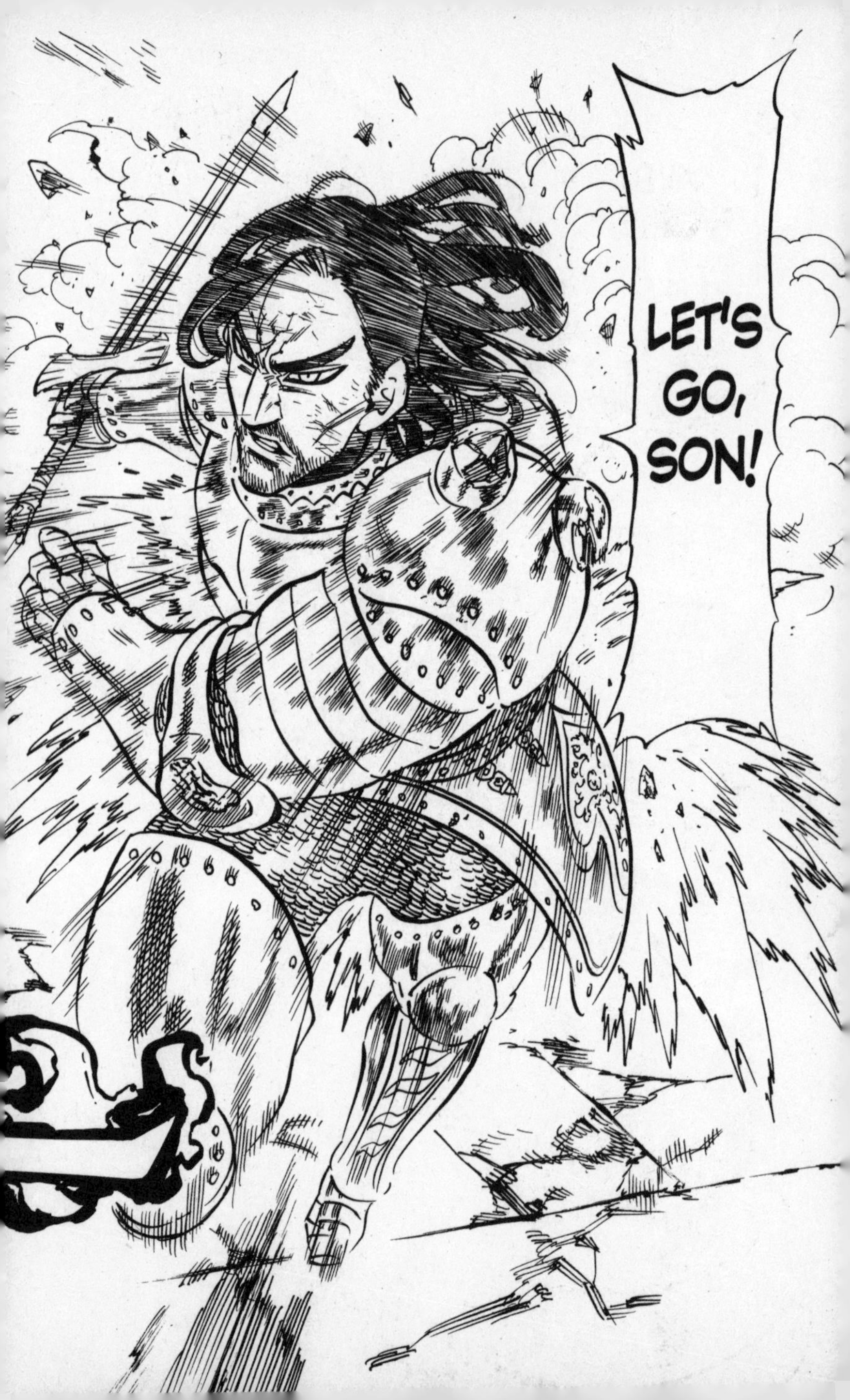
LET'S GO, SON!

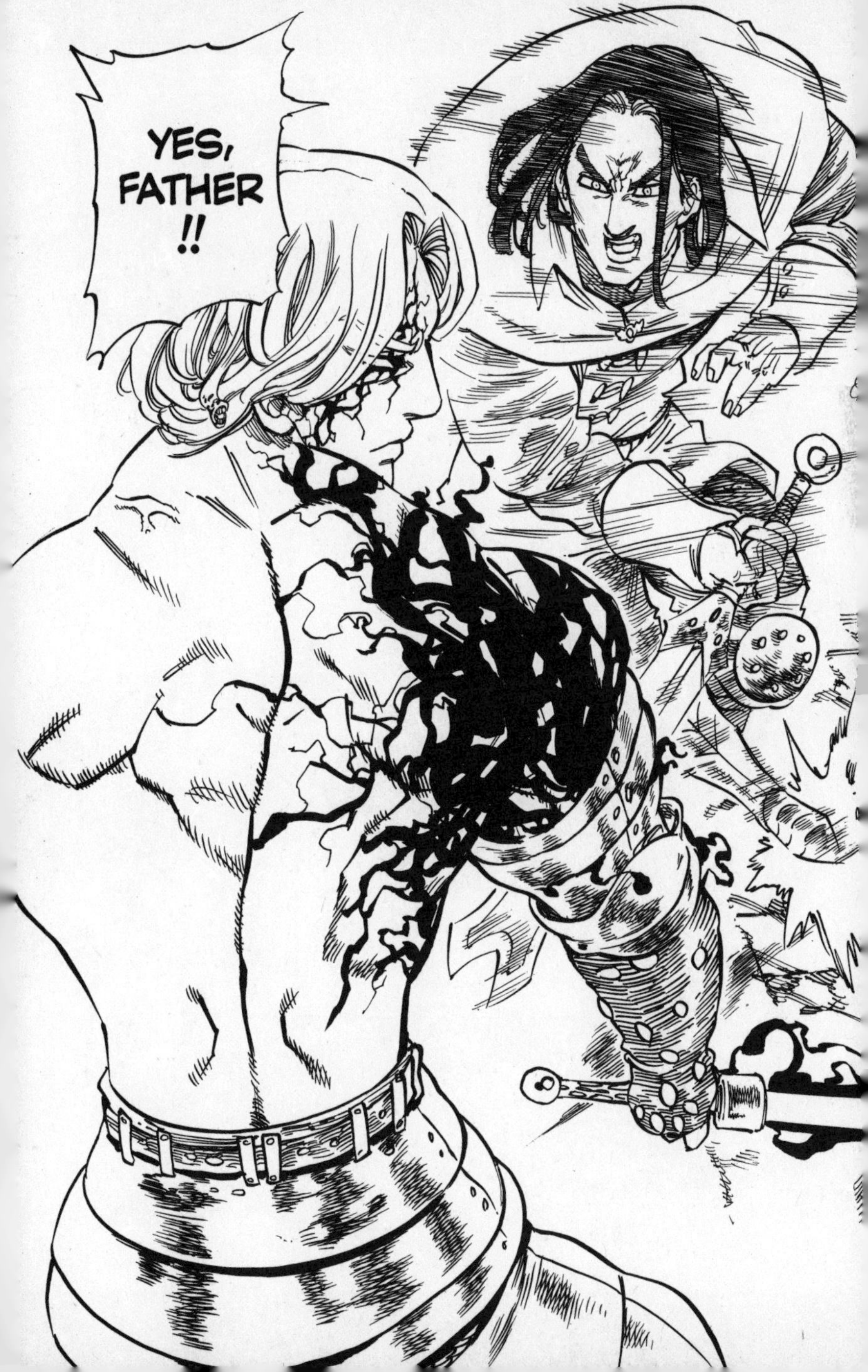
YES, FATHER !!

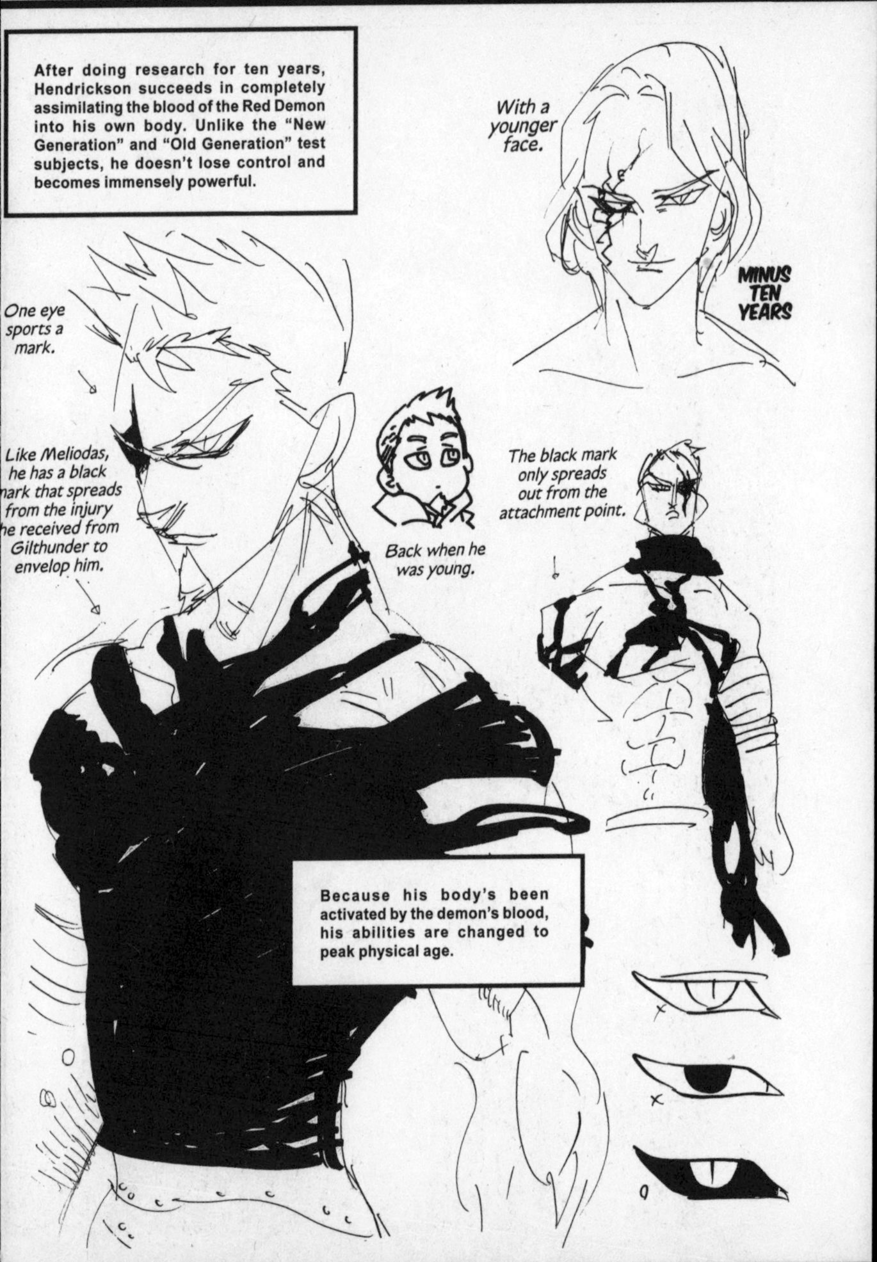
After doing research for ten years, Hendrickson succeeds in completely assimilating the blood of the Red Demon into his own body. Unlike the "New Generation" and "Old Generation" test subjects, he doesn't lose control and becomes immensely powerful.
With a younger face.
MINUS TEN YEARS
One eye sports a mark.
Like Meliodas, he has a black nark that spreads from the injury he received from Gilthunder to envelop him.
Back when he was young.
The black mark only spreads out from the attachment point.
Because his body's been activated by the demon's blood, his abilities are changed to peak physical age.

Chapter 89 - Earnest Hope

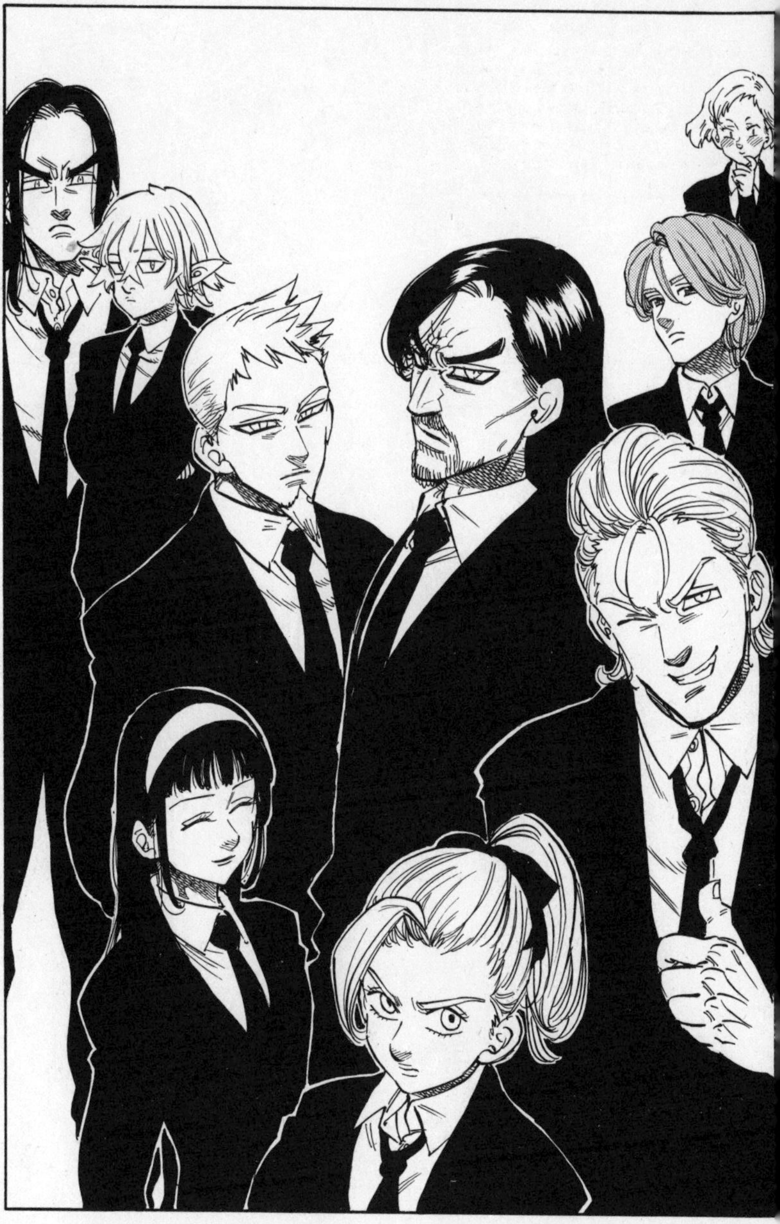

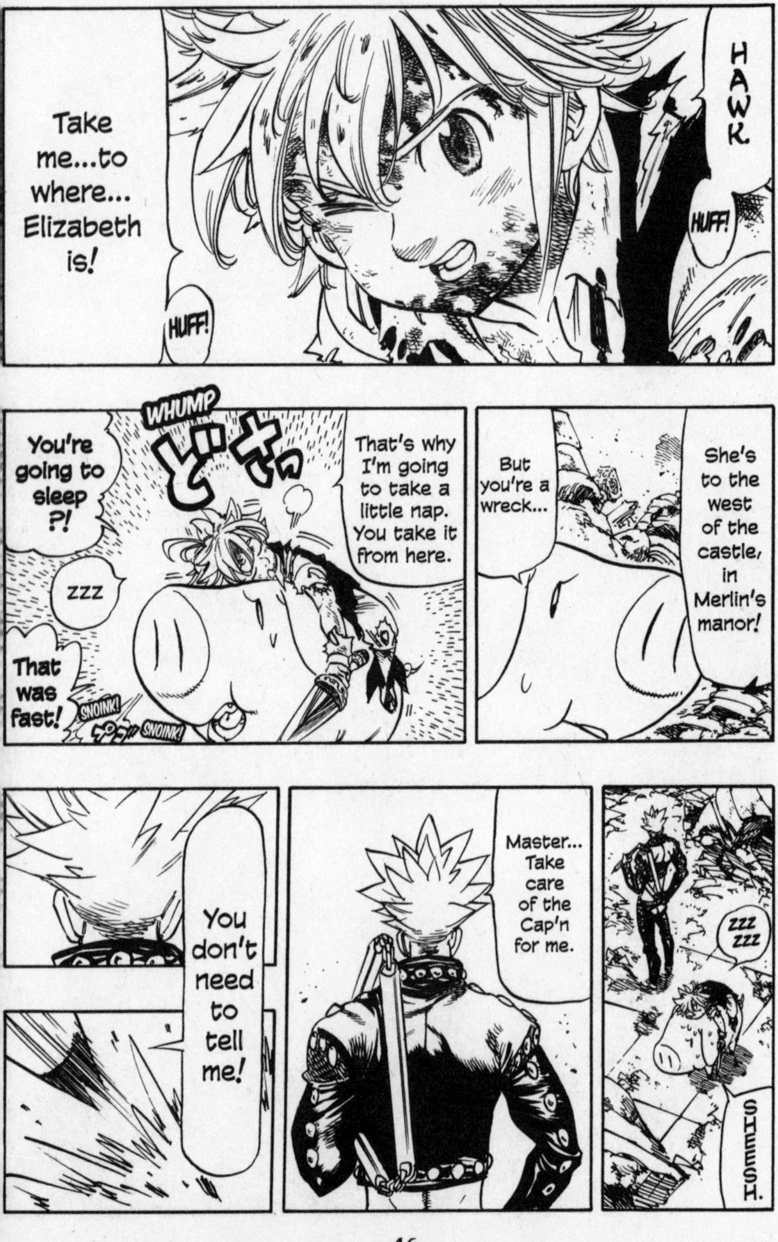
HAWK
HUFF!
Take me...to where... Elizabeth is!
HUFF!
She's to the west of the castle, in Merlin's manor!
But you're a wreck...
That's why I'm going to take a little nap. You take it from here.
WHUMP
You're going to sleep?!
ZZZ
That was fast!
SNOINK!
SNOINK!
ZZZ ZZZ
SHEESH.
Master... Take care of the Cap'n for me.
You don't need to tell me!

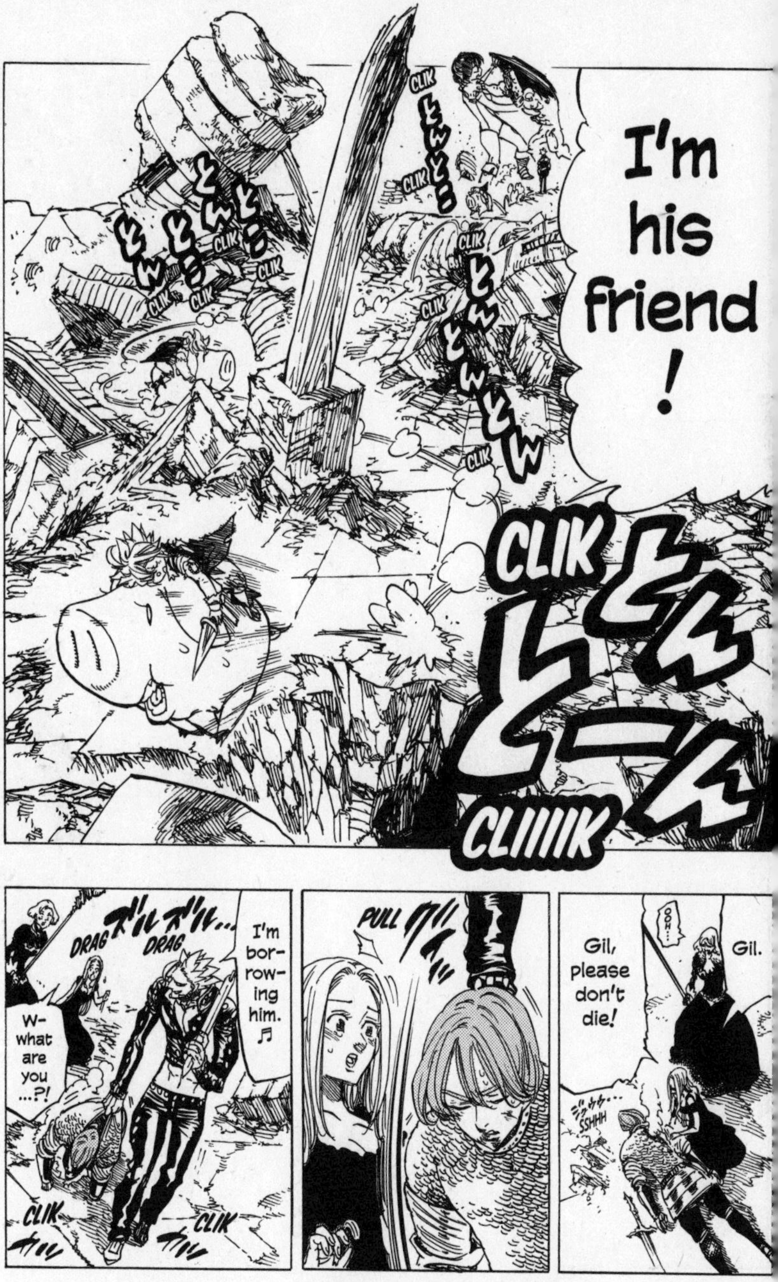
I'm his friend!
CLIK
CLIK
CLIIIIK
Gil.
OOH...
Gil, please don't die!
ジュウウ...
SSHHH
PULL
I'm borrowing him. ♫
DRAG
DRAG
W-what are you ...?!
CLIK
CLIK

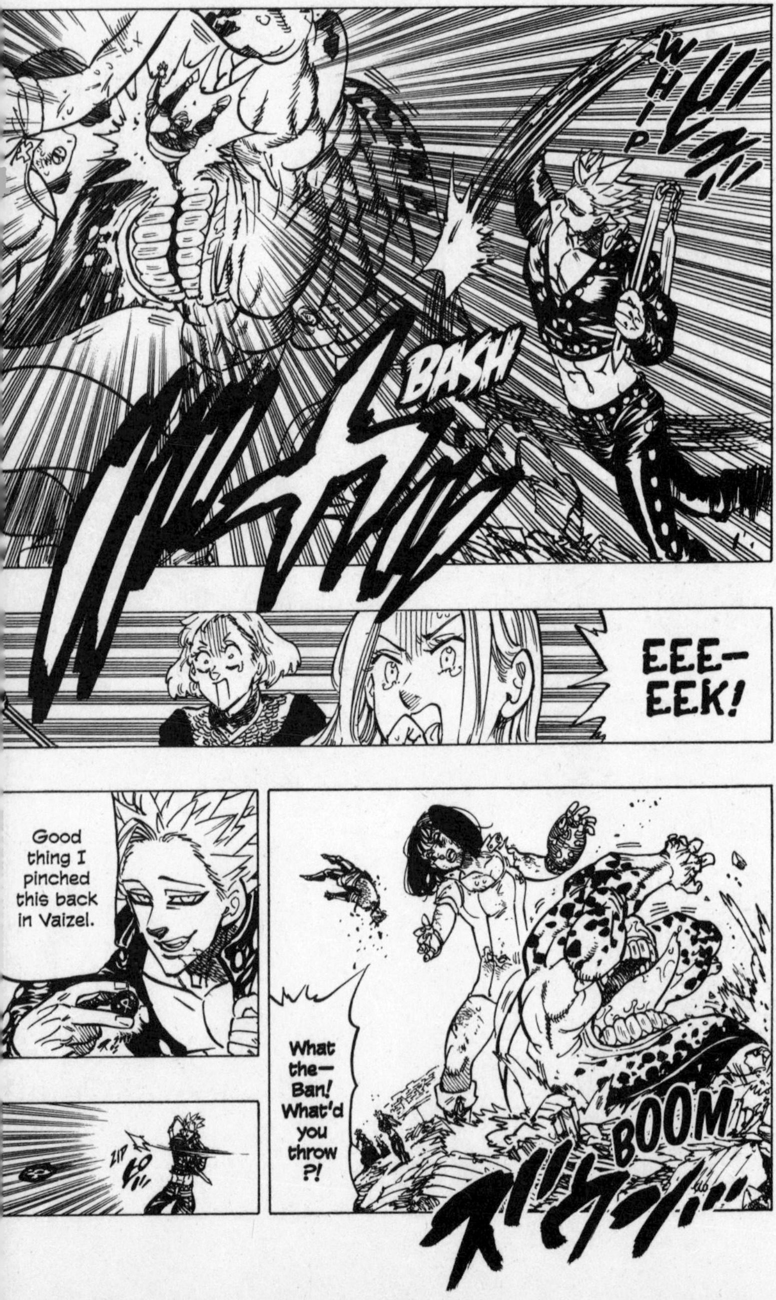
WHIP
BASH
EEE-EEK!
What the— Ban! What'd you throw?!
BOOM
Good thing I pinched this back in Vaizel.
ZIP

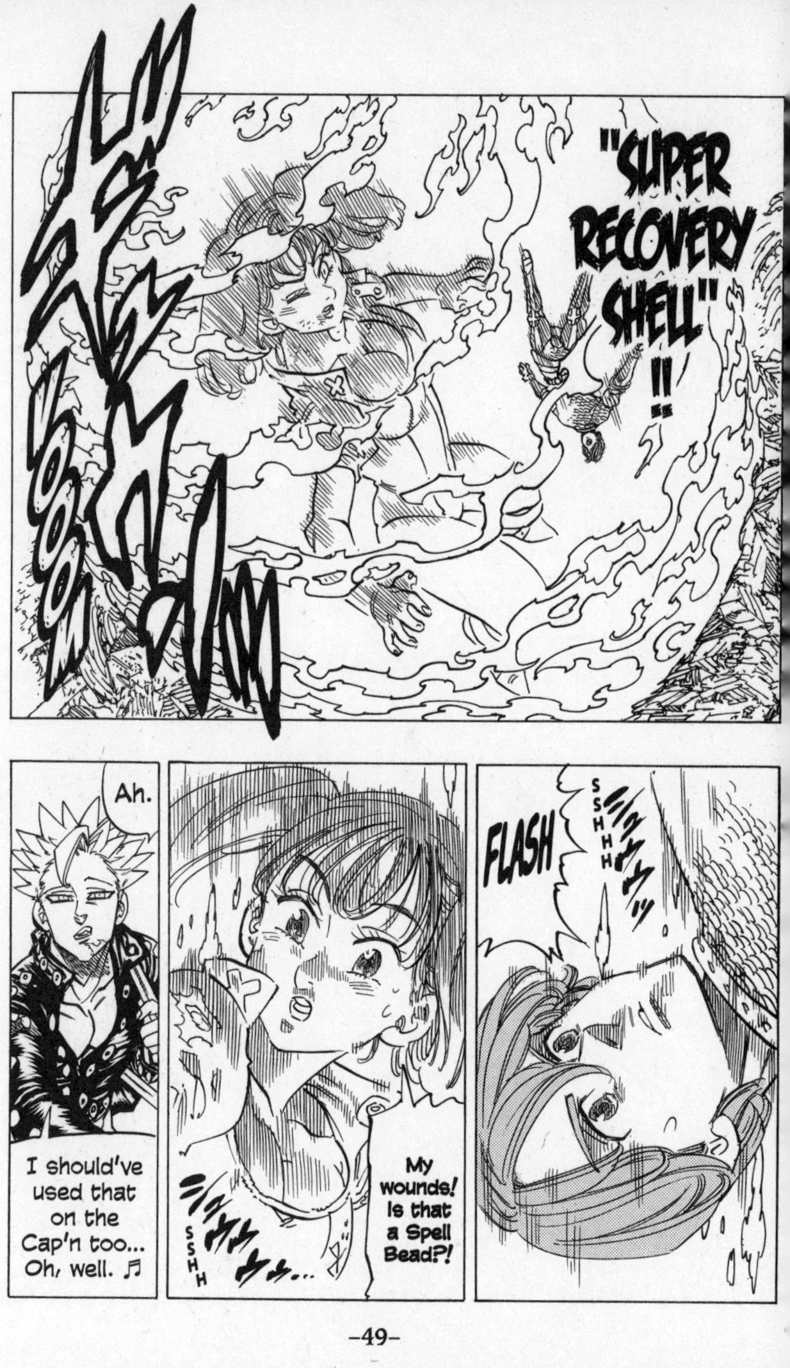
"SUPER RECOVERY SHELL"!!
FLASH
SSHHH
My wounds! Is that a Spell Bead?!
SSHH
Ah.
I should've used that on the Cap'n too... Oh, well. ♬

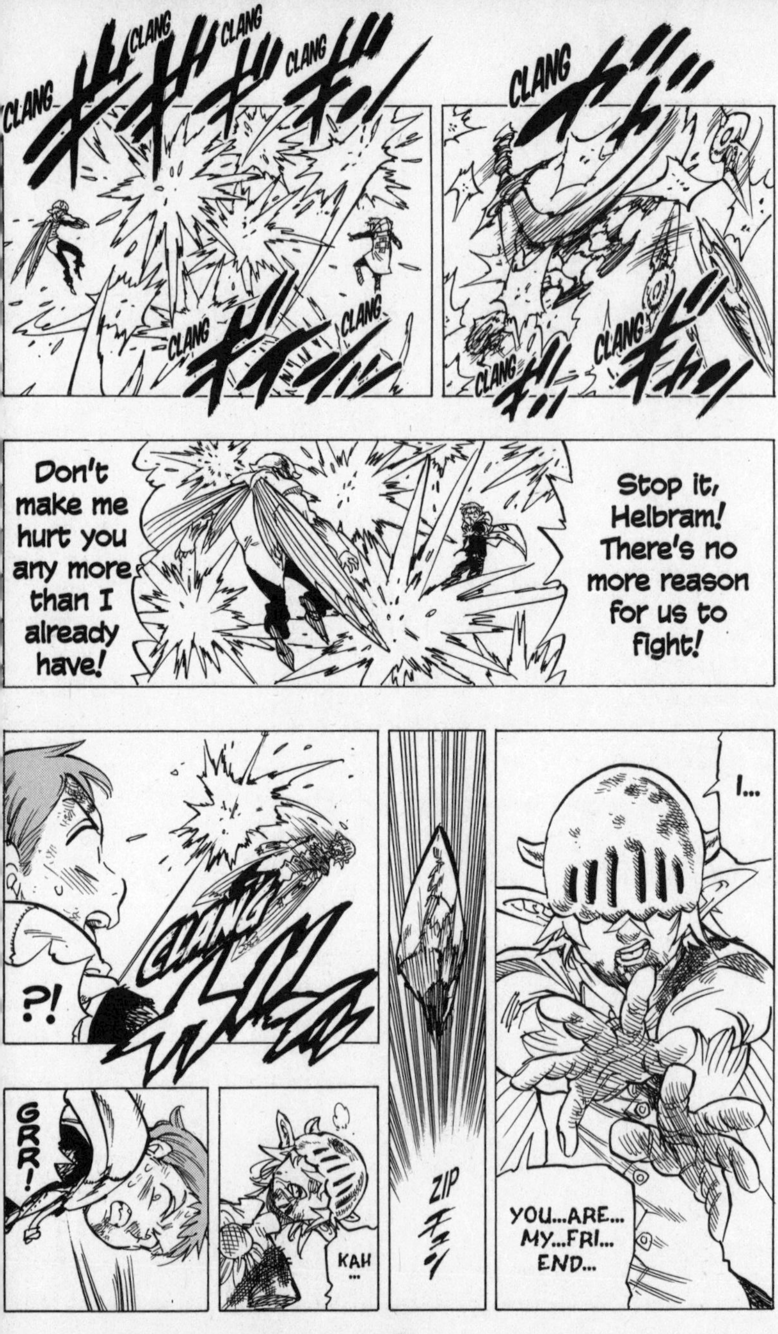
CLANG
CLANG
CLANG
CLANG
CLANG
CLANG
CLANG
CLANG
CLANG
CLANG
Stop it, Helbram! There's no more reason for us to fight!
Don't make me hurt you any more than I already have!
I...
YOU...ARE... MY...FRI... END...
ZIP
CLANG
?!
KAH...
GRR!

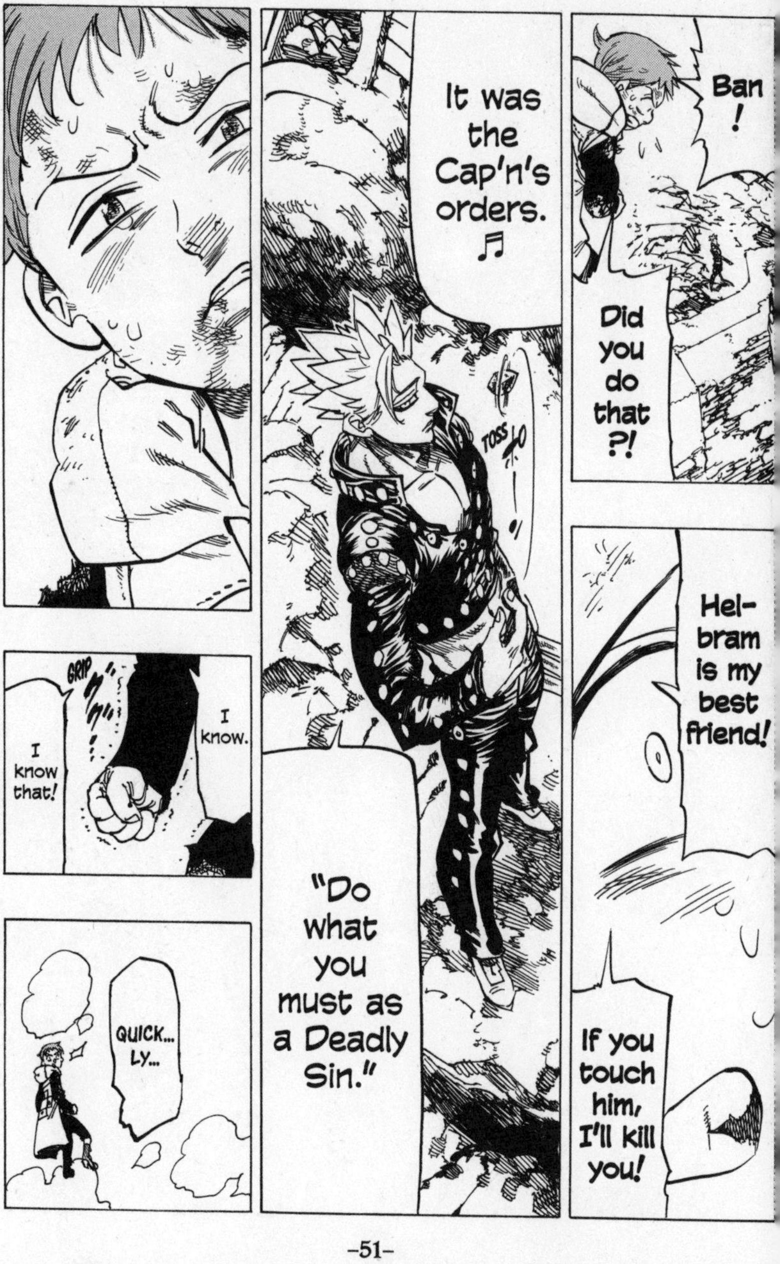
Ban!
Did you do that?!
Hel-bram is my best friend!
If you touch him, I'll kill you!
It was the Cap'n's orders. ♬
TOSS
"Do what you must as a Deadly Sin."
GRIP
I know.
I know that!
QUICK... LY...

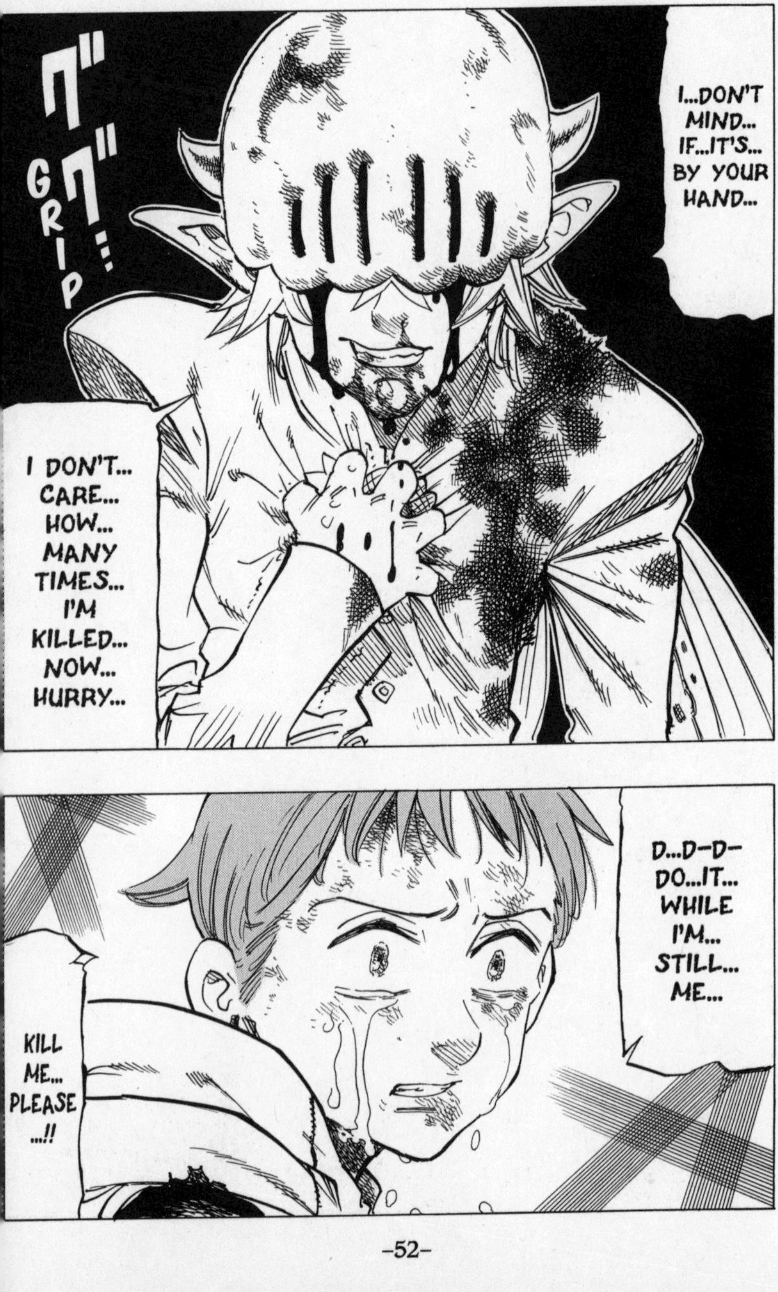
I...DON'T MIND... IF...IT'S... BY YOUR HAND...
I DON'T... CARE... HOW... MANY TIMES... I'M KILLED... NOW... HURRY...
GRIP
D...D-D-DO...IT... WHILE I'M... STILL... ME...
KILL ME... PLEASE ...!!

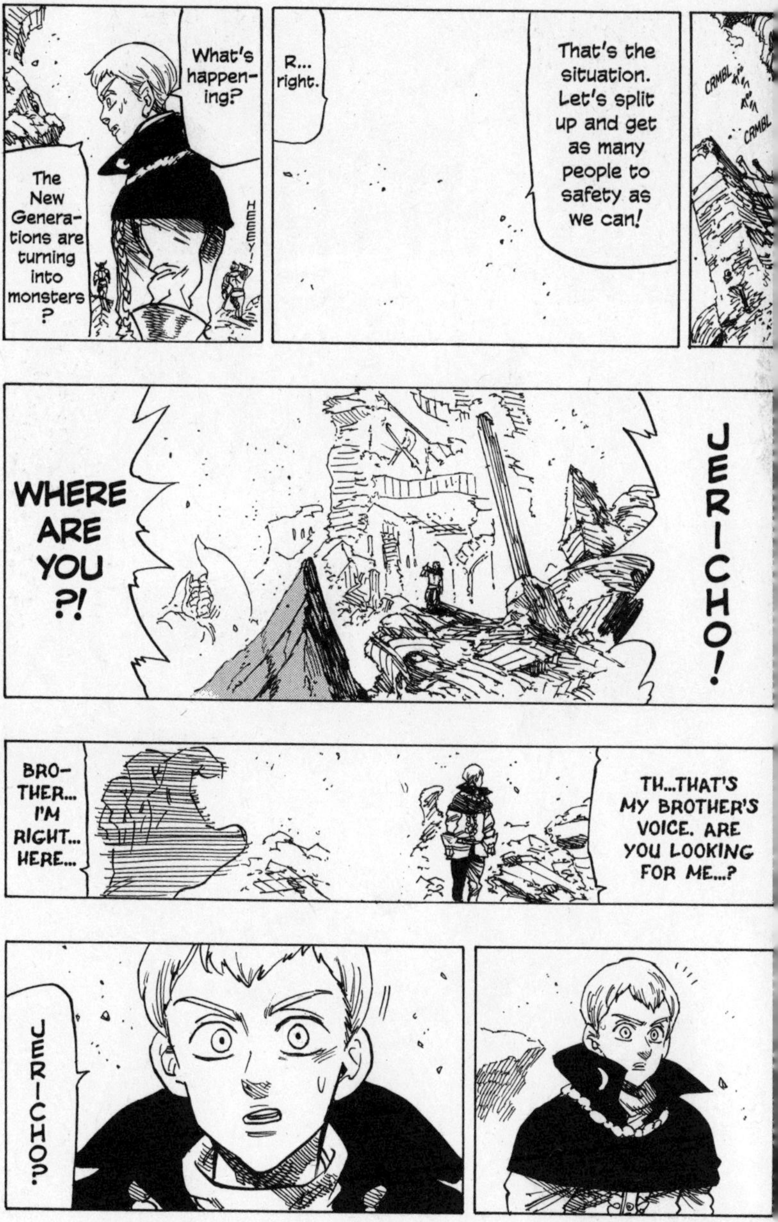
CRMBL
CRMBL
That's the situation. Let's split up and get as many people to safety as we can!
R... right.
What's happening?
HEEEY!
The New Generations are turning into monsters?
JERICHO!
WHERE ARE YOU?!
TH...THAT'S MY BROTHER'S VOICE. ARE YOU LOOKING FOR ME...?
BRO-THER... I'M RIGHT... HERE...
JERICHO?

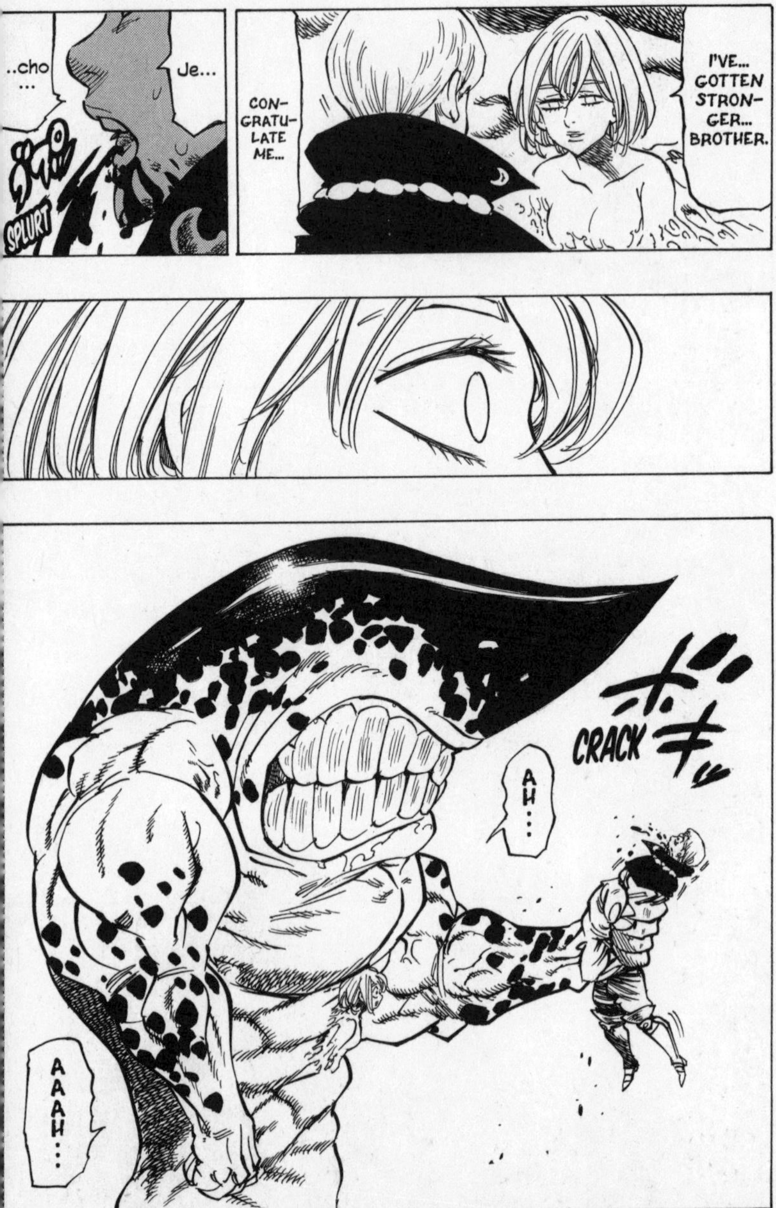
I'VE... GOTTEN STRONGER... BROTHER.
CONGRATULATE ME...
Je...
..cho ...
SPLURT
CRACK
AH...
AAAH...

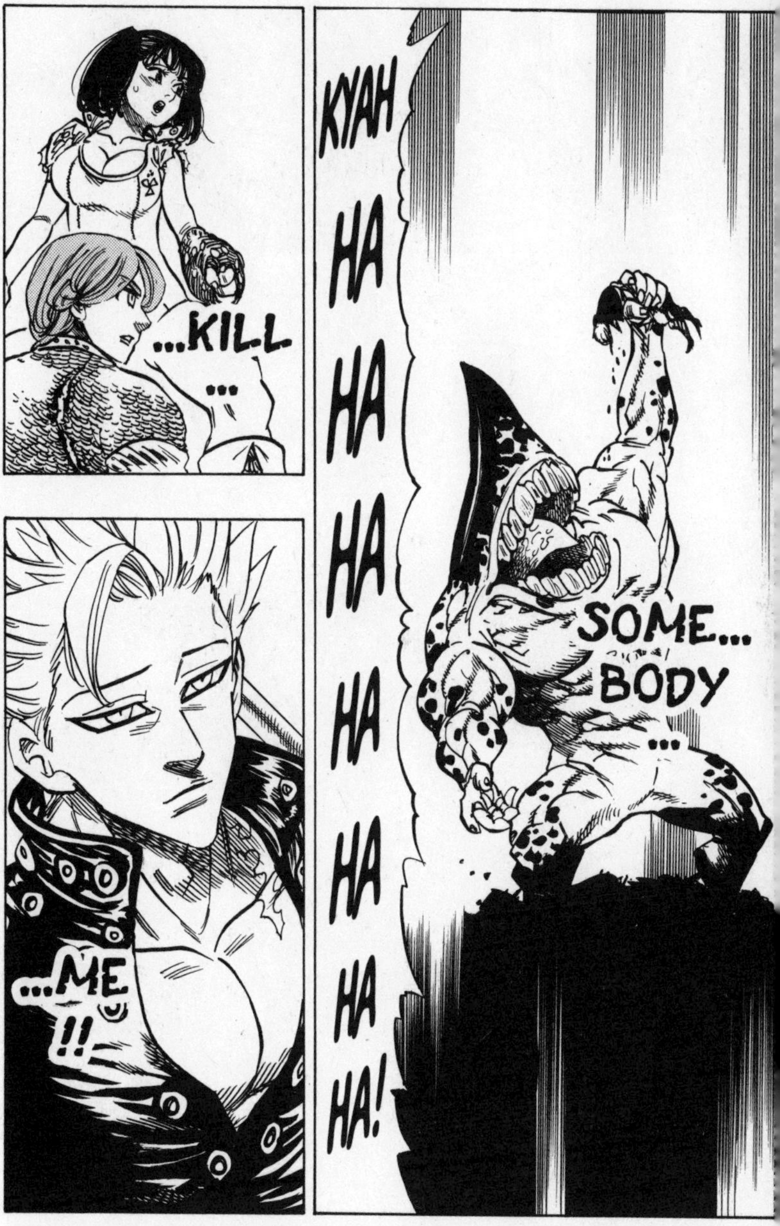
KYAH HA HA HA HA HA HA HA HA!
SOME... BODY...
...KILL...
...ME!!

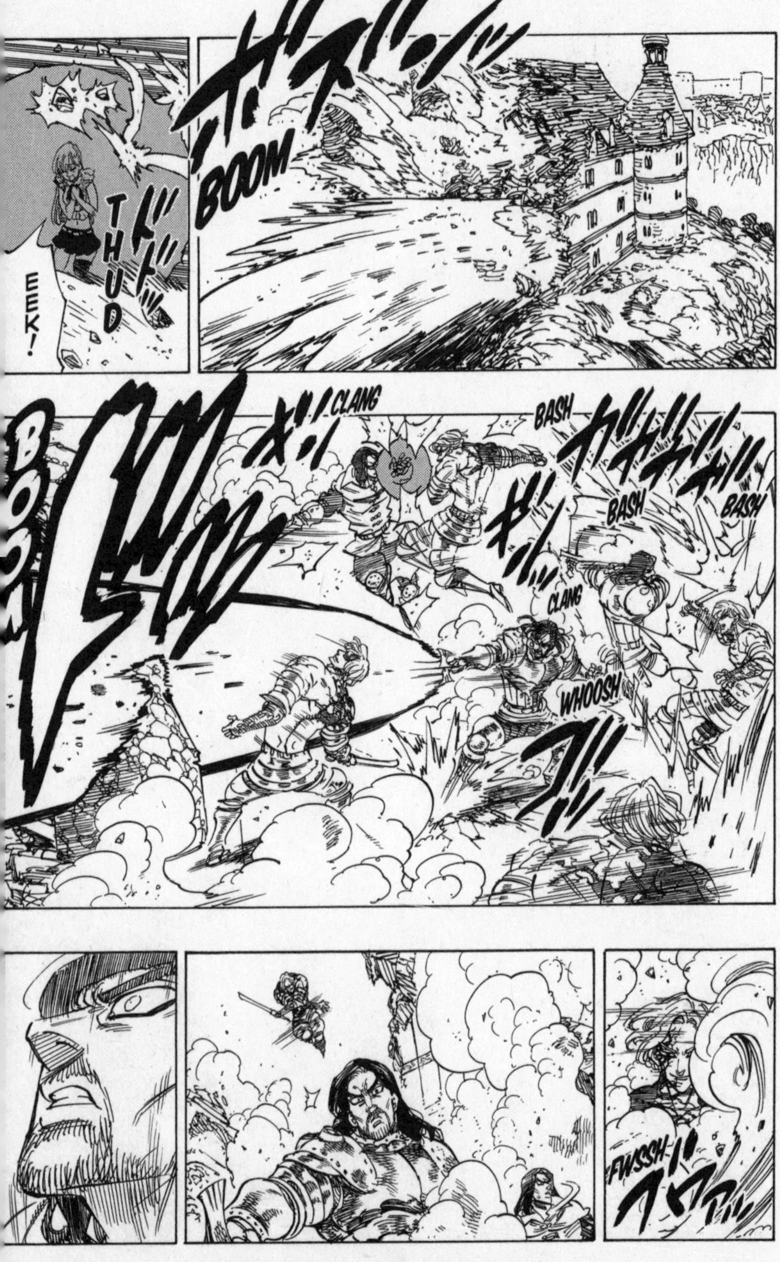
BOOM
THUD
EEK!
BASH
BASH
BASH
CLANG
CLANG
WHOOSH
BOOM
FWSSH

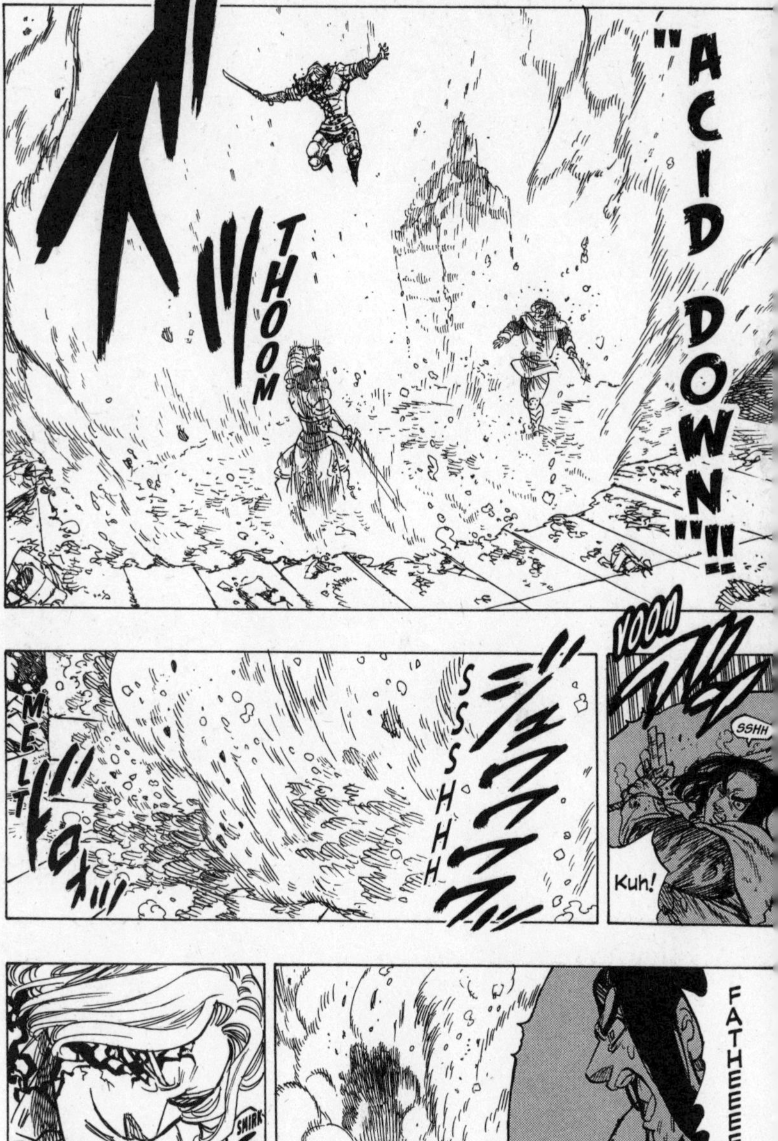
"ACID DOWN"!!
THOOOM
VOOM
SSHH
Kuh!
SSSHHH
MELT
FATHEEEER!!
SHIRK

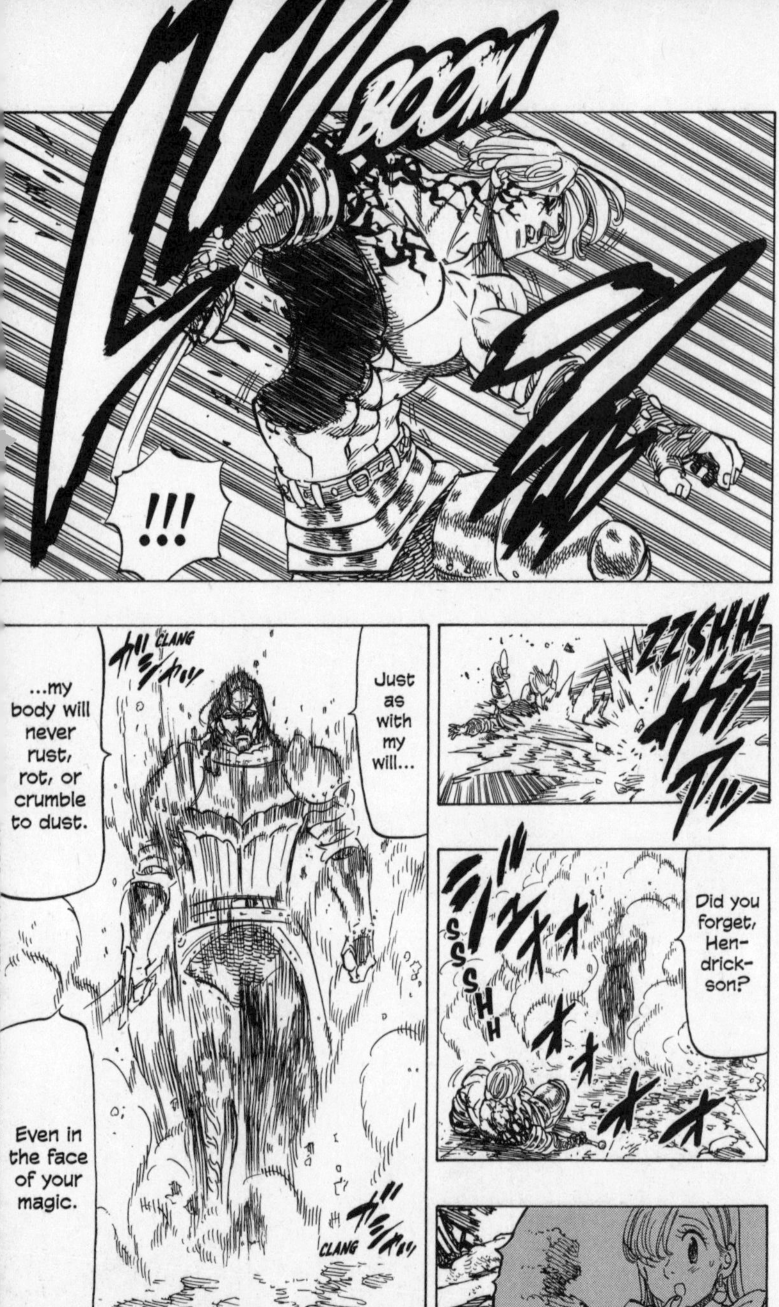
BOOM
!!!
ZZSHH
SSSHH
Did you forget, Hendrickson?
CLANG
Just as with my will...
...my body will never rust, rot, or crumble to dust.
Even in the face of your magic.
CLANG

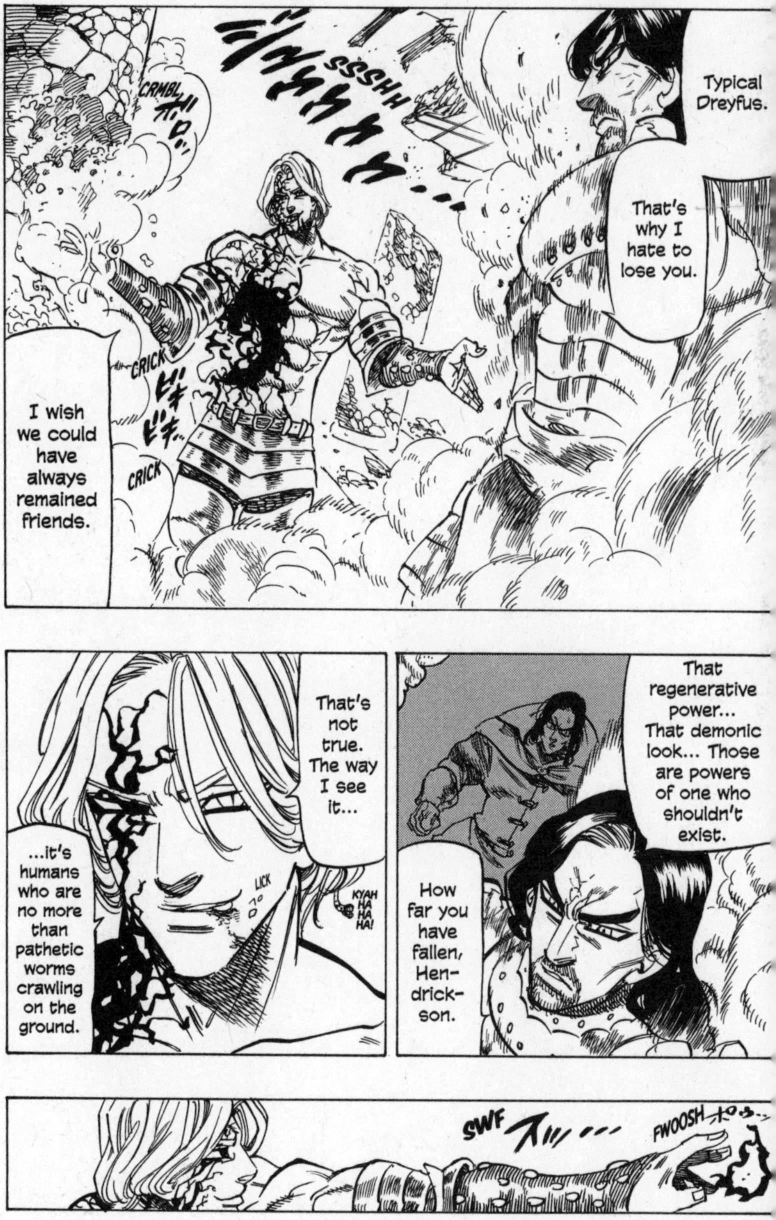
Typical Dreyfus.
That's why I hate to lose you.
HSSSH
CRMBL
CRICK
CRICK
I wish we could have always remained friends.
That regenerative power... That demonic look... Those are powers of one who shouldn't exist.
How far you have fallen, Hendrickson.
That's not true. The way I see it...
KYAH HA HA HA!
LICK
...it's humans who are no more than pathetic worms crawling on the ground.
FWOOSH
SWF

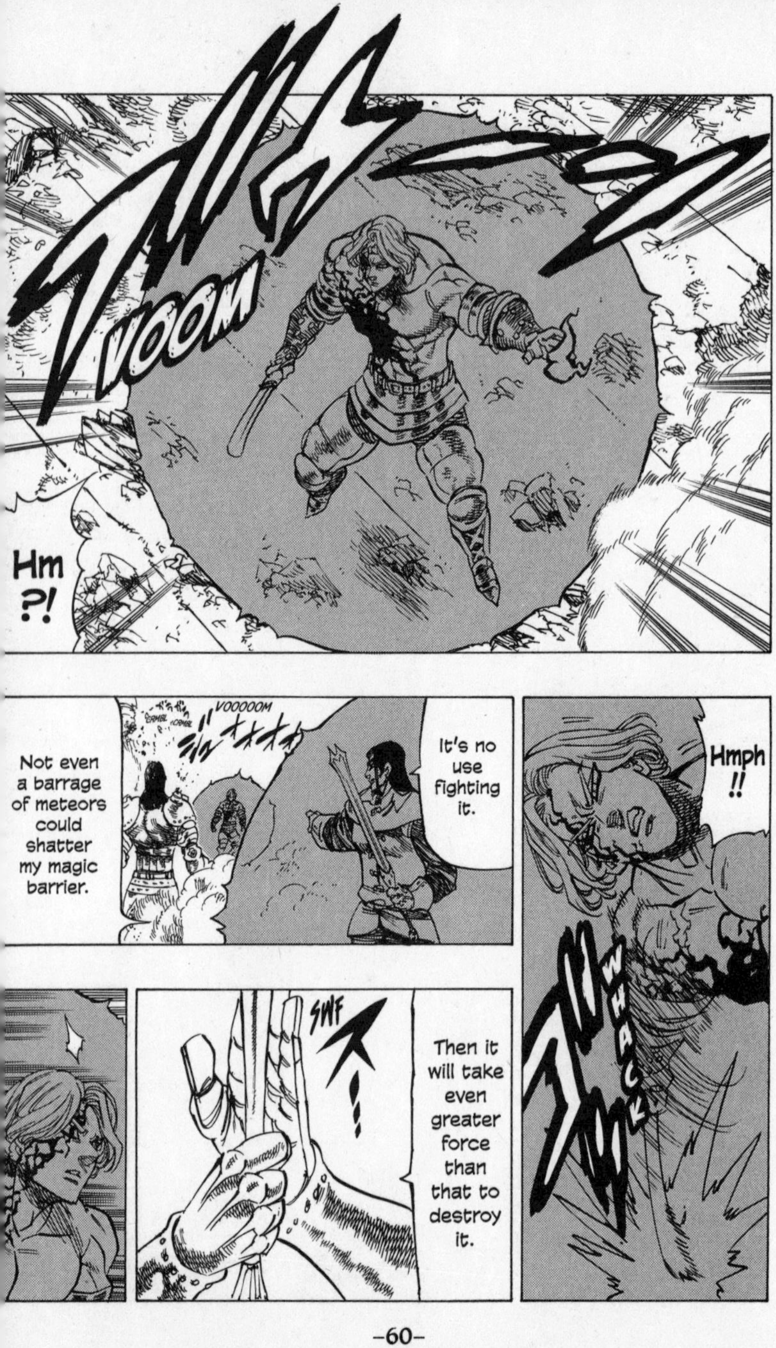
VOOM
Hm ?!
Hmph !!
WHACK
It's no use fighting it.
VOOOOOM
CRMBL CRMBL
Not even a barrage of meteors could shatter my magic barrier.
SWF
Then it will take even greater force than that to destroy it.

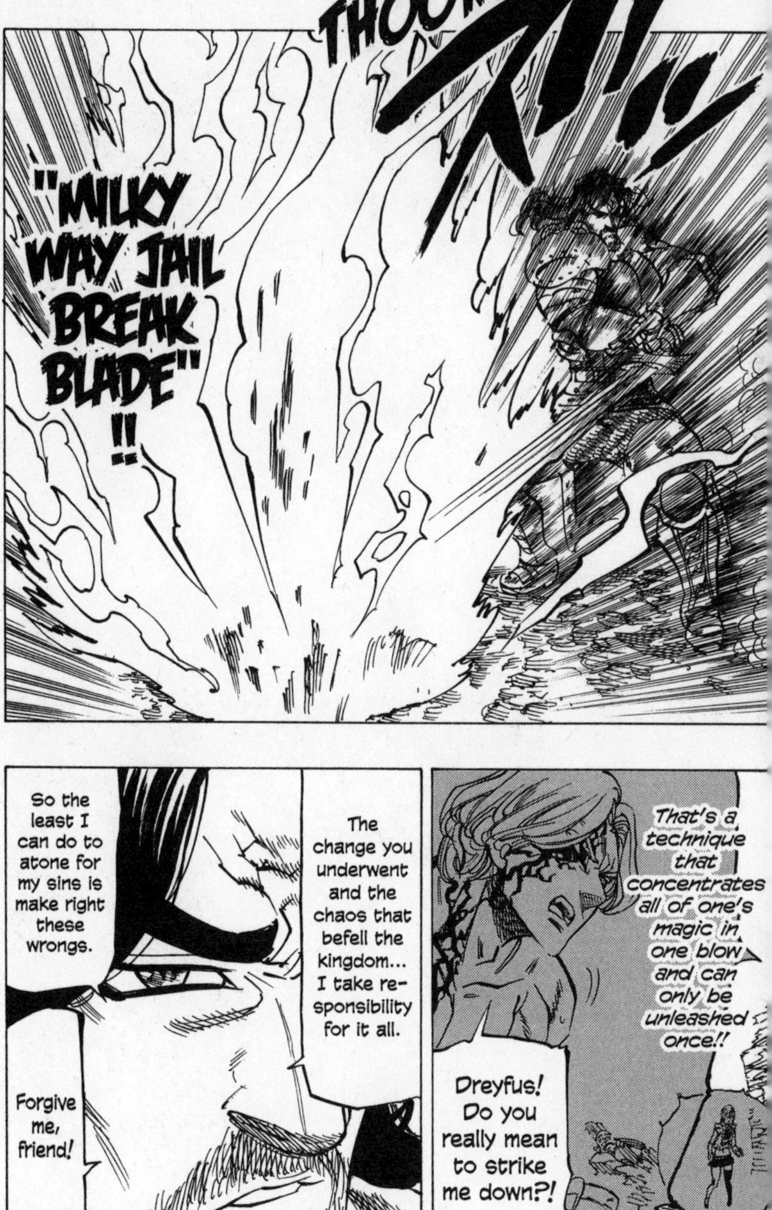
THOOM
"MILKY WAY JAIL BREAK BLADE"!!
That's a technique that concentrates all of one's magic in one blow and can only be unleashed once!!
Dreyfus! Do you really mean to strike me down?!
The change you underwent and the chaos that befell the kingdom... I take responsibility for it all.
So the least I can do to atone for my sins is make right these wrongs.
Forgive me, friend!

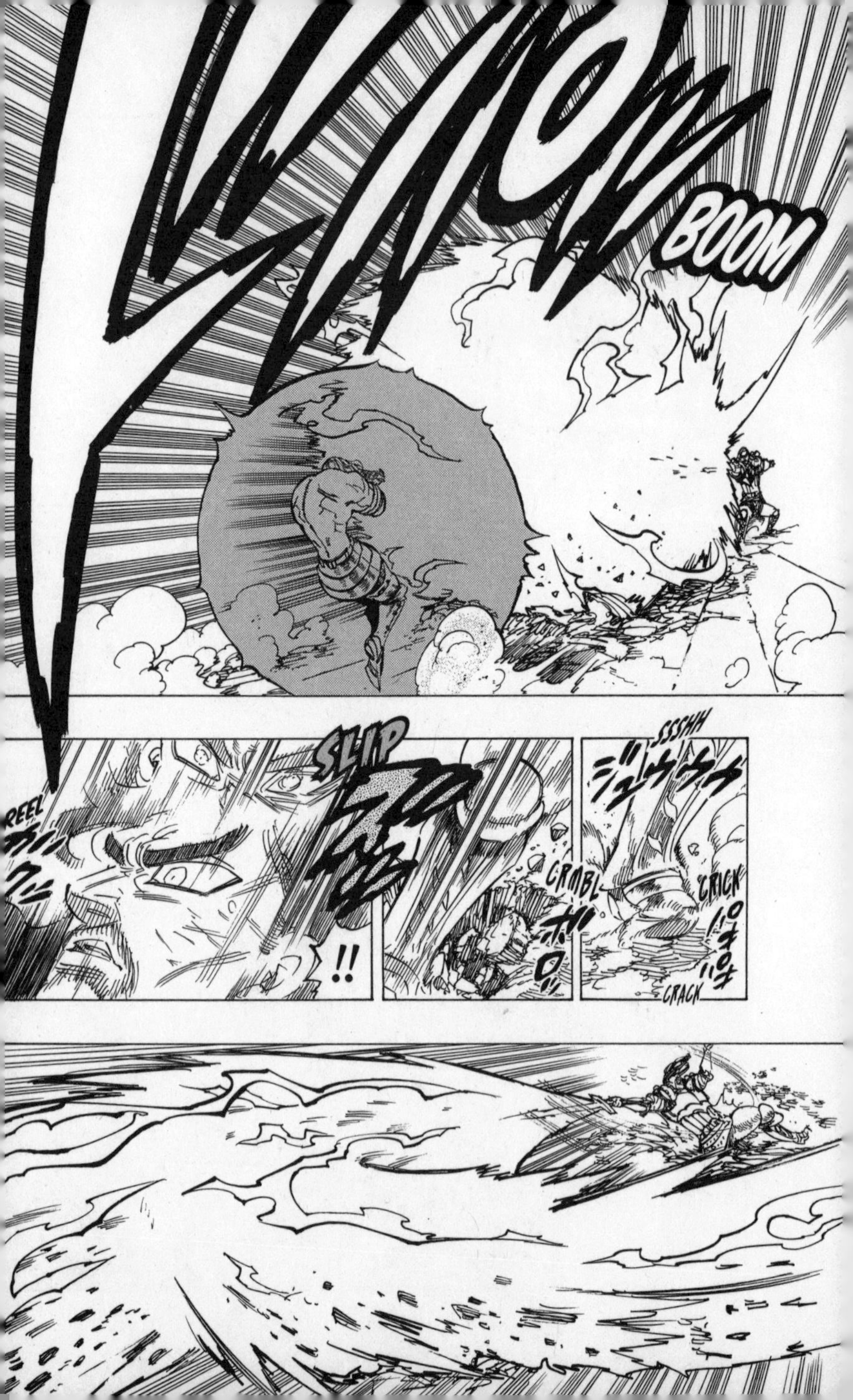
BOOM
SSSHH
CRICK
CRACK
CRMBL
SLIP
REEL
!!

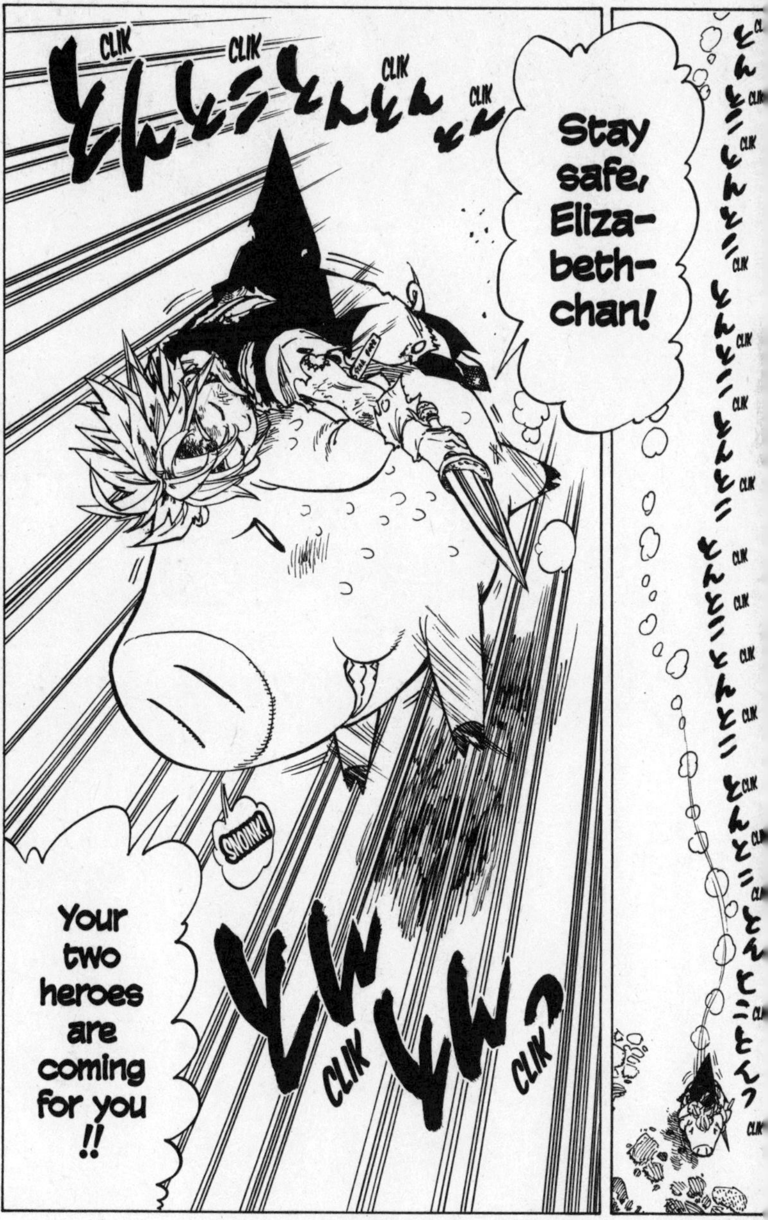
CLIK
CLIK
CLIK
Stay safe, Eliza-beth-chan!
SNOINK!
CLIK
CLIK
Your two heroes are coming for you!!

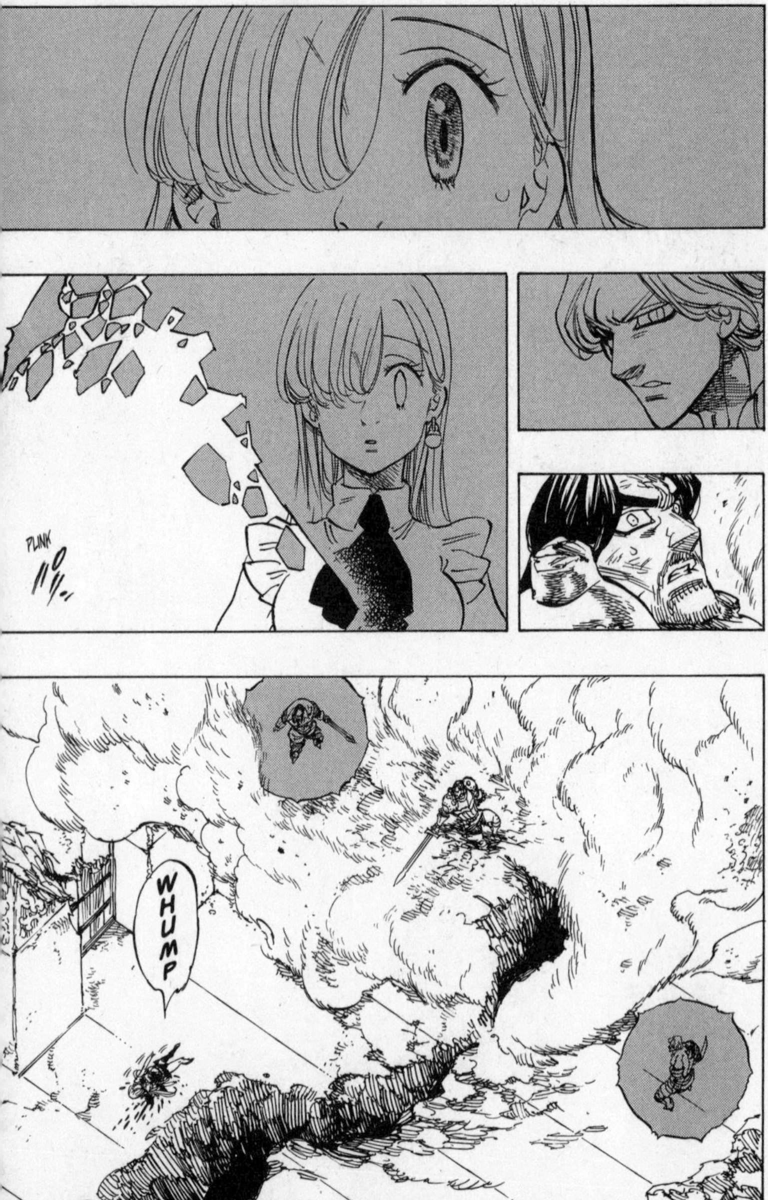
PLINK
WHUMP

Chapter 90 - What I Can Do For You

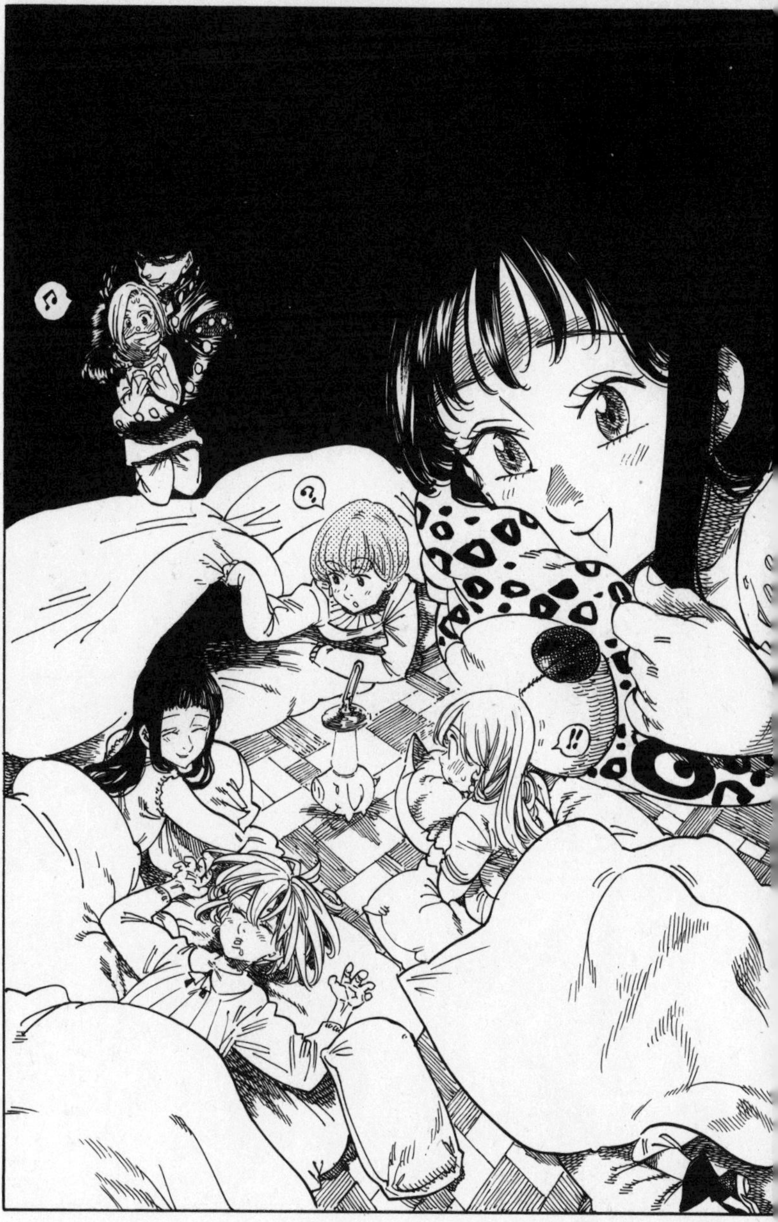
♫
?
!!

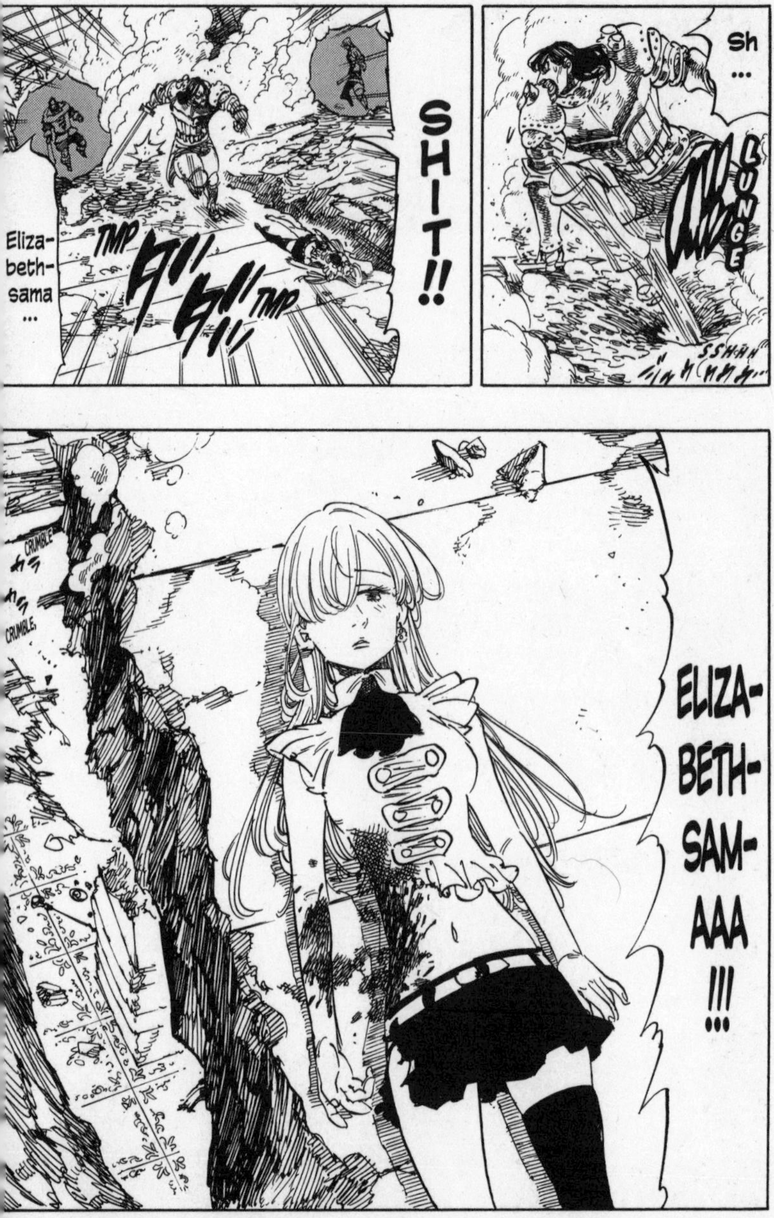
Sh
...
LUNGE
SSHAAN
SHIT!!
TMP
TMP
Eliza-beth-sama
...
ELIZA-BETH-SAM-AAA
!!!
CRUMBLE
CRUMBLE

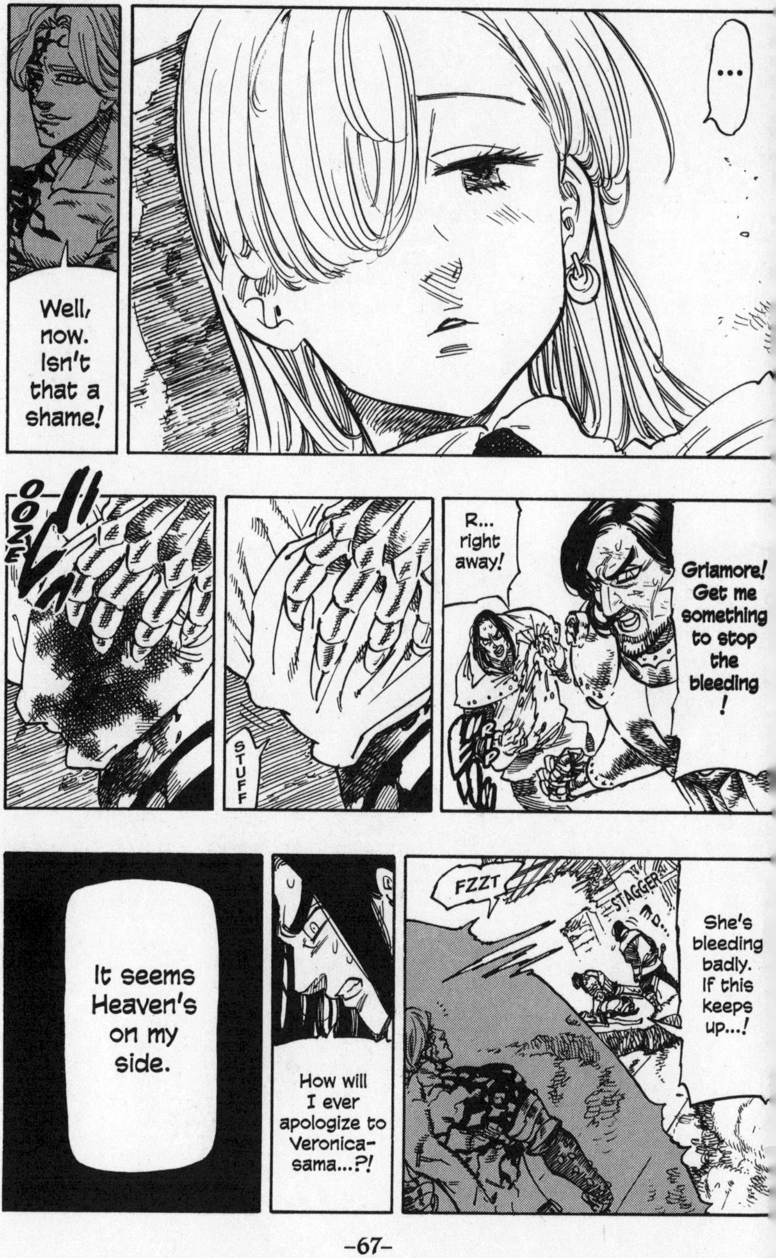
...
Well, now. Isn't that a shame!
Griamore! Get me something to stop the bleeding!
R... right away!
RIP
STUFF
OOZE
She's bleeding badly. If this keeps up...!
STAGGER
FZZT
How will I ever apologize to Veronica-sama...?!
It seems Heaven's on my side.

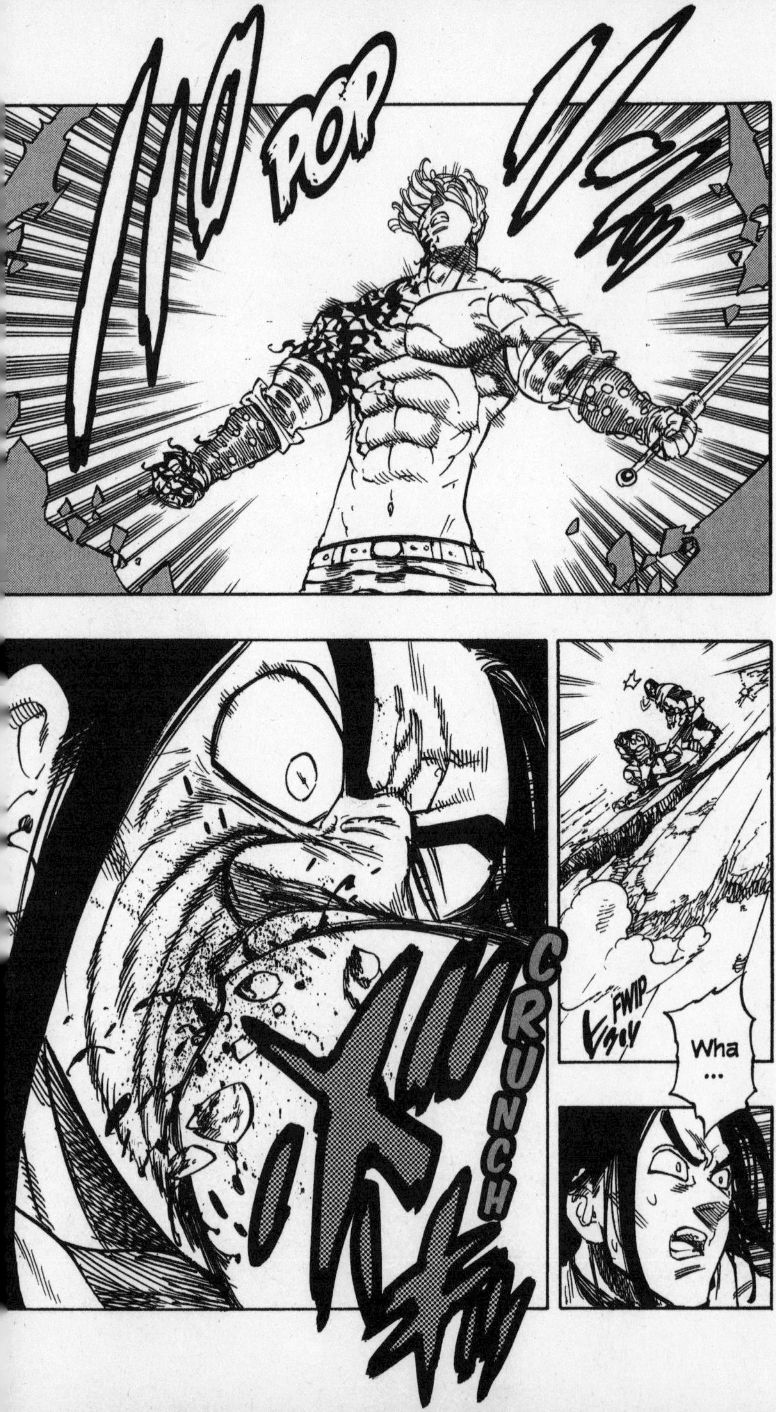
POP
FWIP
Wha...
CRUNCH

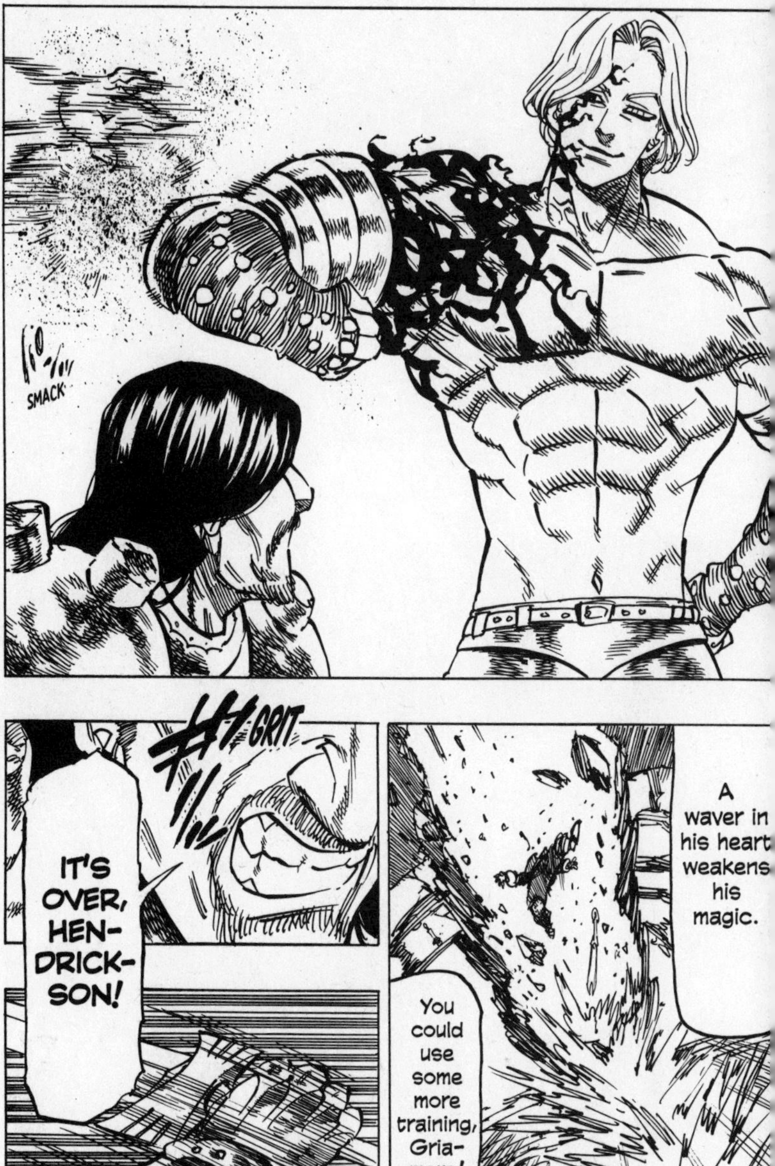
SMACK
A waver in his heart weakens his magic.
You could use some more training, Gria-more!
GRIT
IT'S OVER, HEN-DRICK-SON!

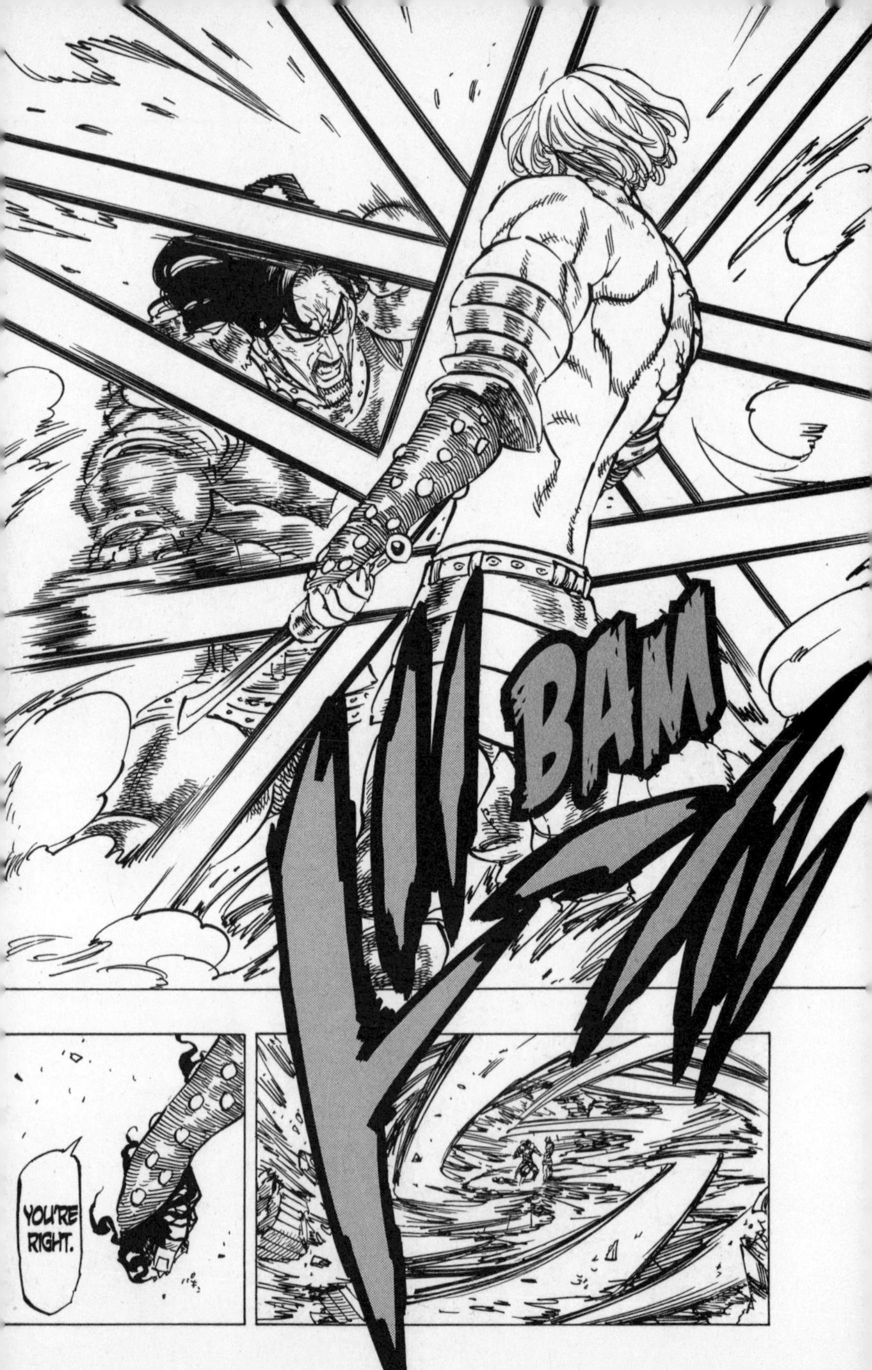
BAM
YOU'RE RIGHT.

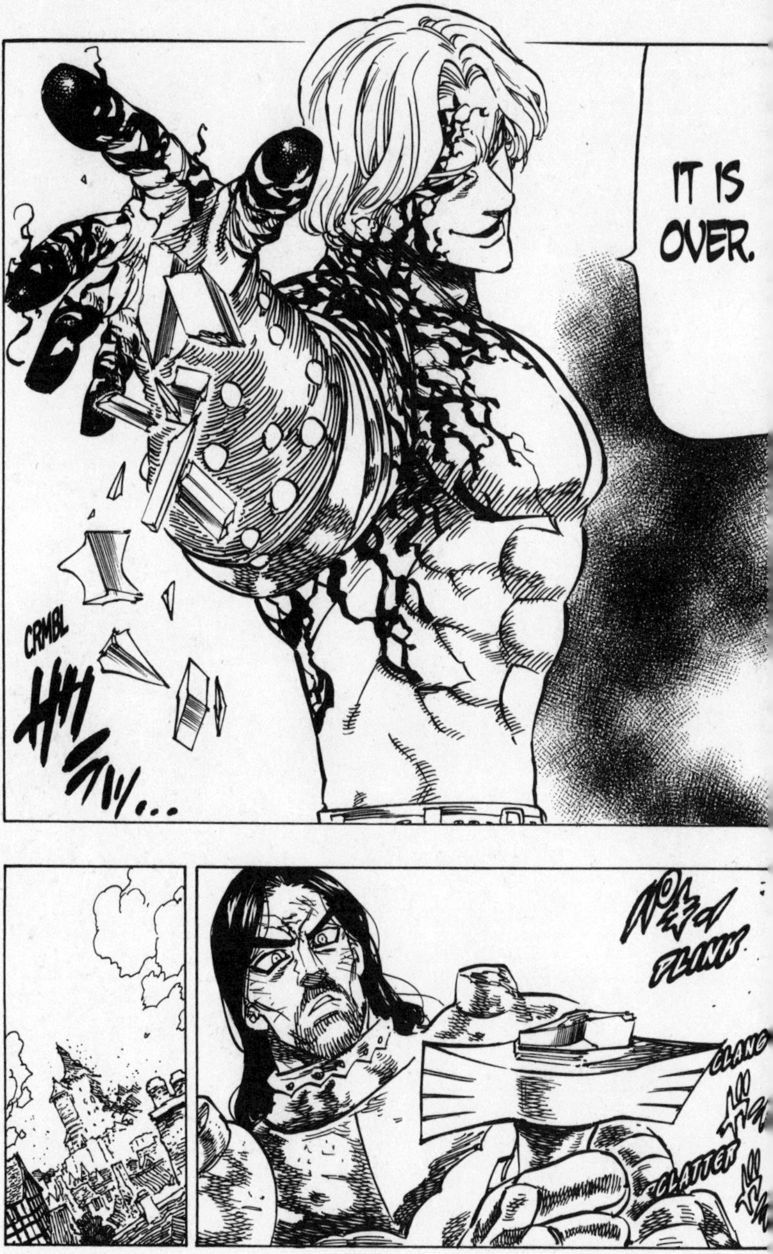
IT IS OVER.
CRMBL
PLINK
CLANG
CLATTER

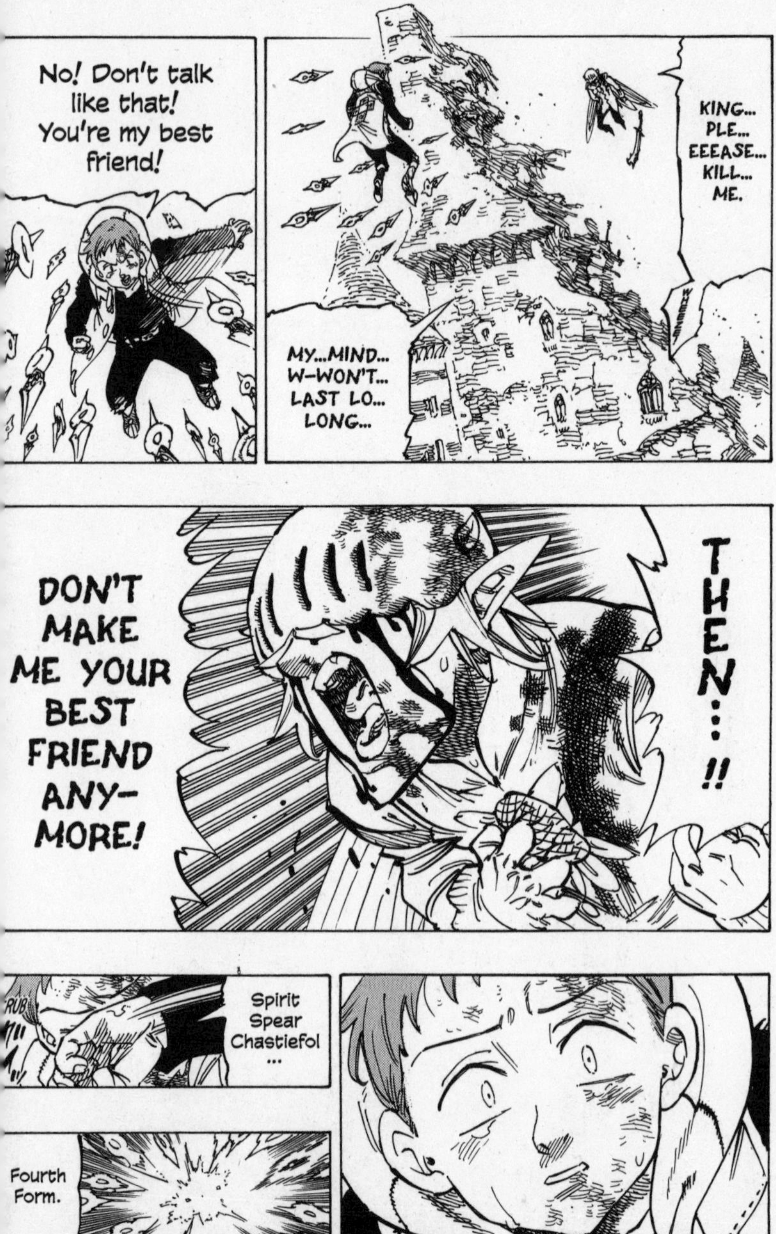
KING... PLE... EEEASE... KILL... ME.
MY...MIND... W-WON'T... LAST LO... LONG...
No! Don't talk like that! You're my best friend!
THEN...!!
DON'T MAKE ME YOUR BEST FRIEND ANY-MORE!
Spirit Spear Chastiefol ...
RUB
Fourth Form.

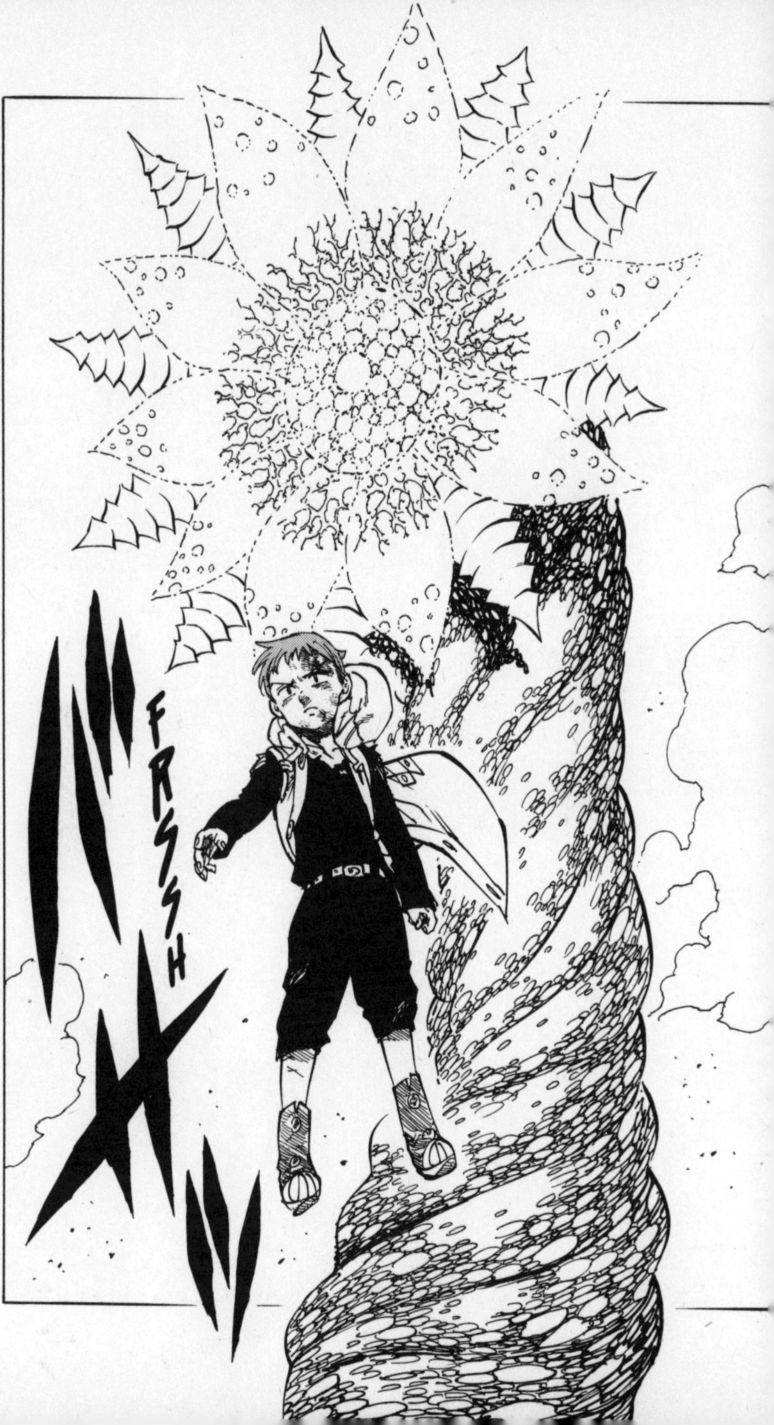
FRSSH

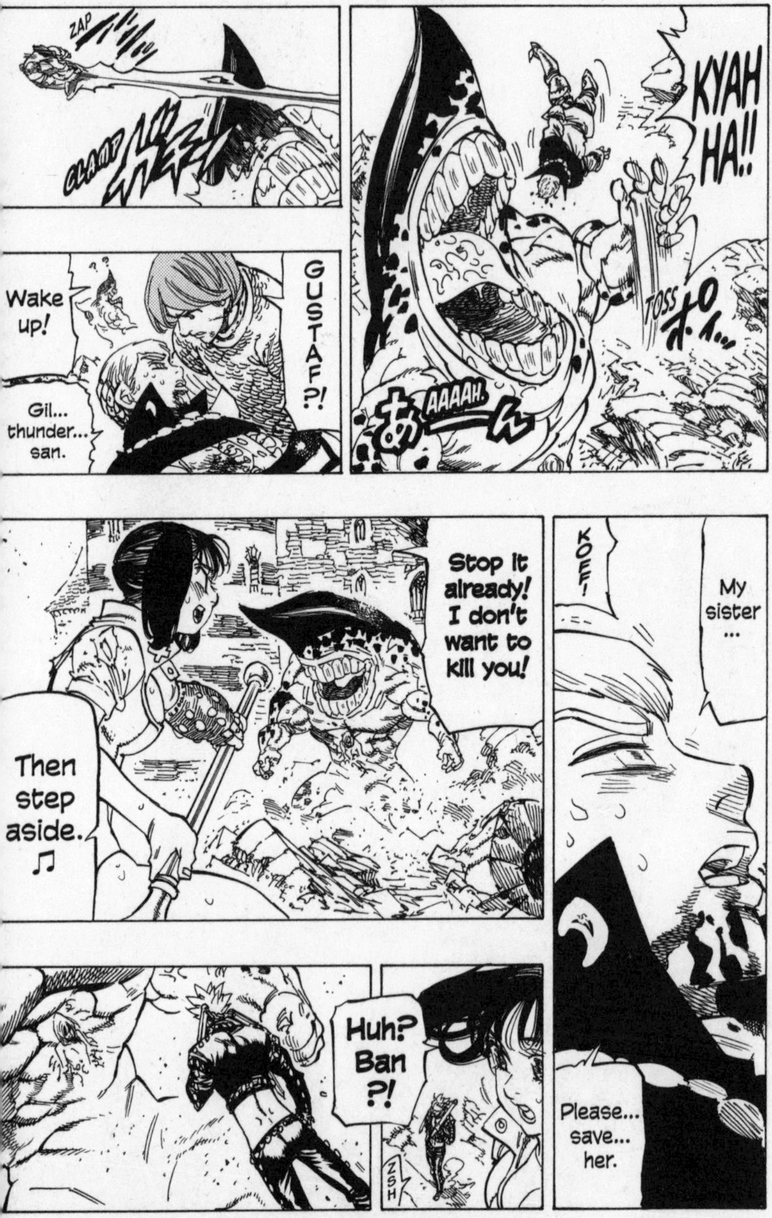
KYAH HA!!
TOSS
AAAAH.
ZAP
CLAMP
GUSTAF?!
Wake up!
Gil... thunder... san.
KOFF!
My sister...
Please... save... her.
Stop it already! I don't want to kill you!
Then step aside. ♫
Huh? Ban?!
ZSH

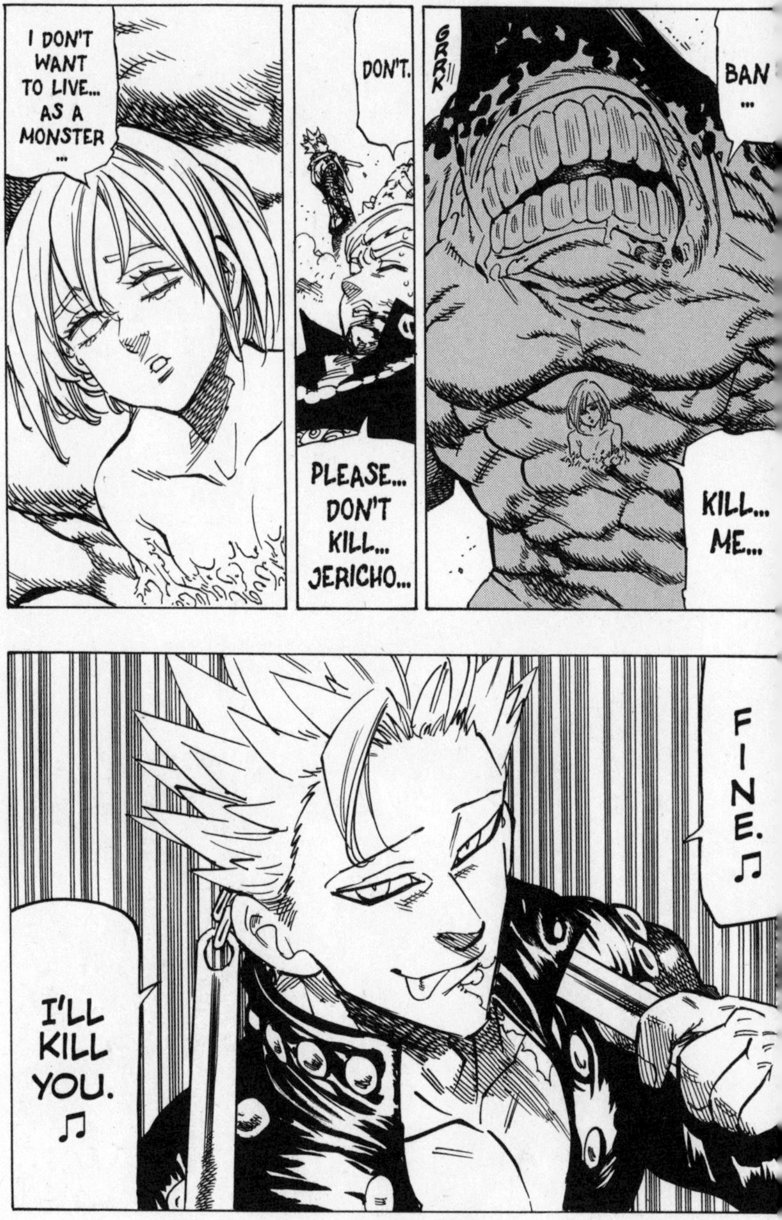
GRRK
BAN ...
KILL... ME...
DON'T.
PLEASE... DON'T KILL... JERICHO...
I DON'T WANT TO LIVE... AS A MONSTER ...
FINE.♫
I'LL KILL YOU. ♫

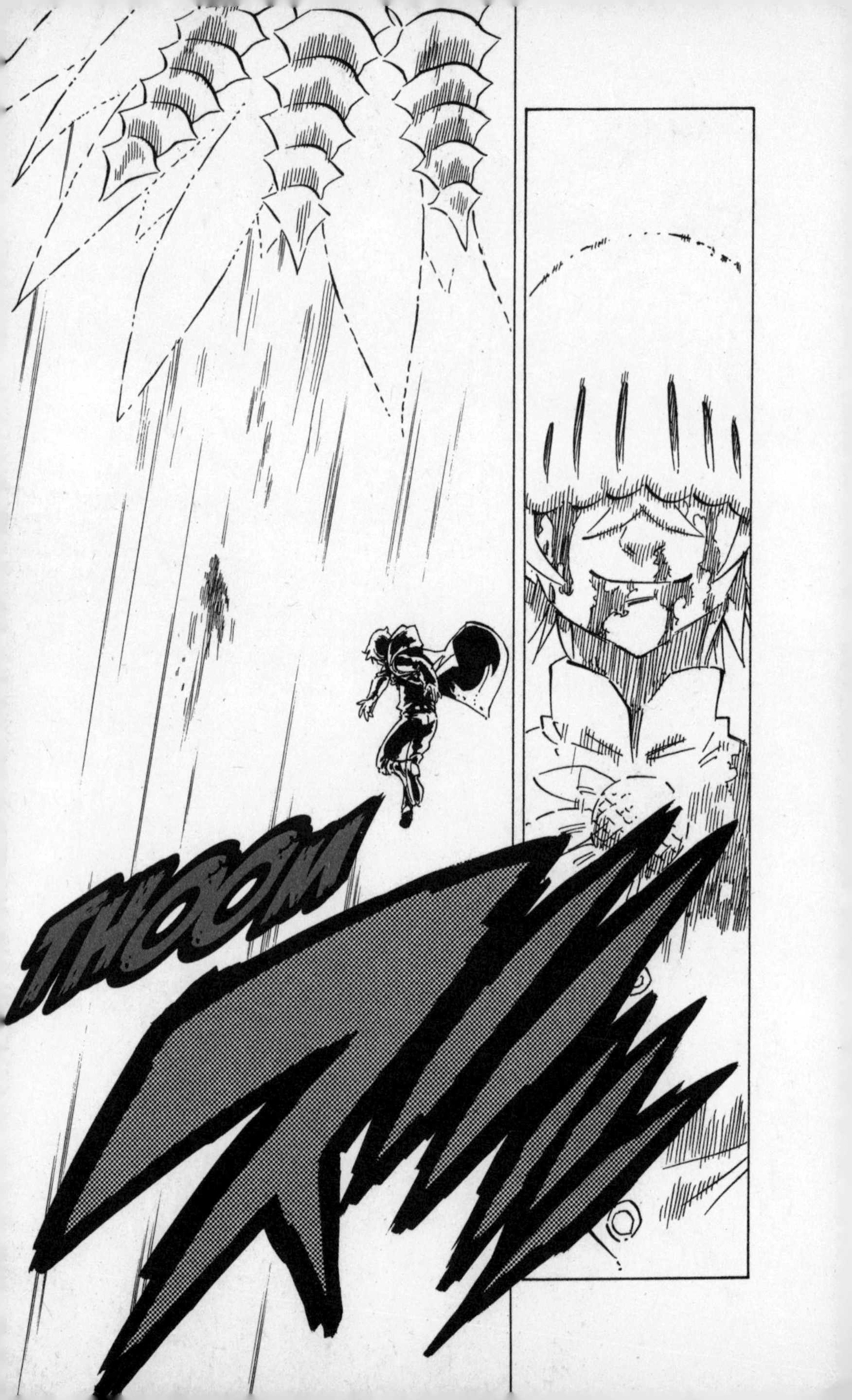
THOOM

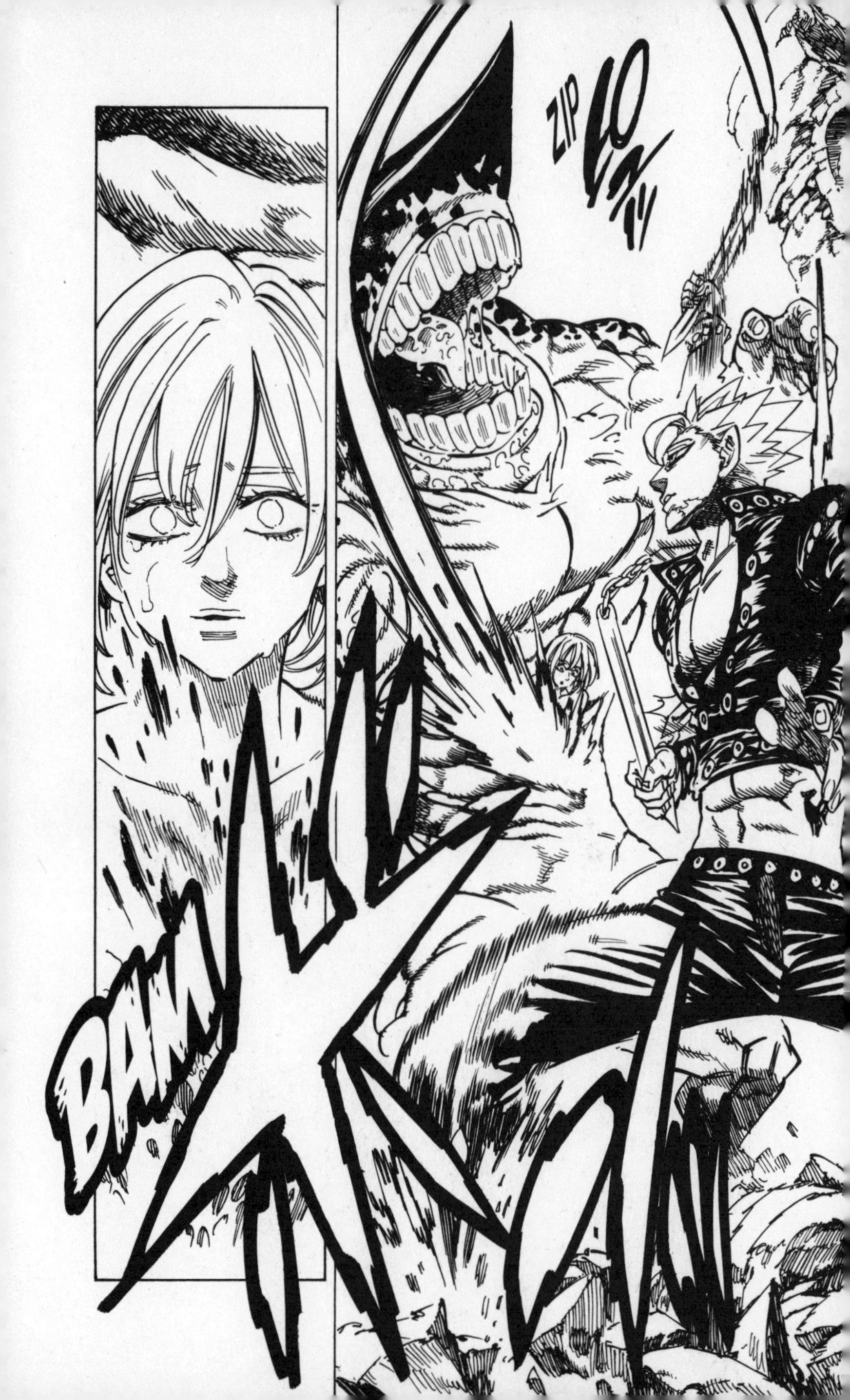
ZIP
BAM

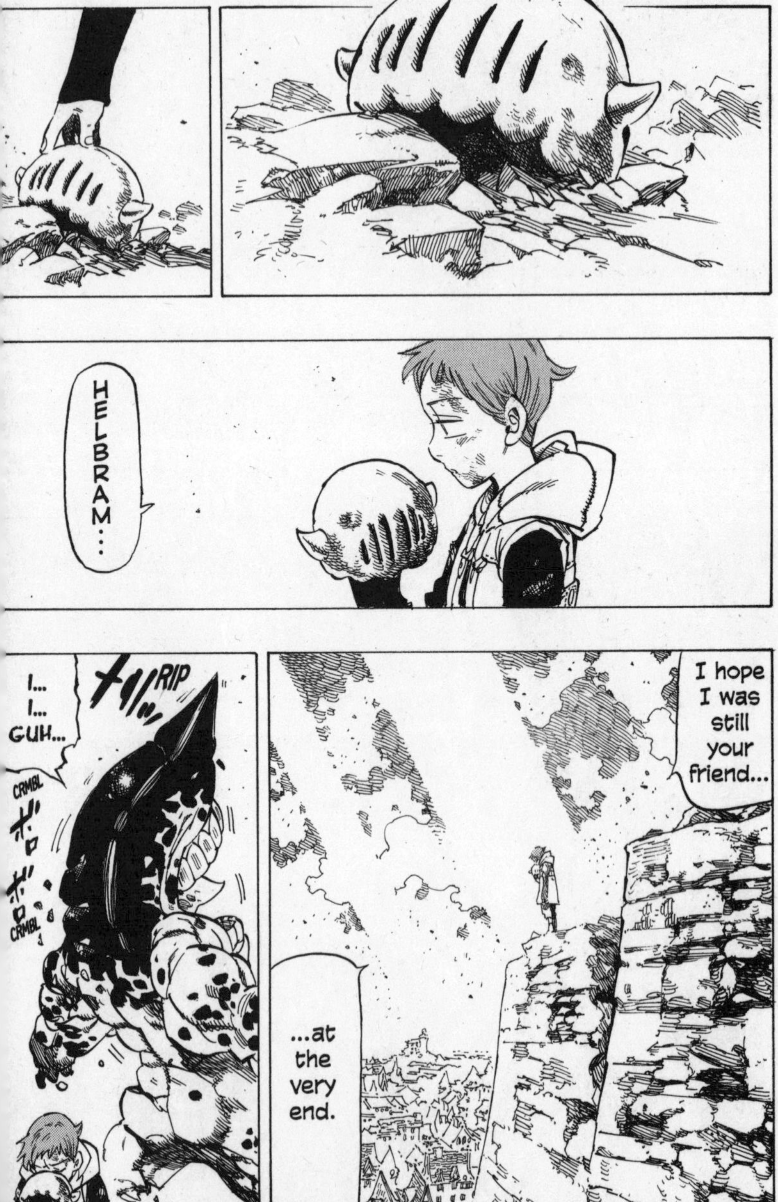
HELBRAM...
I hope I was still your friend...
...at the very end.
I... I... GUH...
RIP
CRMBL
ボロ
ボロ
CRMBL

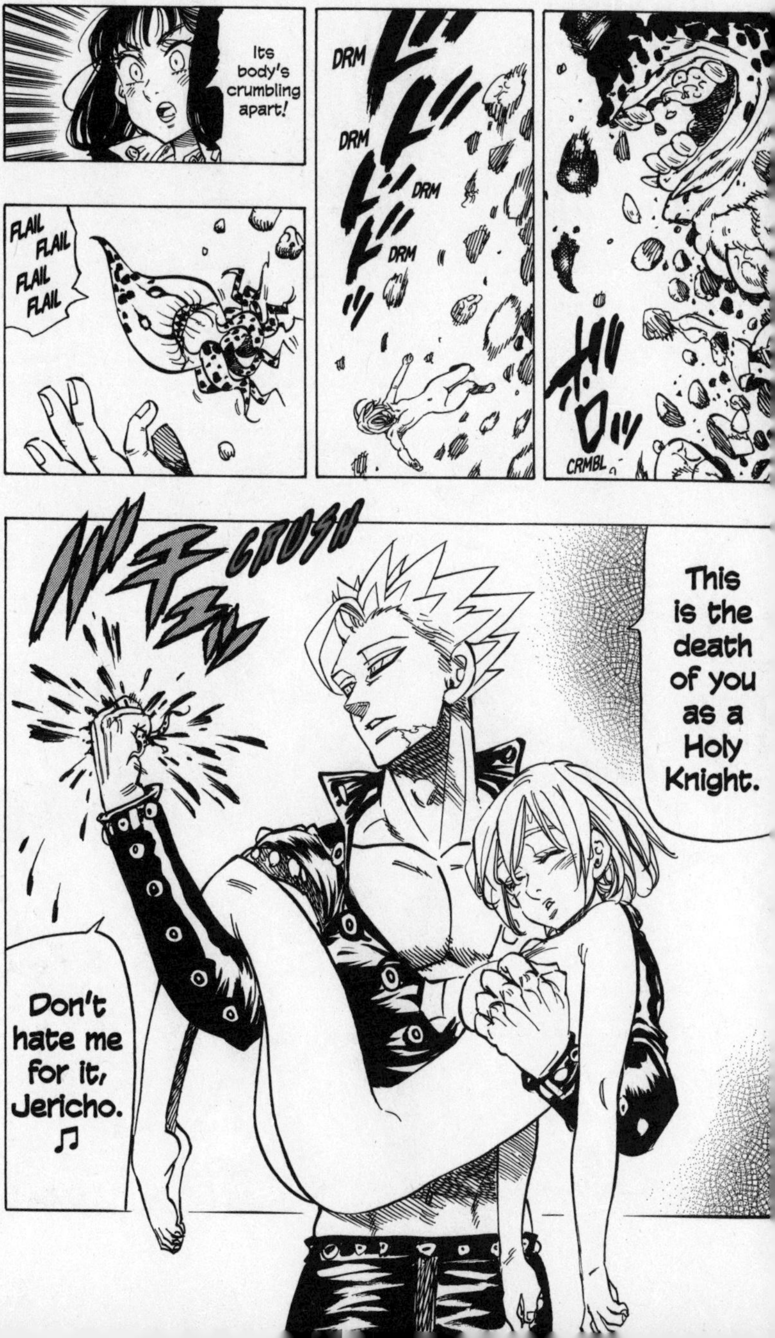
CRMBL
DRM
DRM
DRM
DRM
Its body's crumbling apart!
FLAIL FLAIL FLAIL FLAIL
CRUSH
This is the death of you as a Holy Knight.
Don't hate me for it, Jericho. ♫

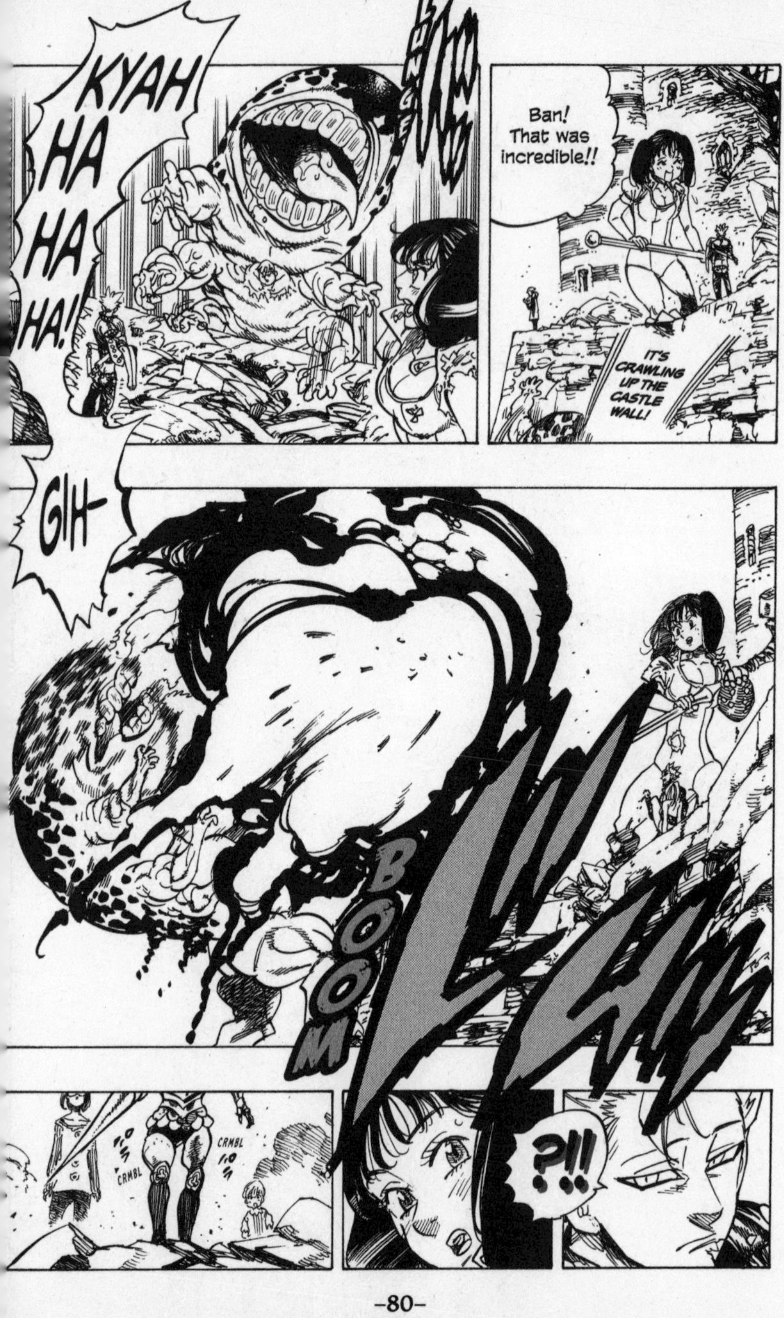
Ban! That was incredible!!
IT'S CRAWLING UP THE CASTLE WALL!
LUNGE
KYAH HA HA HA HA!
GIH
BOOOOM
?!!
CRMBL
CRMBL

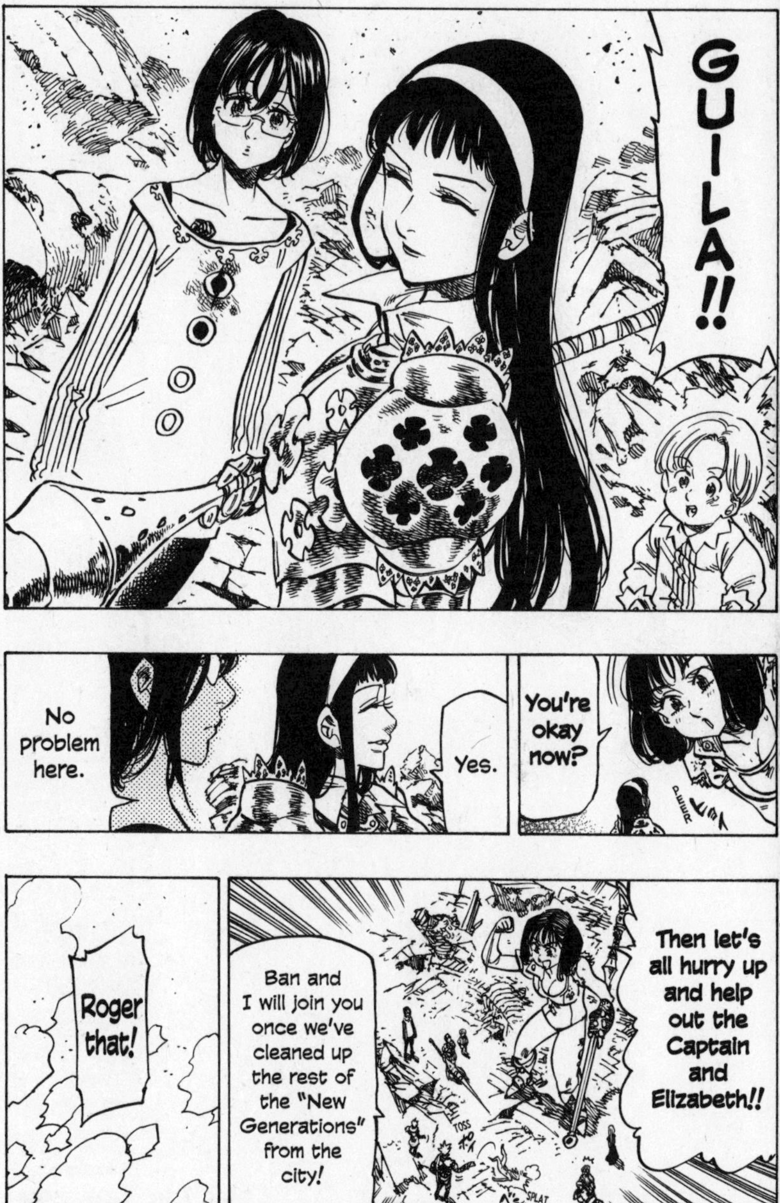
GUILA!!
PEER
You're okay now?
Yes.
No problem here.
Then let's all hurry up and help out the Captain and Elizabeth!!
Ban and I will join you once we've cleaned up the rest of the "New Generations" from the city!
TOSS
SPLAT
Roger that!

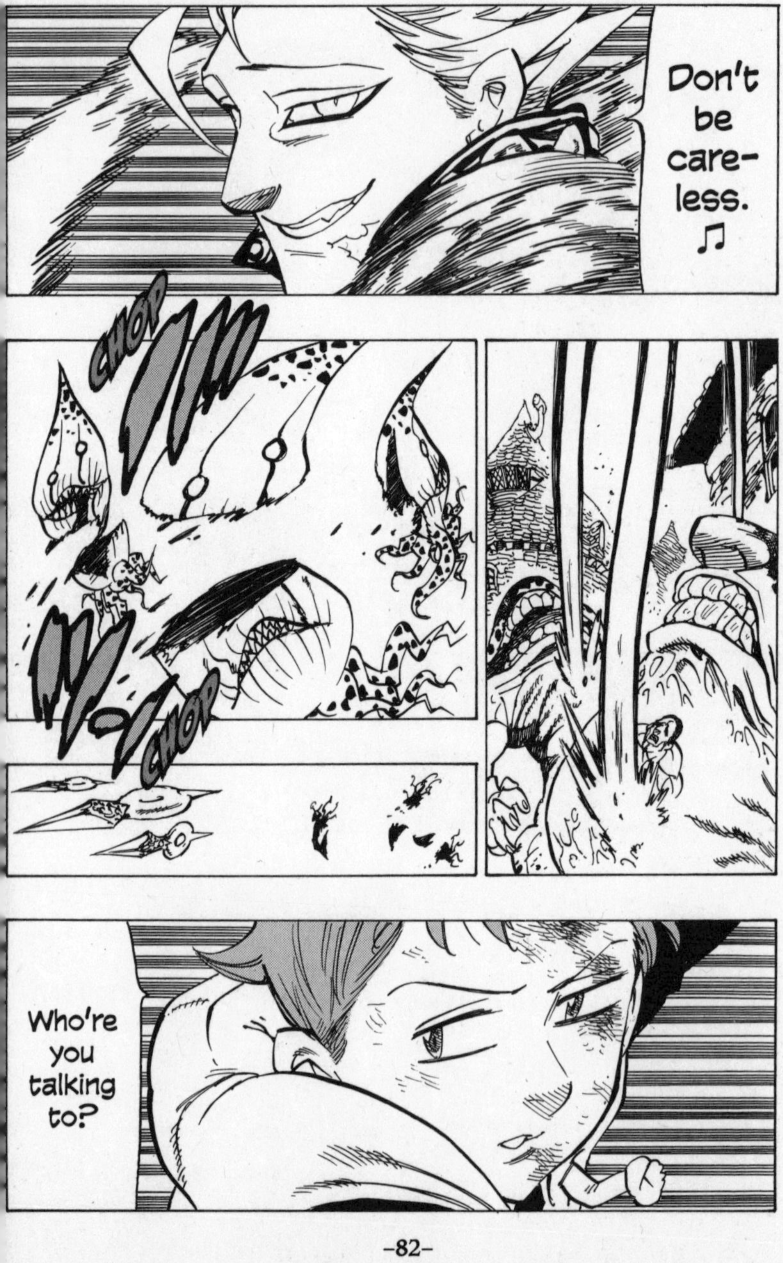
Don't be care-less. ♫
CHOP
CHOP
Who're you talking to?

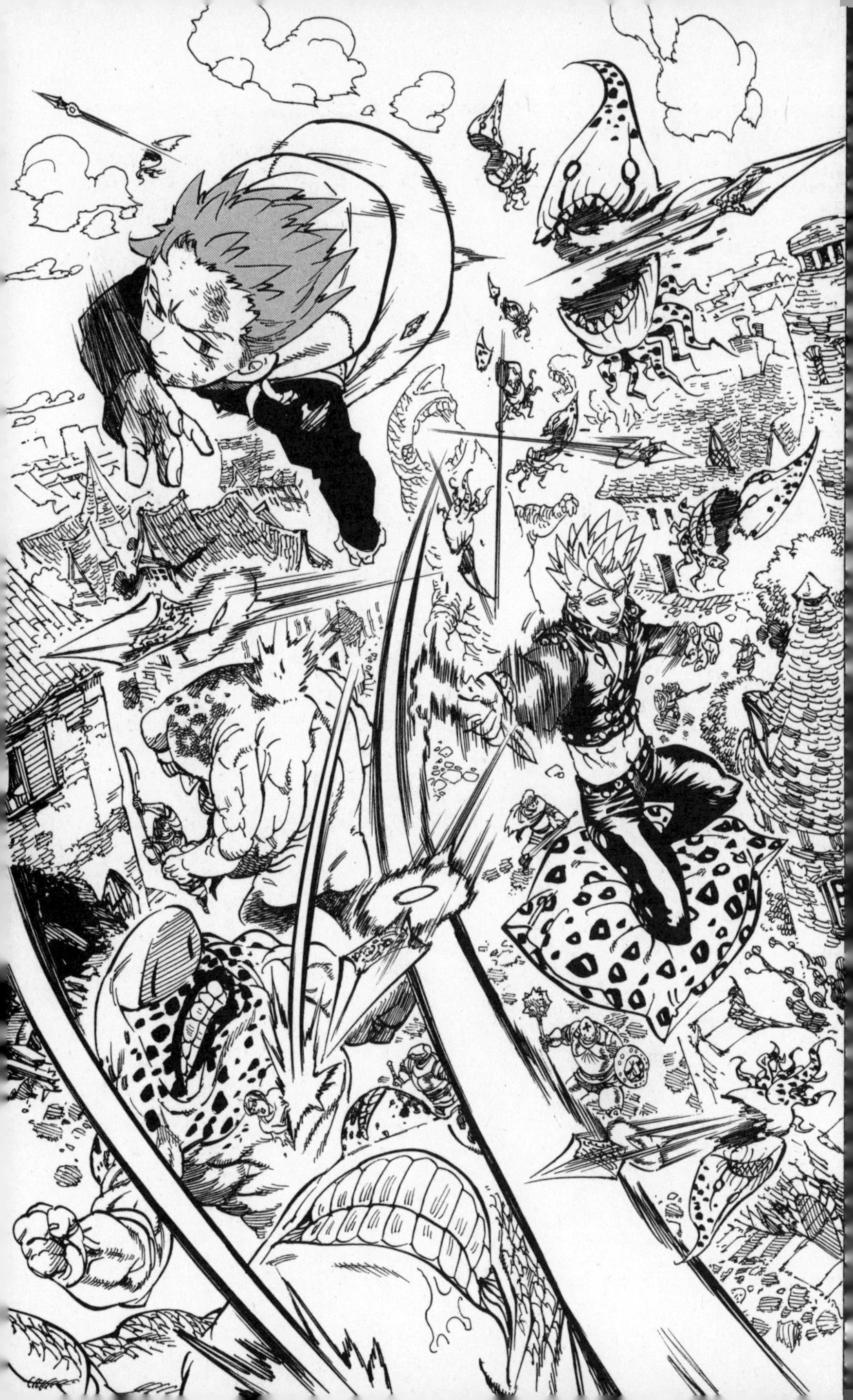

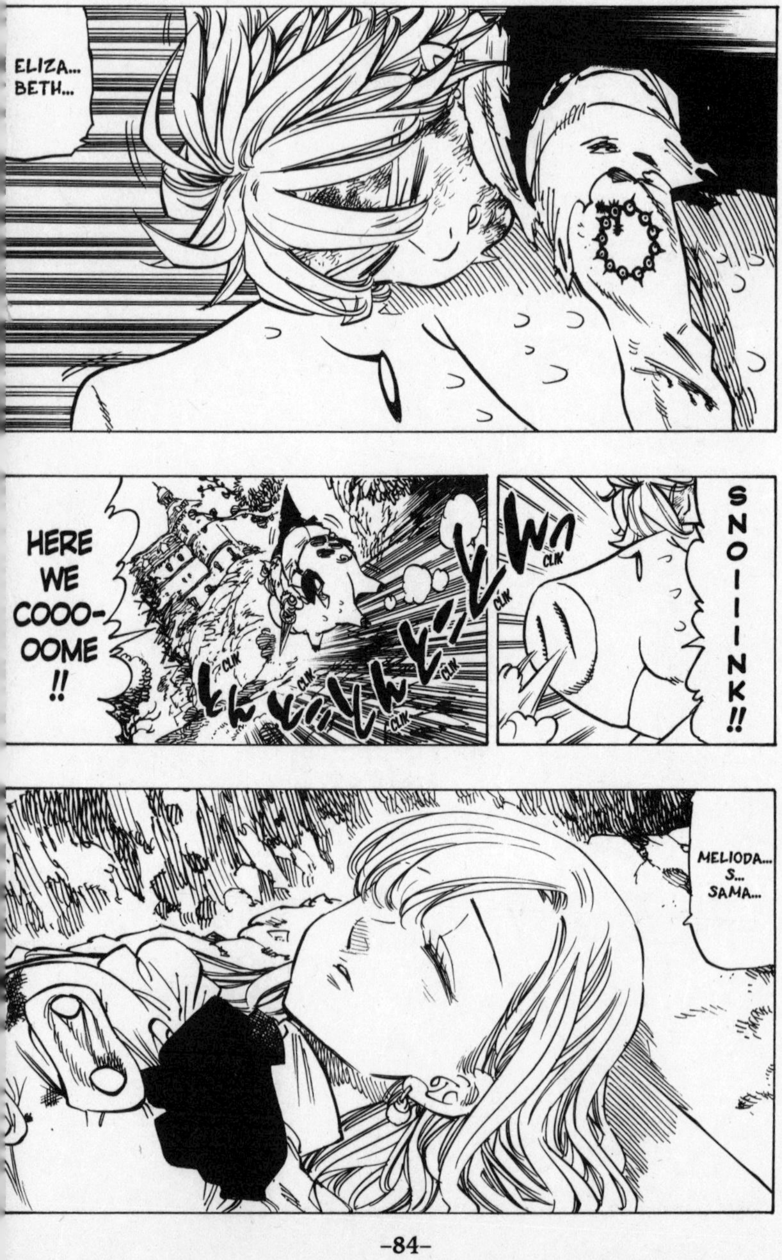
ELIZA... BETH...
SNOIIIINK!!
HERE WE COOOO-OOME!!
CLIK
CLIK
CLIK
CLIK
MELIODA... S... SAMA...

Chapter 91 - A Loathsome Existence

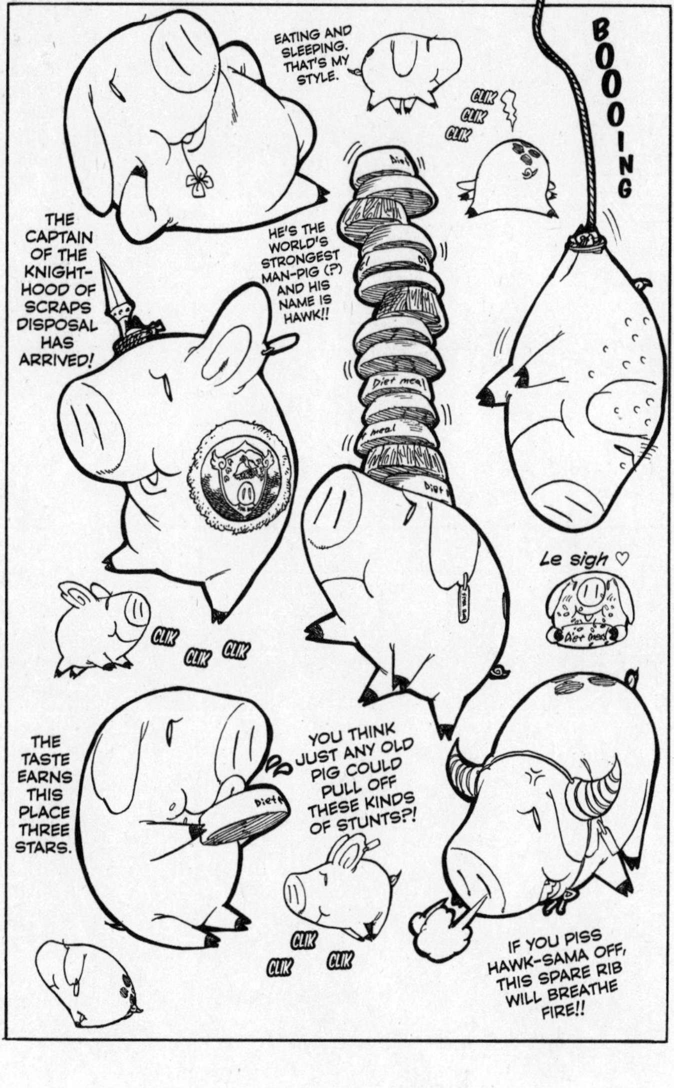

BOOOING
CLIK CLIK CLIK
EATING AND SLEEPING. THAT'S MY STYLE.
HE'S THE WORLD'S STRONGEST MAN-PIG (?) AND HIS NAME IS HAWK!!
THE CAPTAIN OF THE KNIGHT-HOOD OF SCRAPS DISPOSAL HAS ARRIVED!
Le sigh ♡
Diet meal
CLIK CLIK CLIK
IF YOU PISS HAWK-SAMA OFF, THIS SPARE RIB WILL BREATHE FIRE!!
YOU THINK JUST ANY OLD PIG COULD PULL OFF THESE KINDS OF STUNTS?!
THE TASTE EARNS THIS PLACE THREE STARS.
CLIK CLIK CLIK

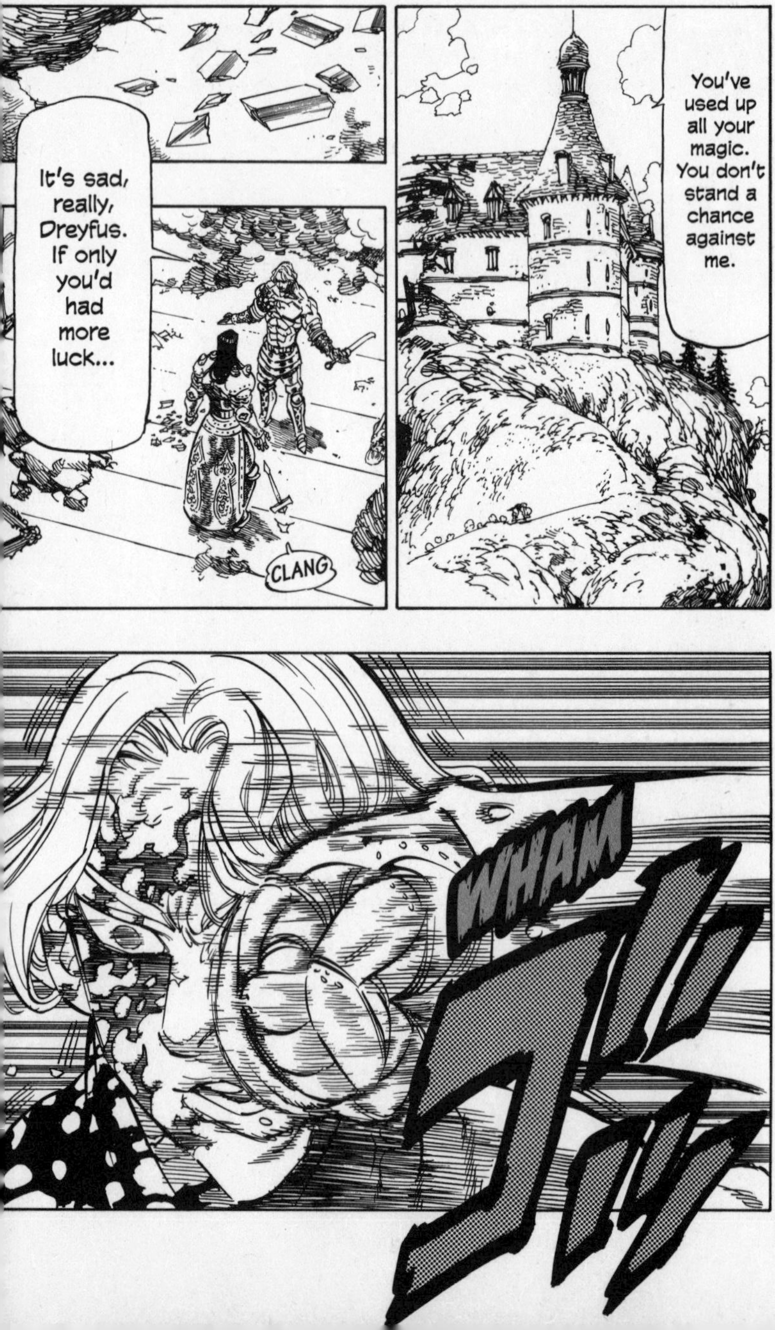
You've used up all your magic. You don't stand a chance against me.
It's sad, really, Dreyfus. If only you'd had more luck...
CLANG
WHAM

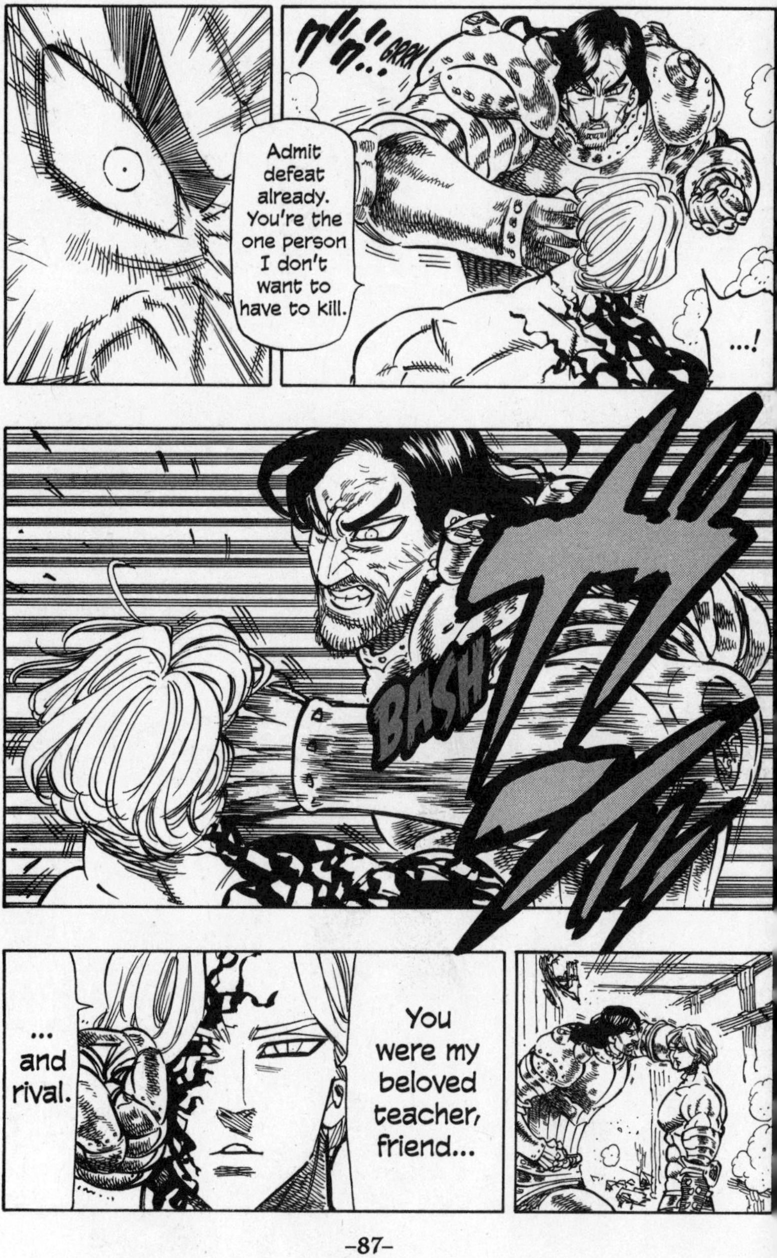
GRRK
Admit defeat already. You're the one person I don't want to have to kill.
...!
BASH
You were my beloved teacher, friend...
... and rival.

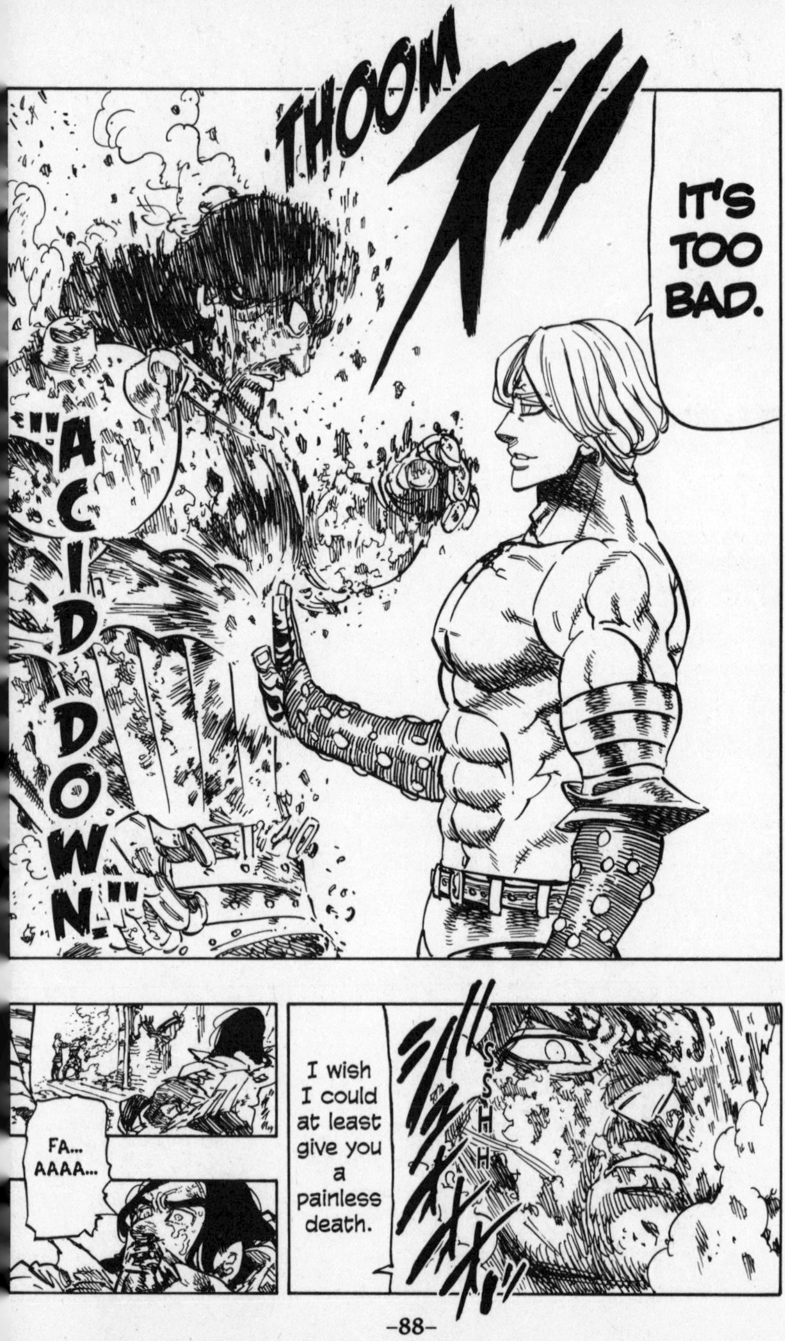
THOOM
IT'S TOO BAD.
"ACID DOWN"
I wish I could at least give you a painless death.
SSHH
FA... AAAA...

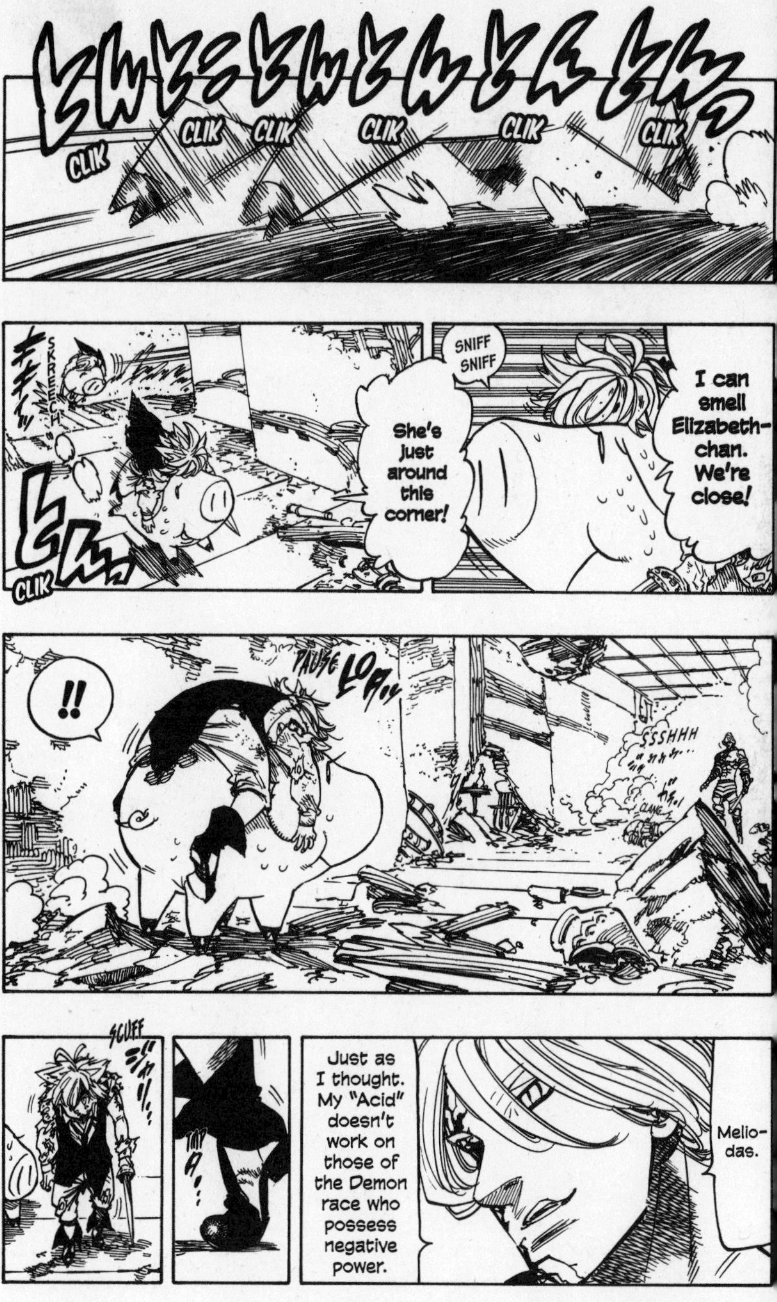
CLIK
CLIK
CLIK
CLIK
CLIK
CLIK
SNIFF SNIFF
I can smell Elizabeth-chan. We're close!
She's just around this corner!
SKREECH
CLIK
PAUSE
!!
SSSHHH
CLANG
Melio-das.
Just as I thought. My "Acid" doesn't work on those of the Demon race who possess negative power.
SCUFF

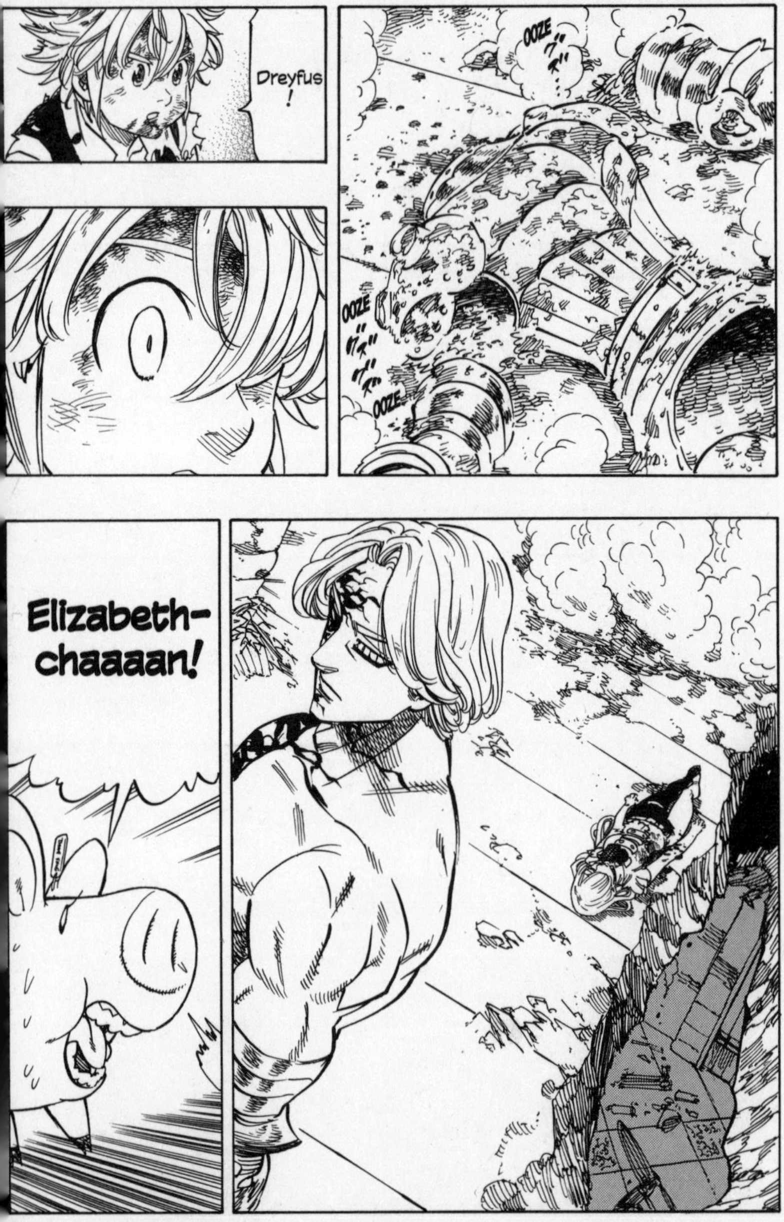
OOZE
OOZE
OOZE
Dreyfus!
Elizabeth-chaaaan!

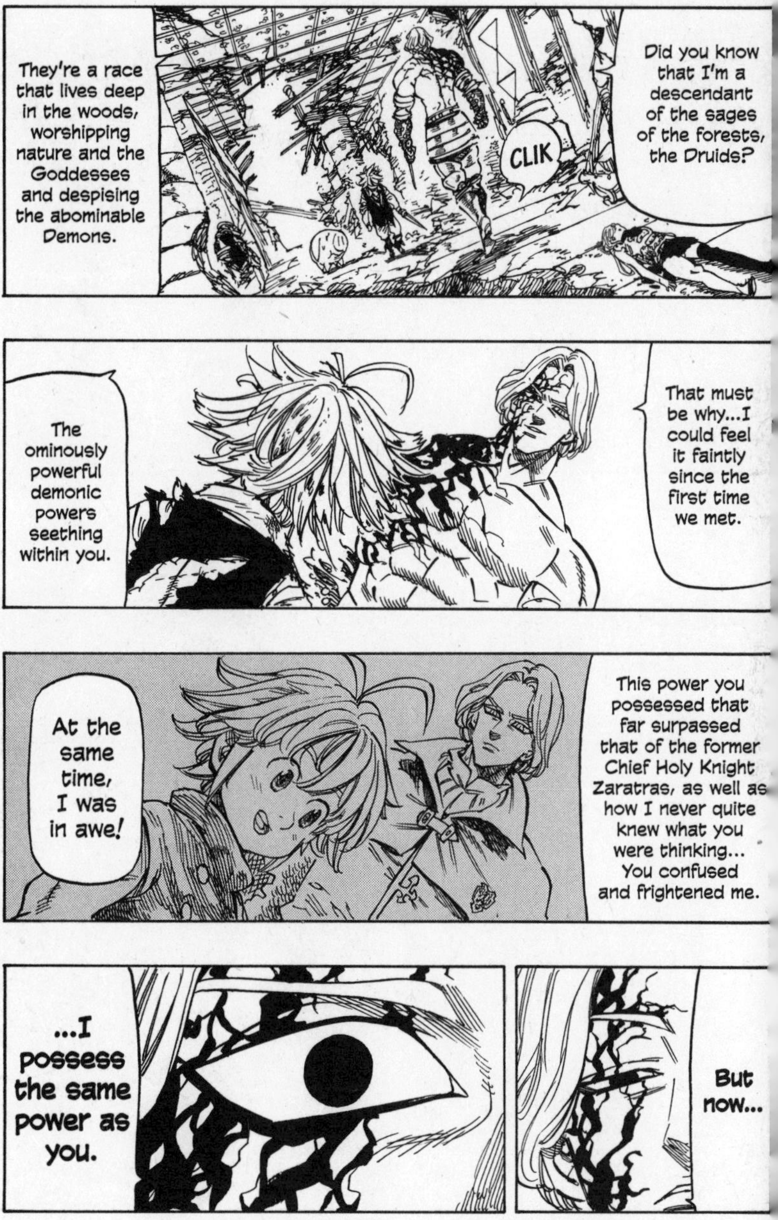
Did you know that I'm a descendant of the sages of the forests, the Druids?
CLIK
They're a race that lives deep in the woods, worshipping nature and the Goddesses and despising the abominable Demons.
That must be why...I could feel it faintly since the first time we met.
The ominously powerful demonic powers seething within you.
This power you possessed that far surpassed that of the former Chief Holy Knight Zaratras, as well as how I never quite knew what you were thinking... You confused and frightened me.
At the same time, I was in awe!
But now...
...I possess the same power as you.

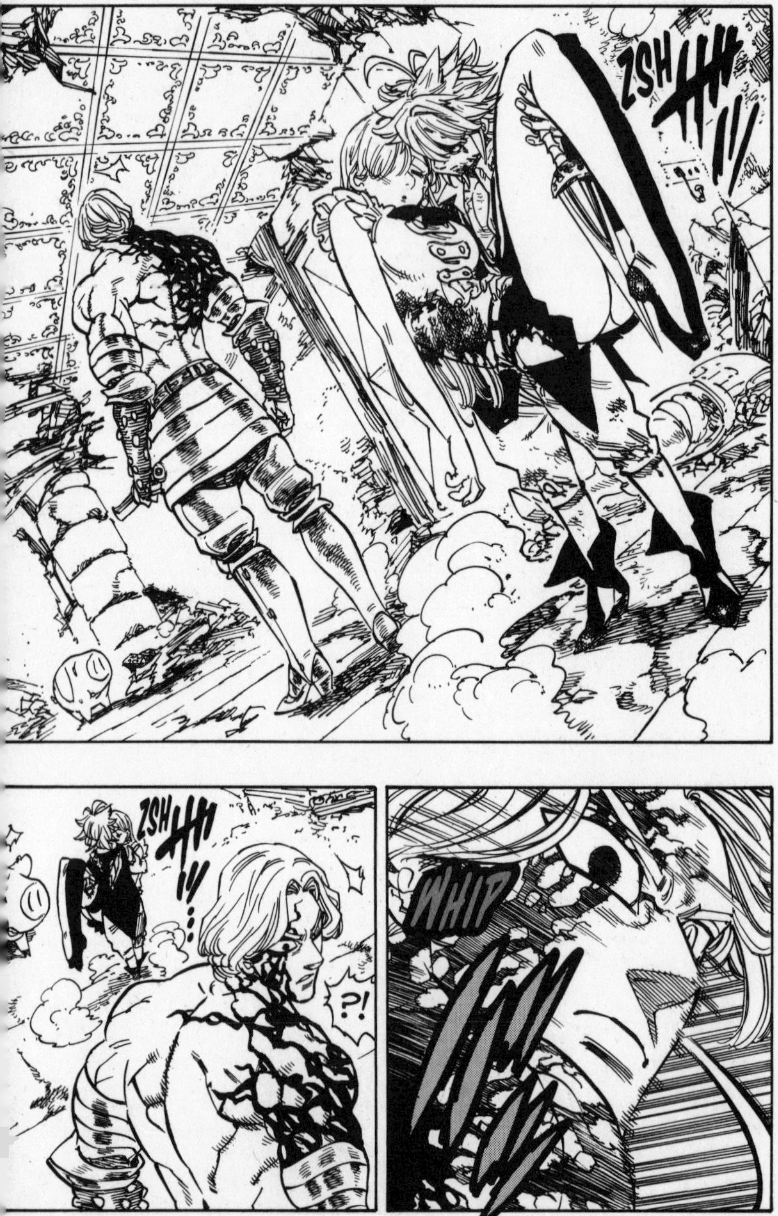
ZSHHH
...
WHIP
ZSHHH
...
?!

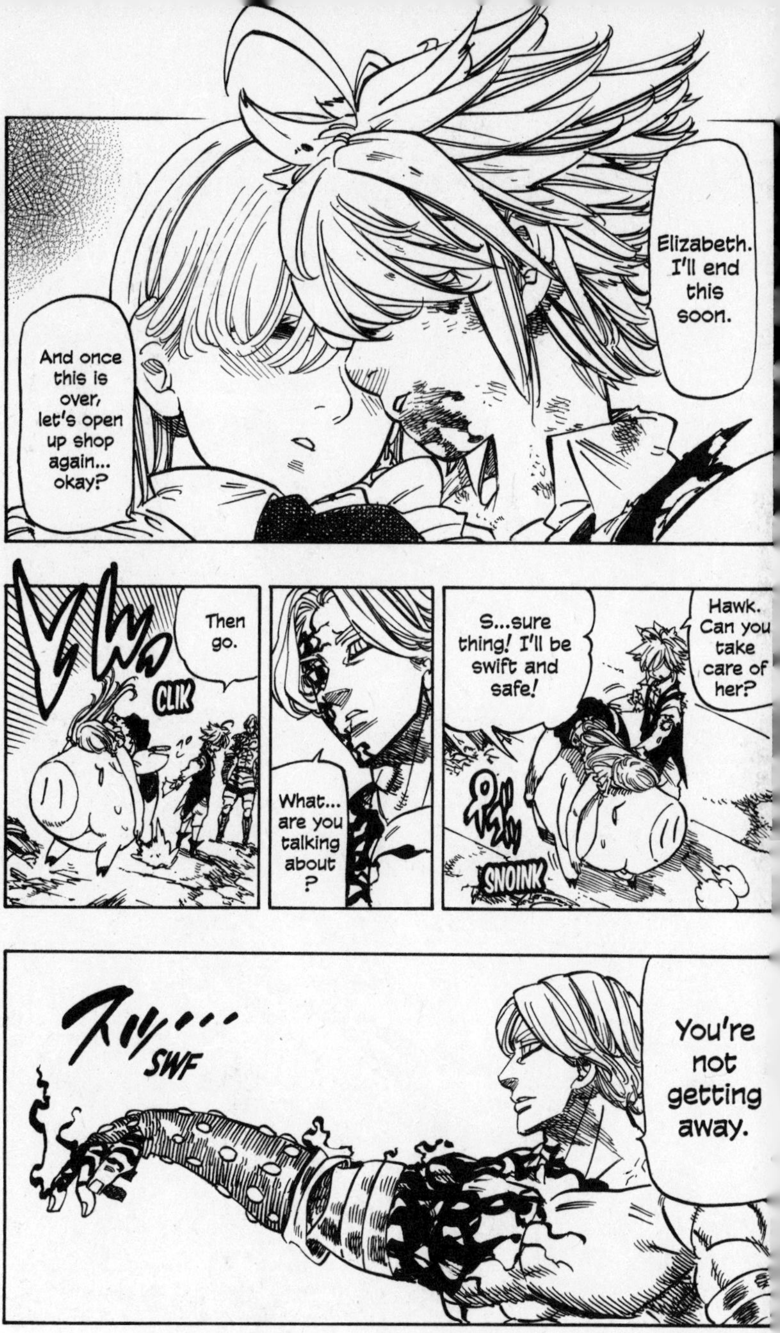
Elizabeth. I'll end this soon.
And once this is over, let's open up shop again... okay?
Hawk. Can you take care of her?
S...sure thing! I'll be swift and safe!
SNOINK
What... are you talking about?
Then go.
CLIK
You're not getting away.
SWF

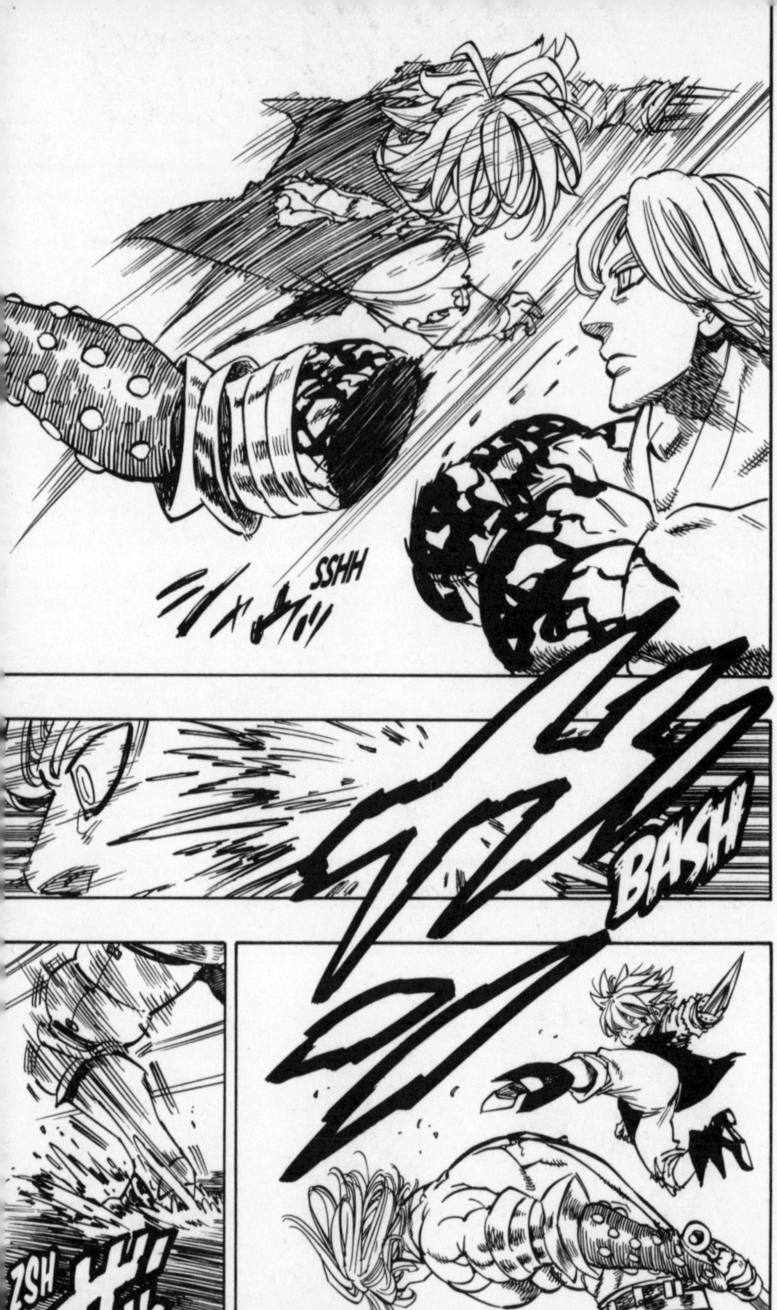
SSHH
BASH
ZSH

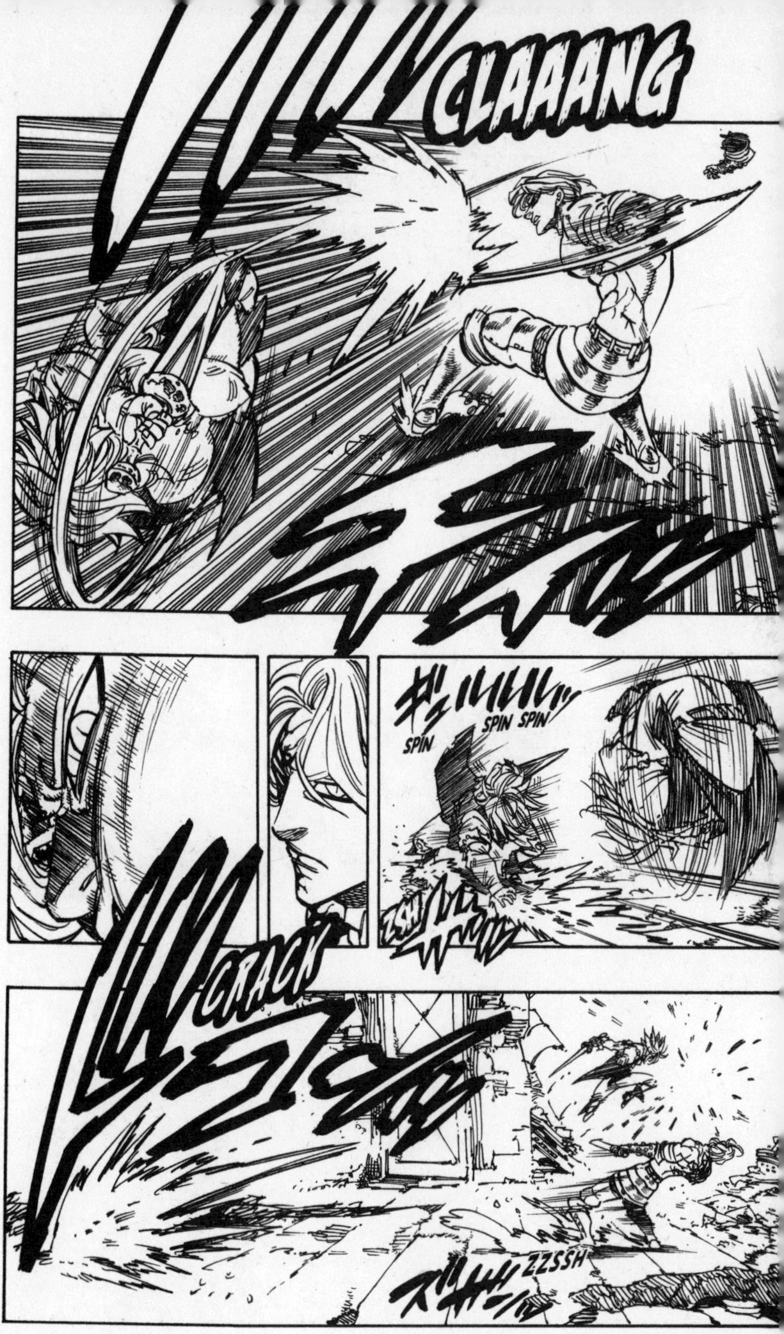
CLAAANG
SPIN SPIN
SPIN
ZSH
CRACK
ZZSSH

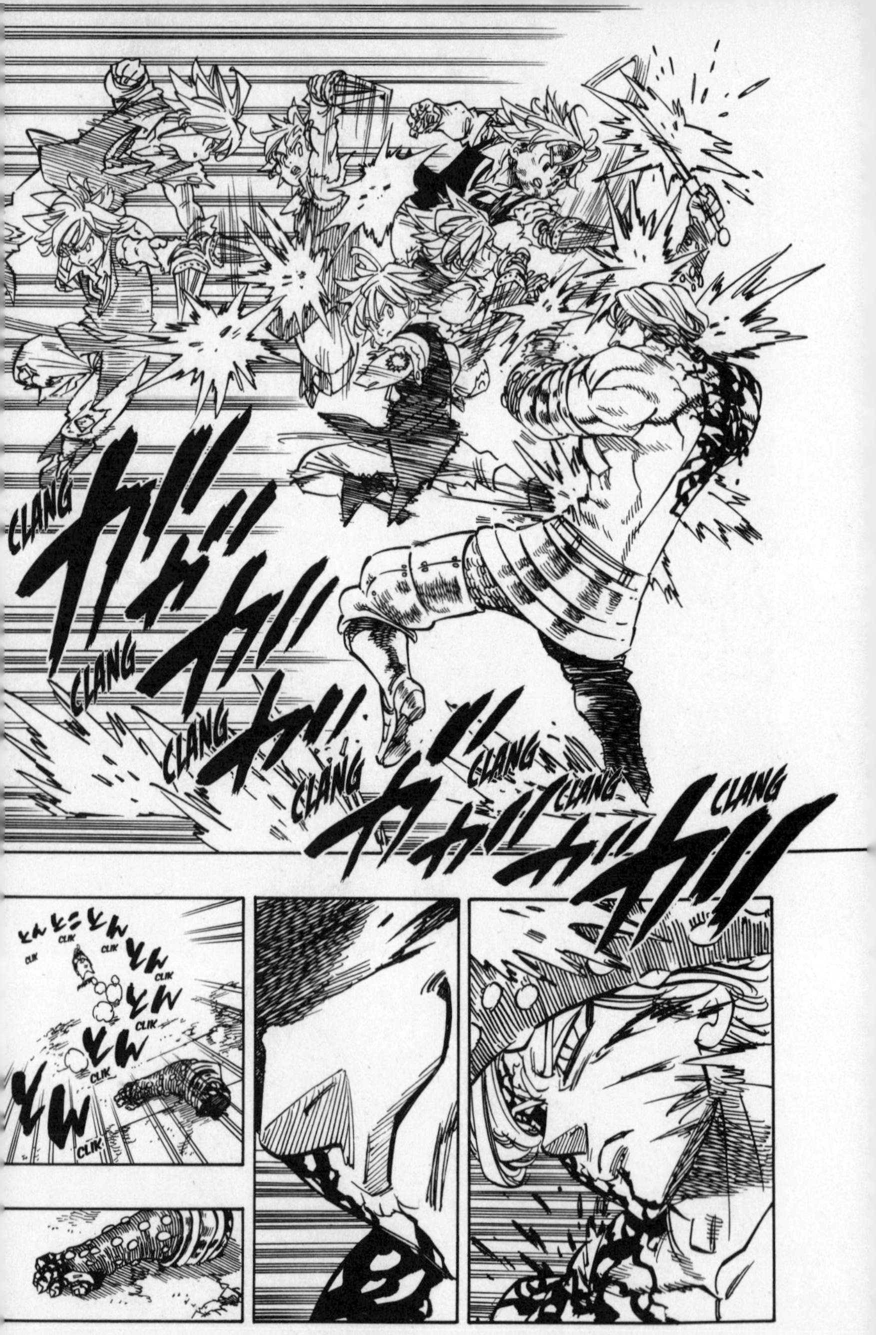
CLANG
CLANG
CLANG
CLANG
CLANG
CLANG
CLANG
CLIK
CLIK
CLIK
CLIK
CLIK
CLIK
CLIK

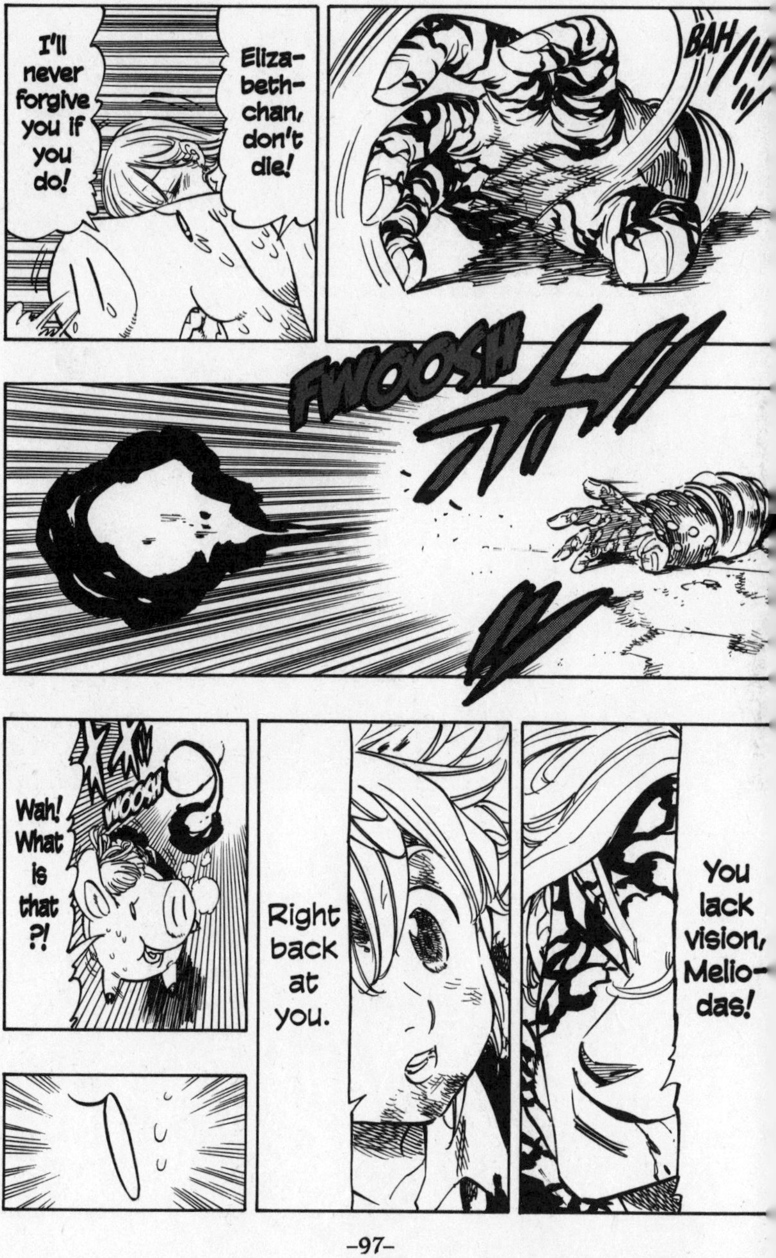
BAH
Eliza-beth-chan, don't die!
I'll never forgive you if you do!
FWOOSH
You lack vision, Melio-das!
Right back at you.
WOOSH
Wah! What is that?!

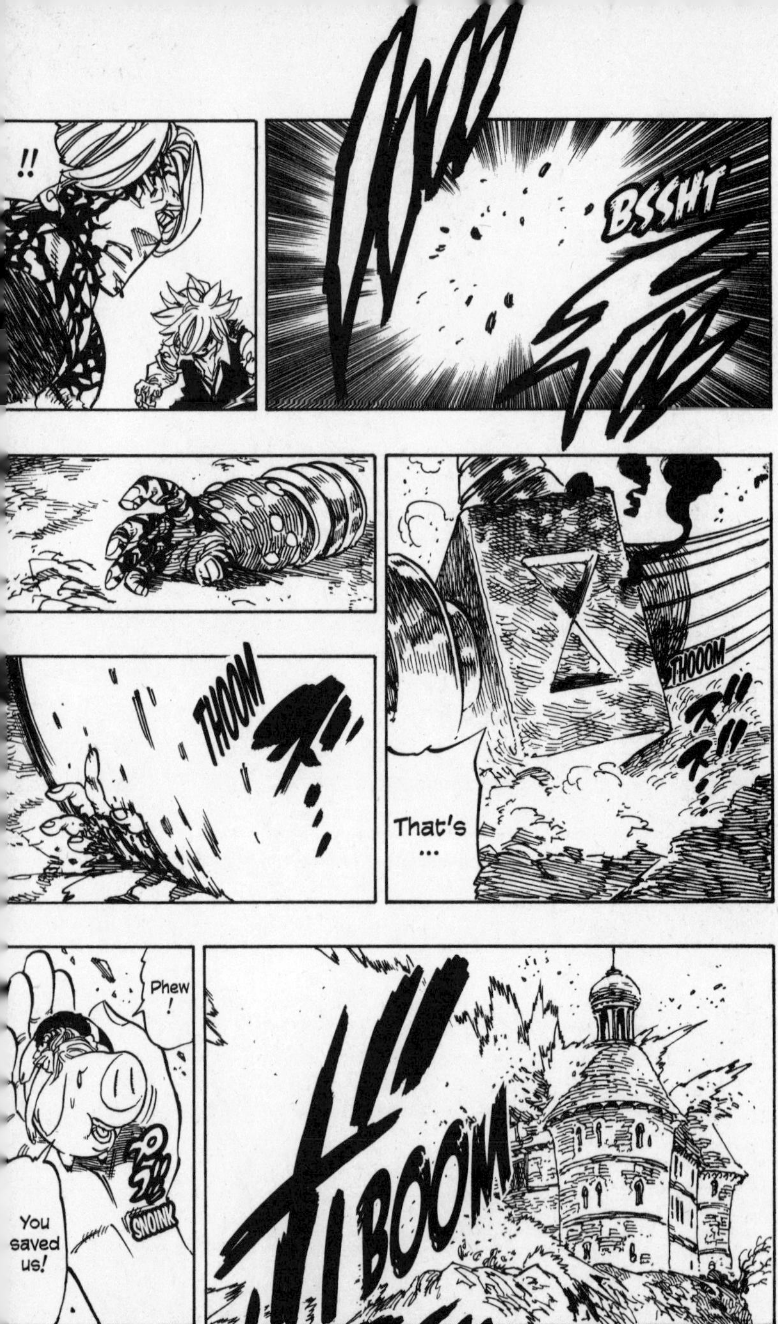
BSSHT
!!
THOOOM
That's ...
THOOM
BOOM
Phew!
SNOINK
You saved us!

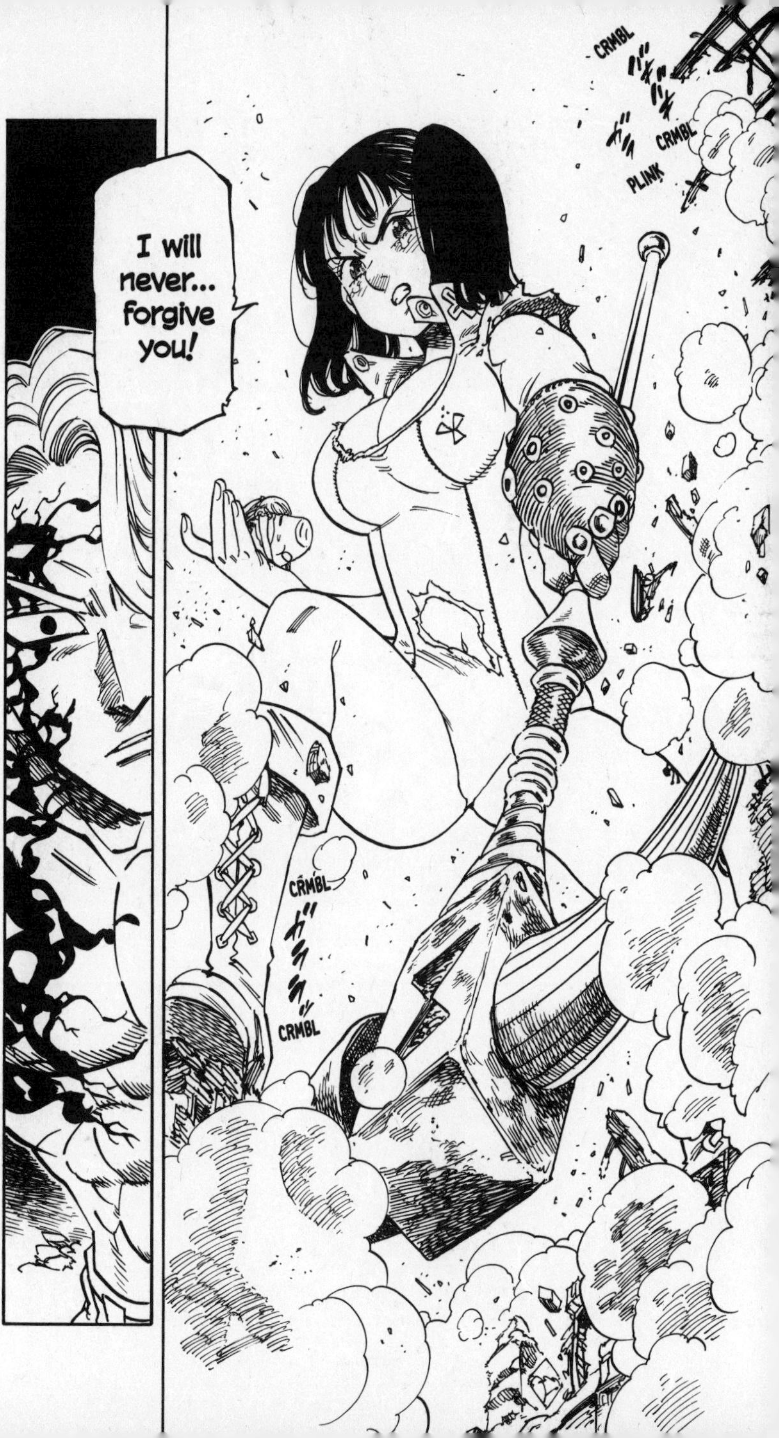
CRMBL
CRMBL
PLINK
I will never... forgive you!
CRMBL
CRMBL

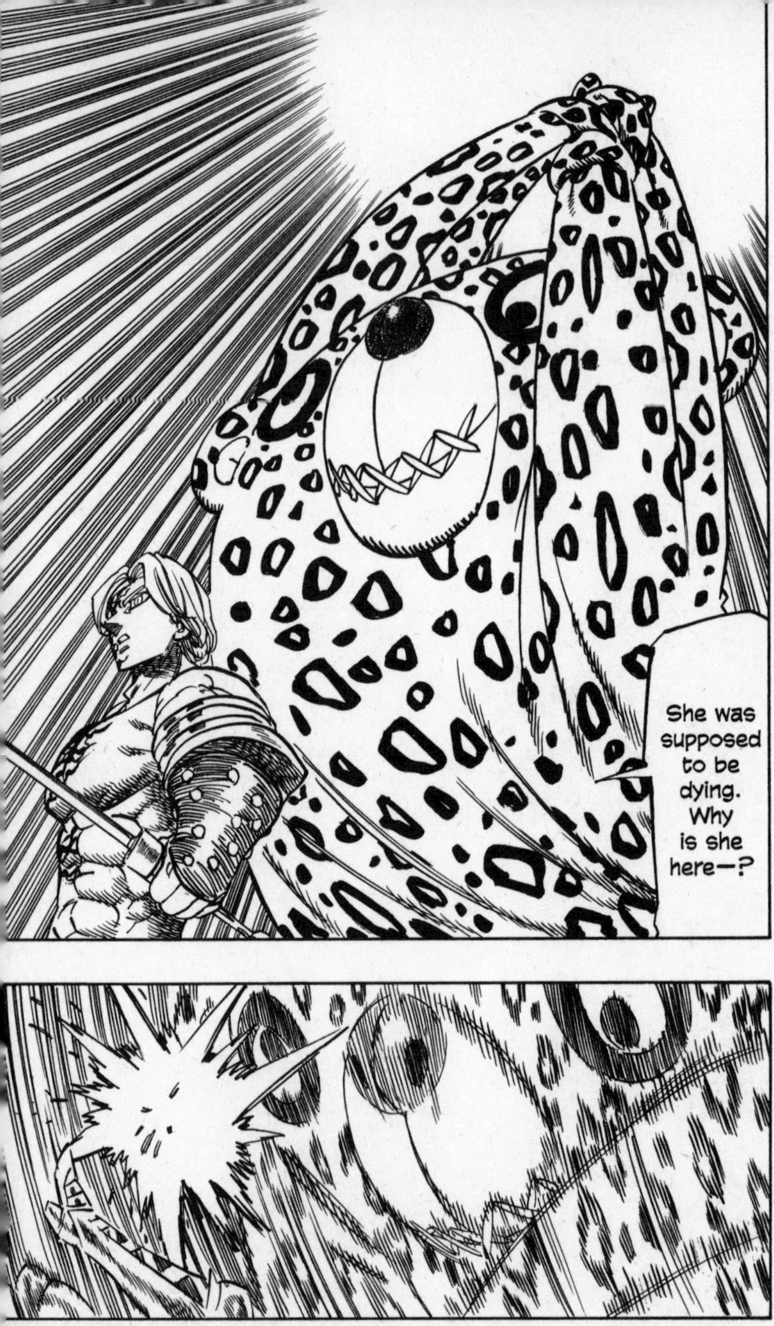
She was supposed to be dying. Why is she here—?

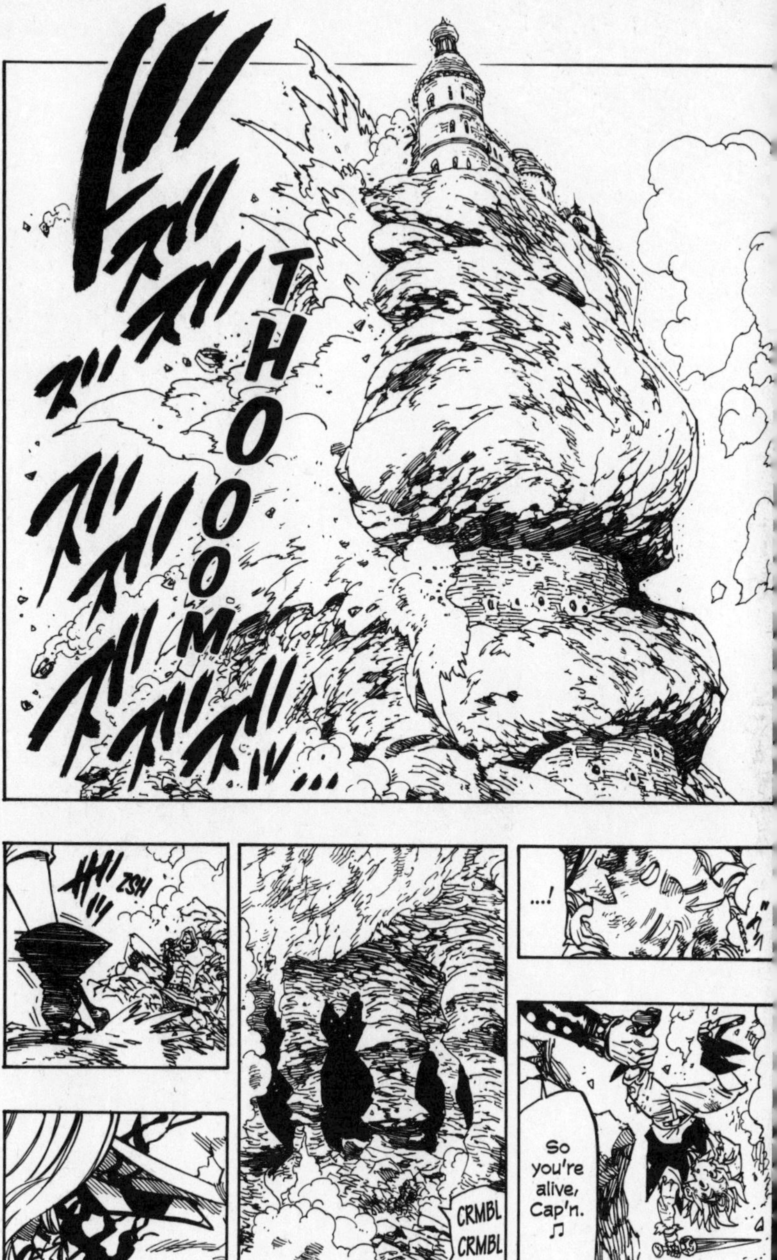
THOOOOM
...!
So you're alive, Cap'n. ♫
CRMBL CRMBL
ZSH

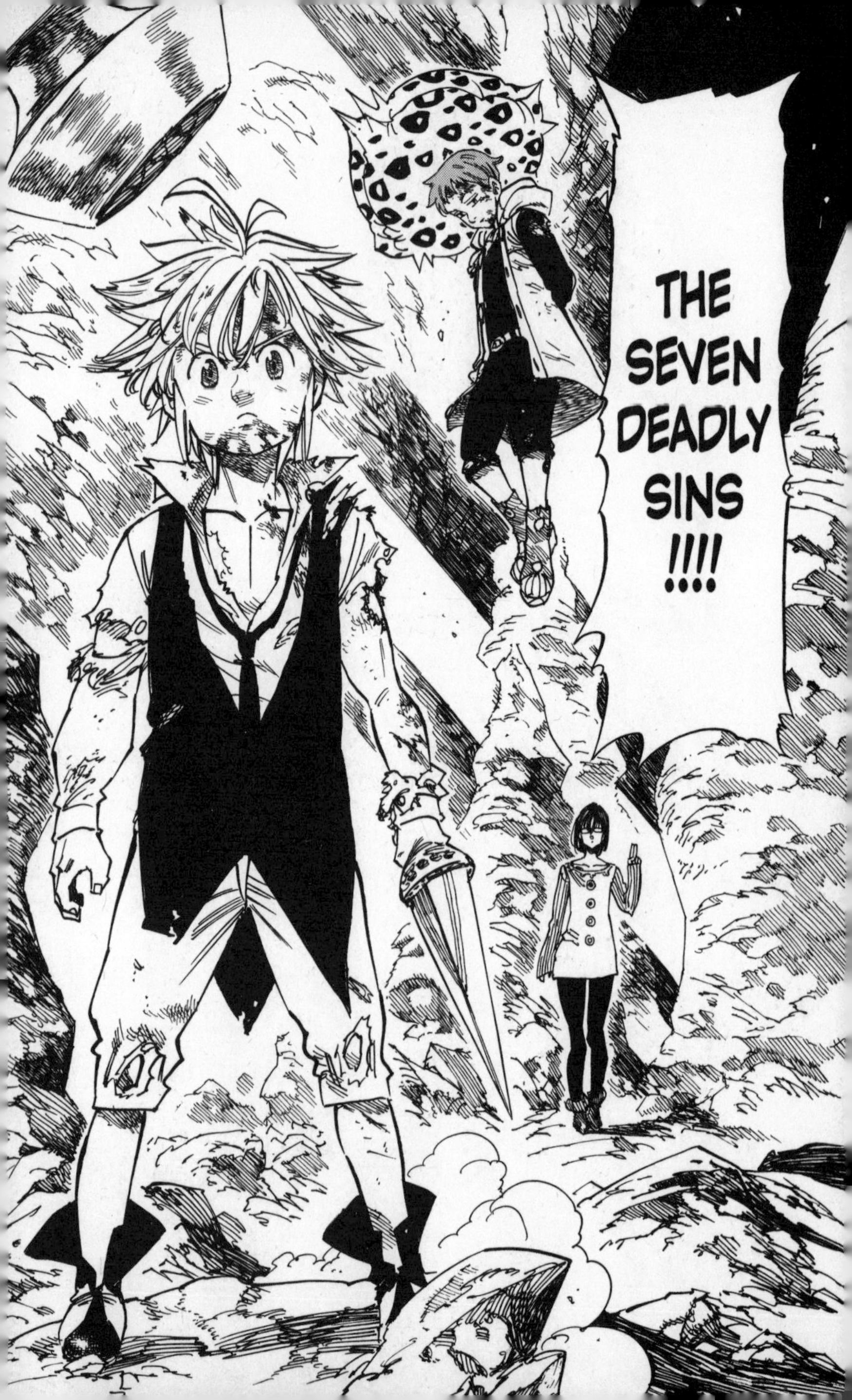
THE SEVEN DEADLY SINS !!!!

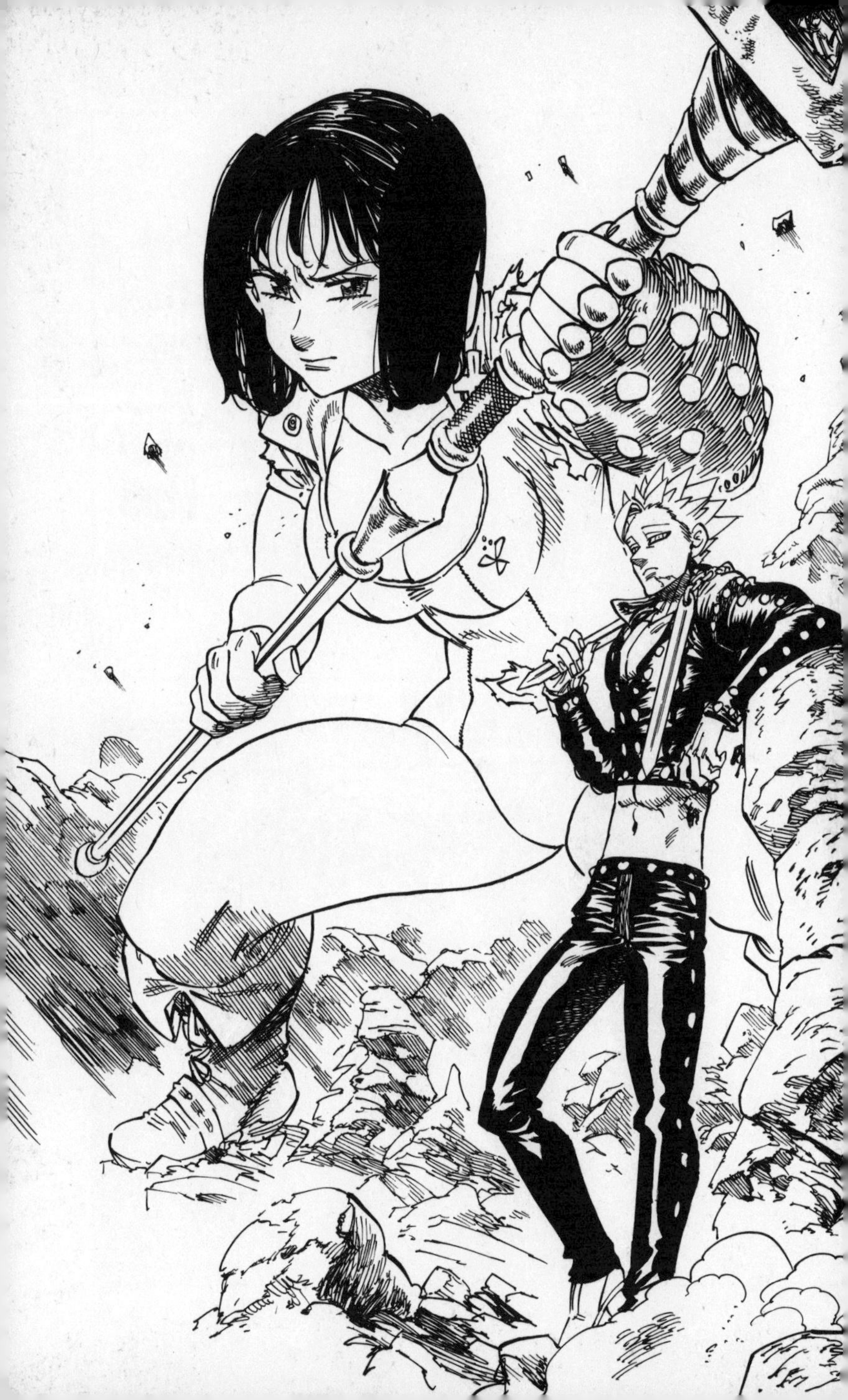

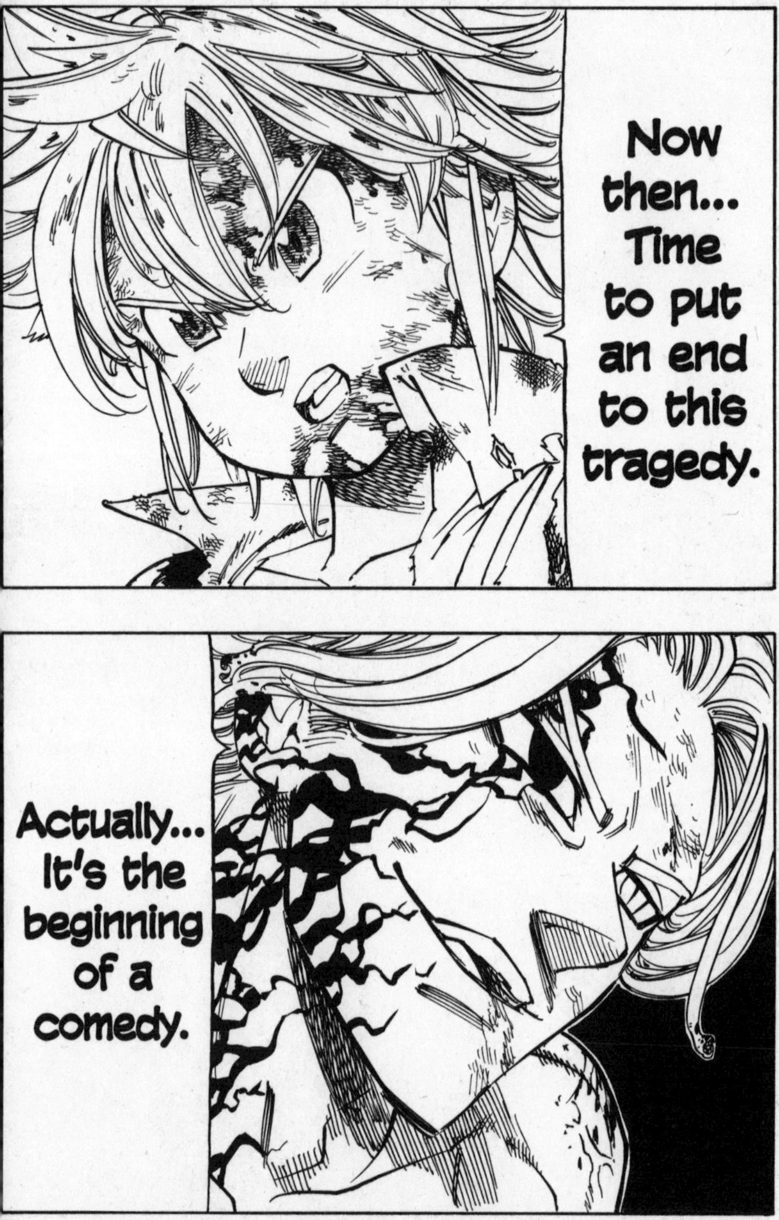
Now then... Time to put an end to this tragedy.
Actually... It's the beginning of a comedy.

Chapter 92 - The Final Decisive Battle Begins

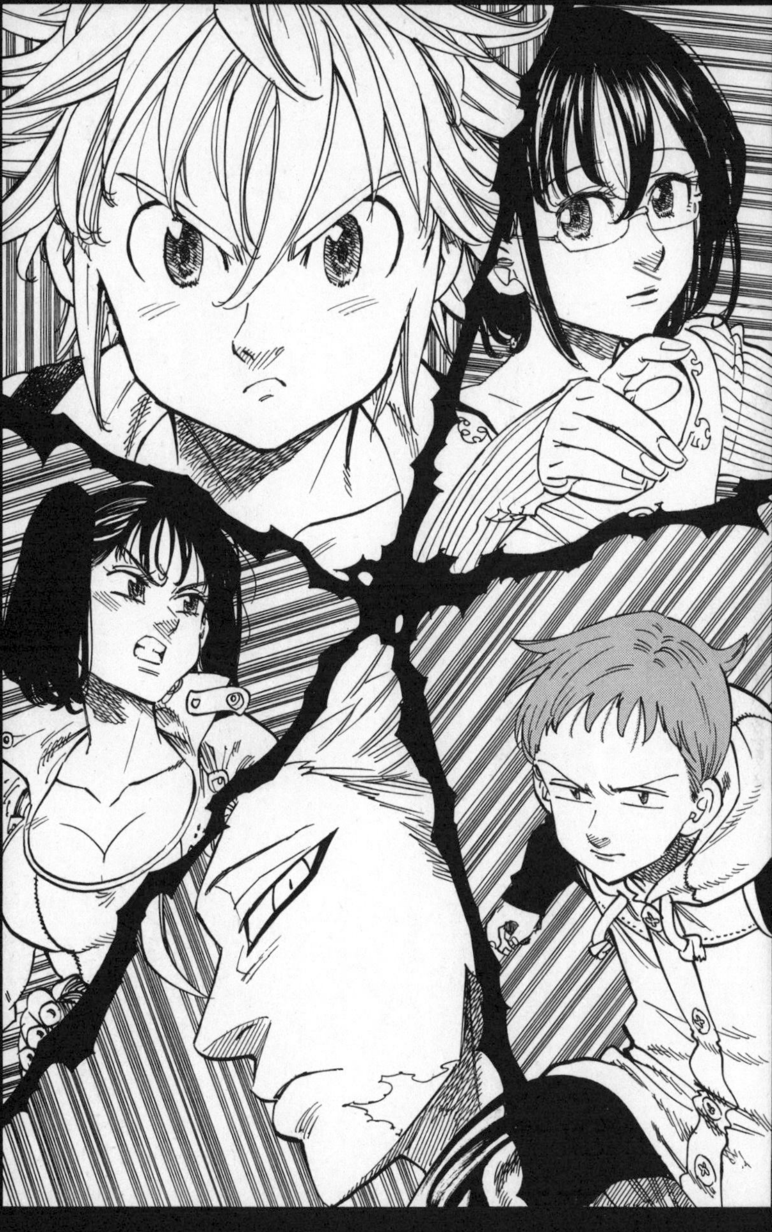

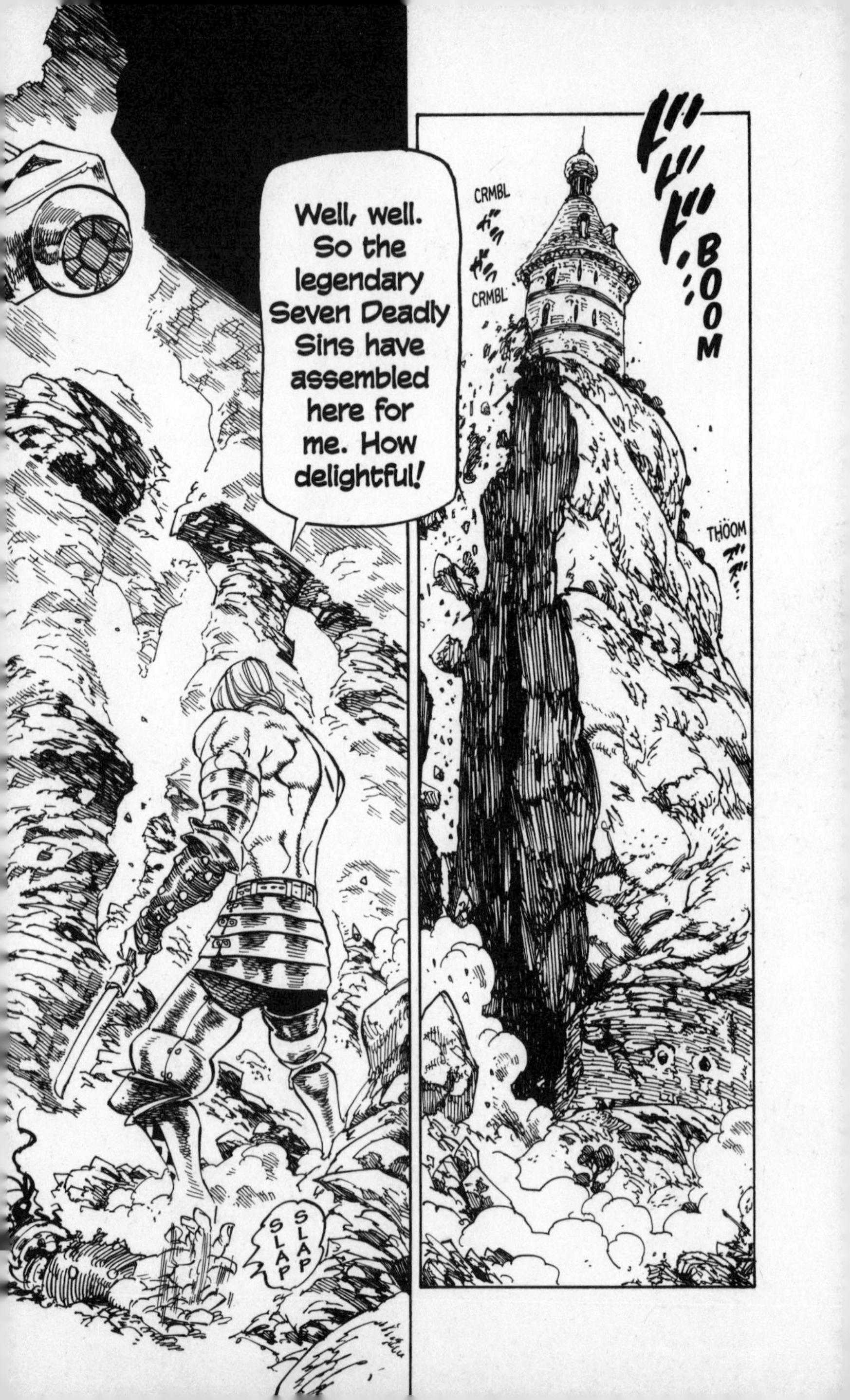
BOOM
CRMBL
CRMBL
THOOM
Well, well. So the legendary Seven Deadly Sins have assembled here for me. How delightful!
SLAP SLAP

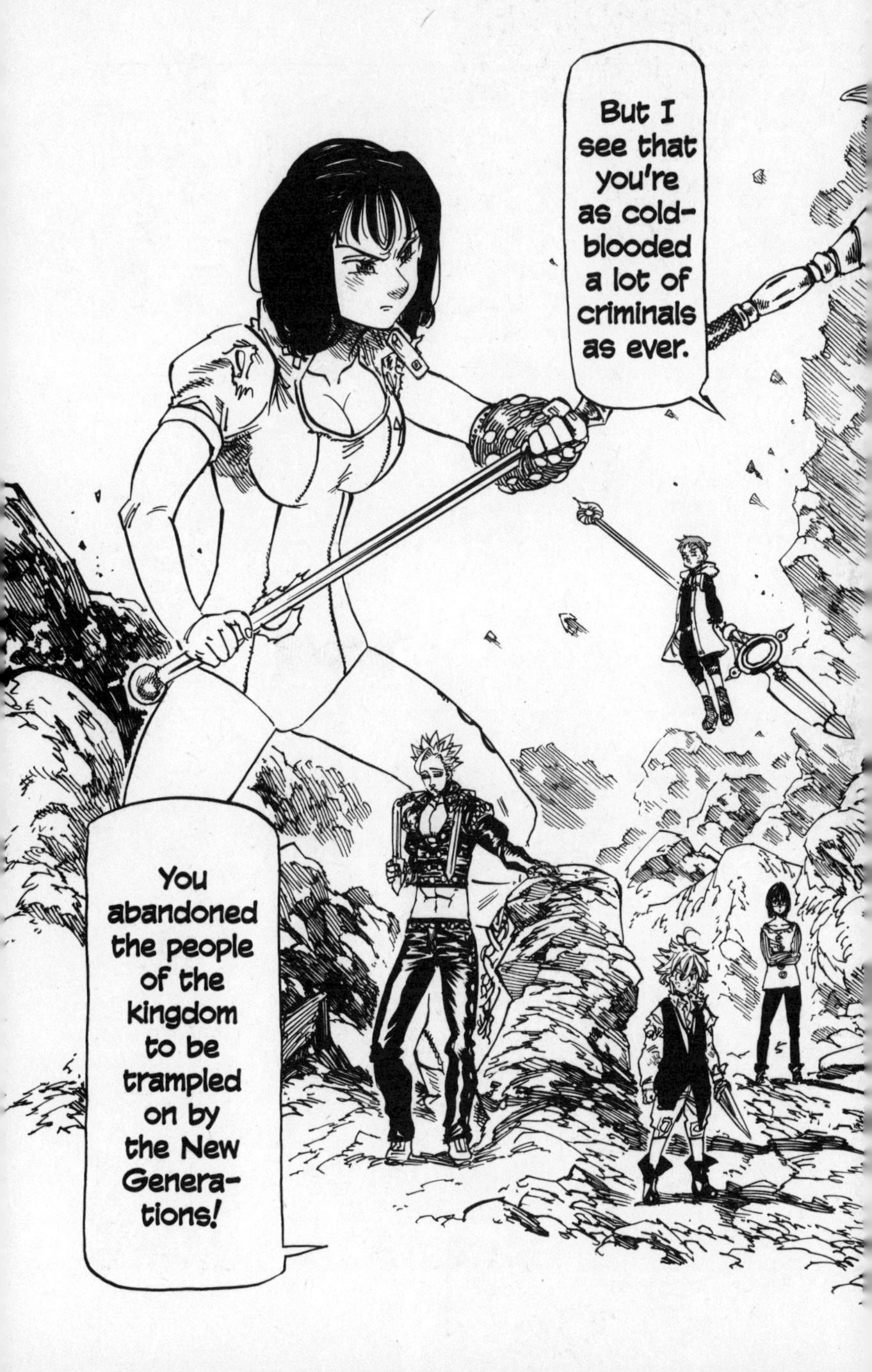
But I see that you're as cold-blooded a lot of criminals as ever.
You abandoned the people of the kingdom to be trampled on by the New Generations!

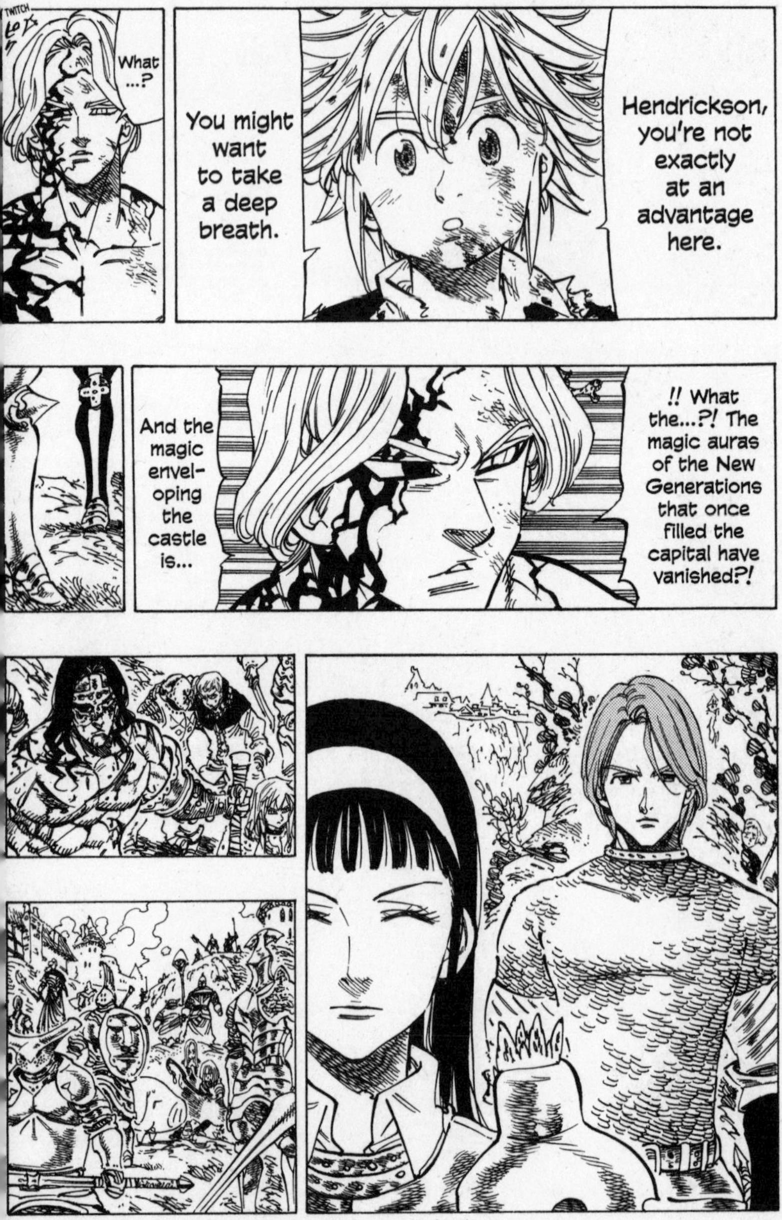
Hendrickson, you're not exactly at an advantage here.
You might want to take a deep breath.
TWITCH
What ...?
!! What the...?! The magic auras of the New Generations that once filled the capital have vanished?!
And the magic enveloping the castle is...

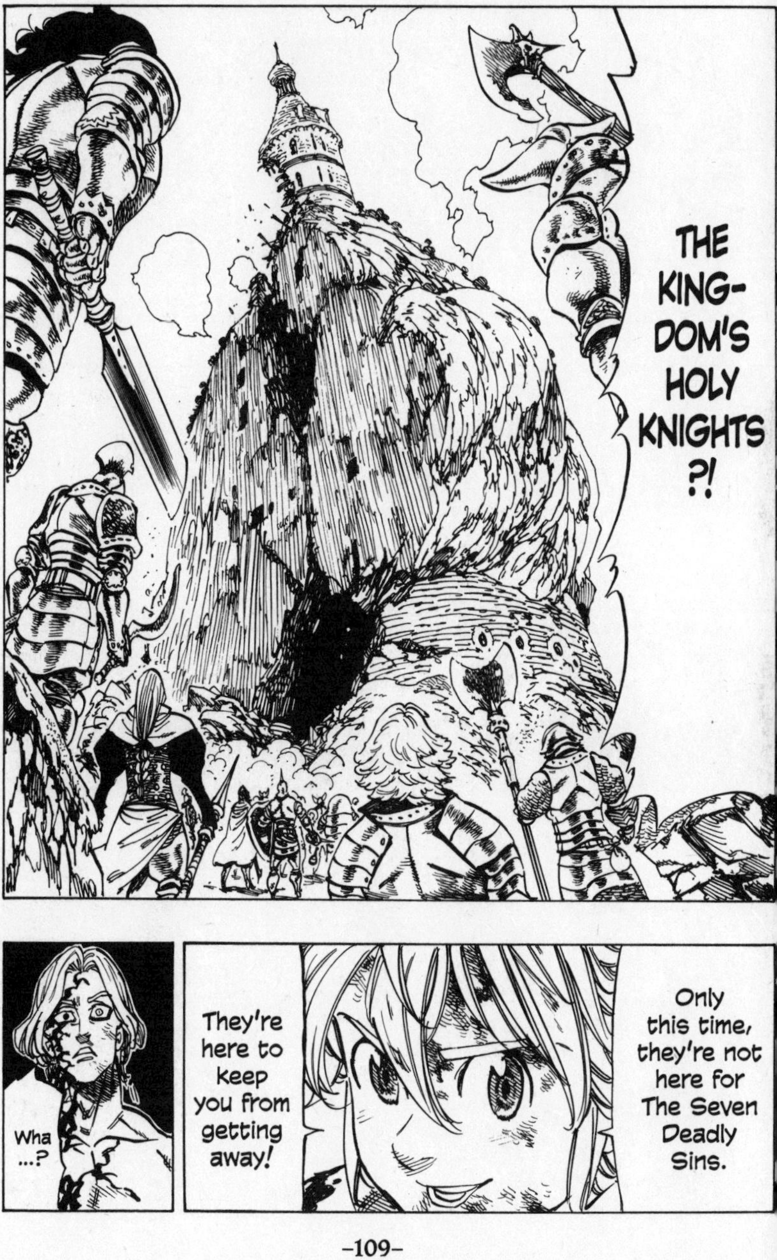
THE KING-DOM'S HOLY KNIGHTS?!
Only this time, they're not here for The Seven Deadly Sins.
They're here to keep you from getting away!
Wha ...?

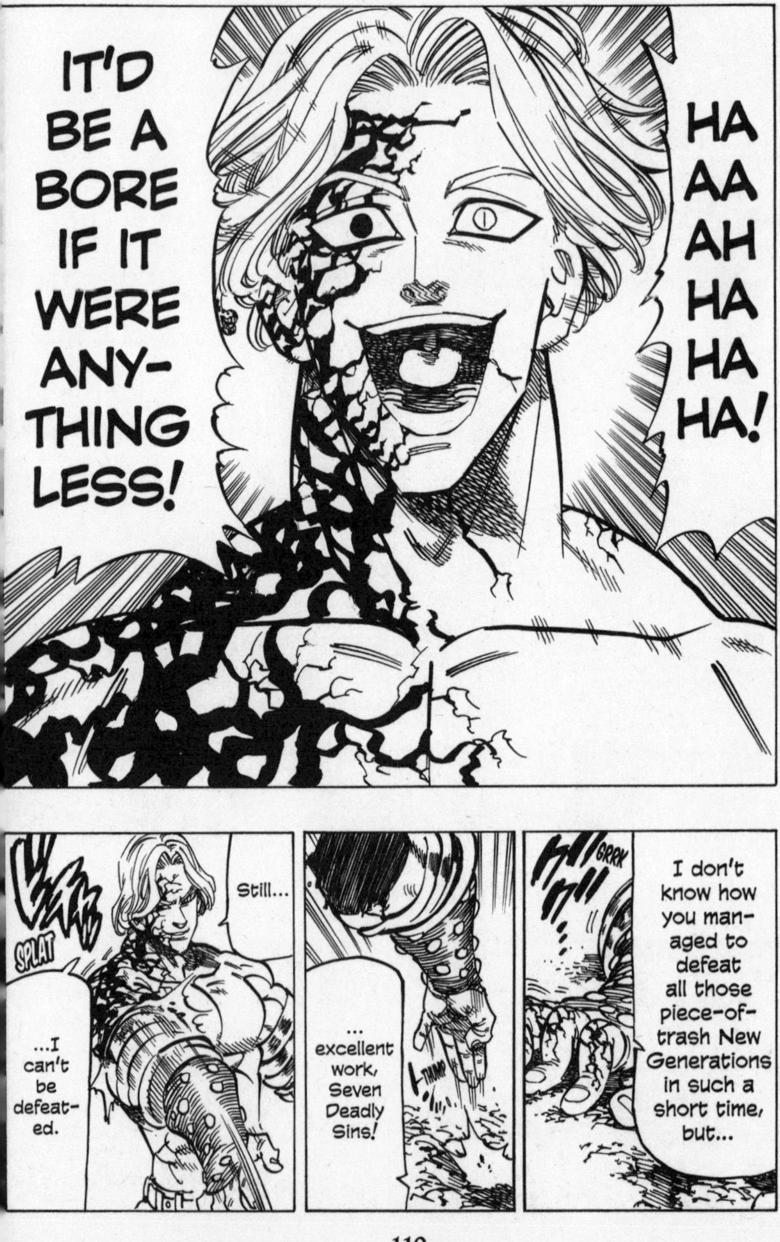
HA AA AH HA HA HA!
IT'D BE A BORE IF IT WERE ANYTHING LESS!
GRRK
I don't know how you managed to defeat all those piece-of-trash New Generations in such a short time, but...
THUMP
...excellent work, Seven Deadly Sins!
Still...
SPLAT
...I can't be defeated.

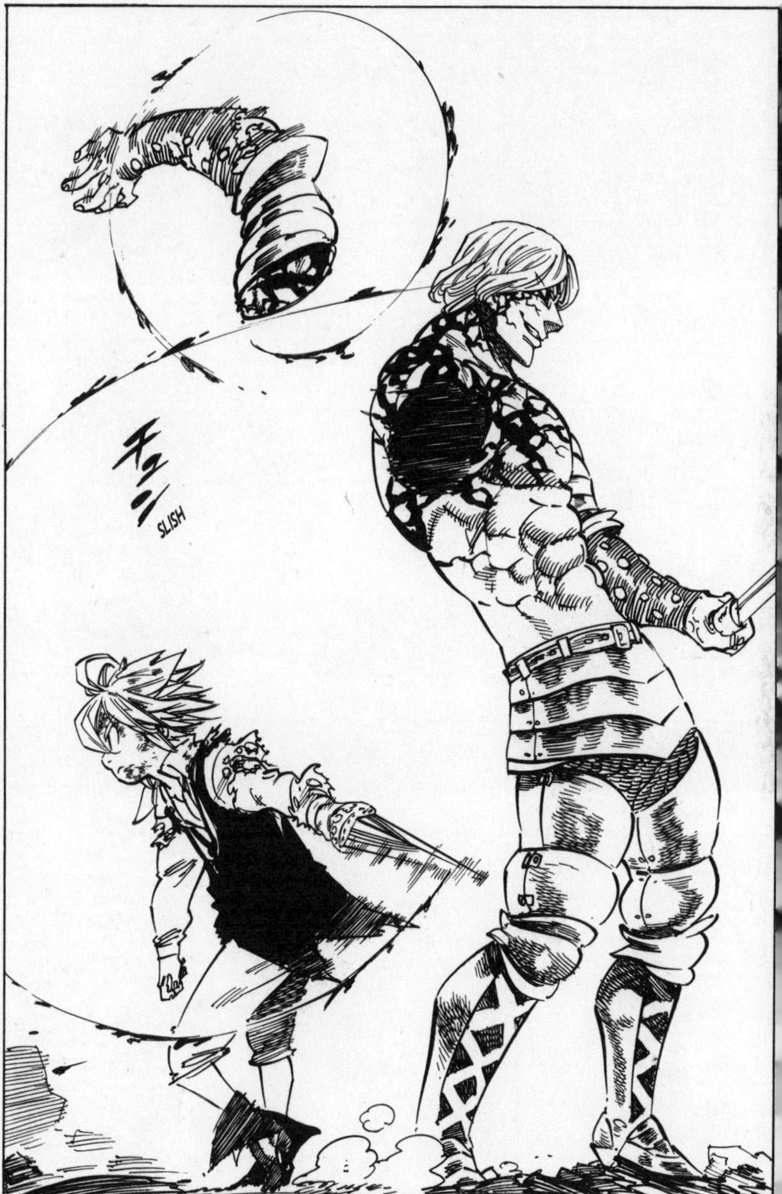
チュン
SLISH

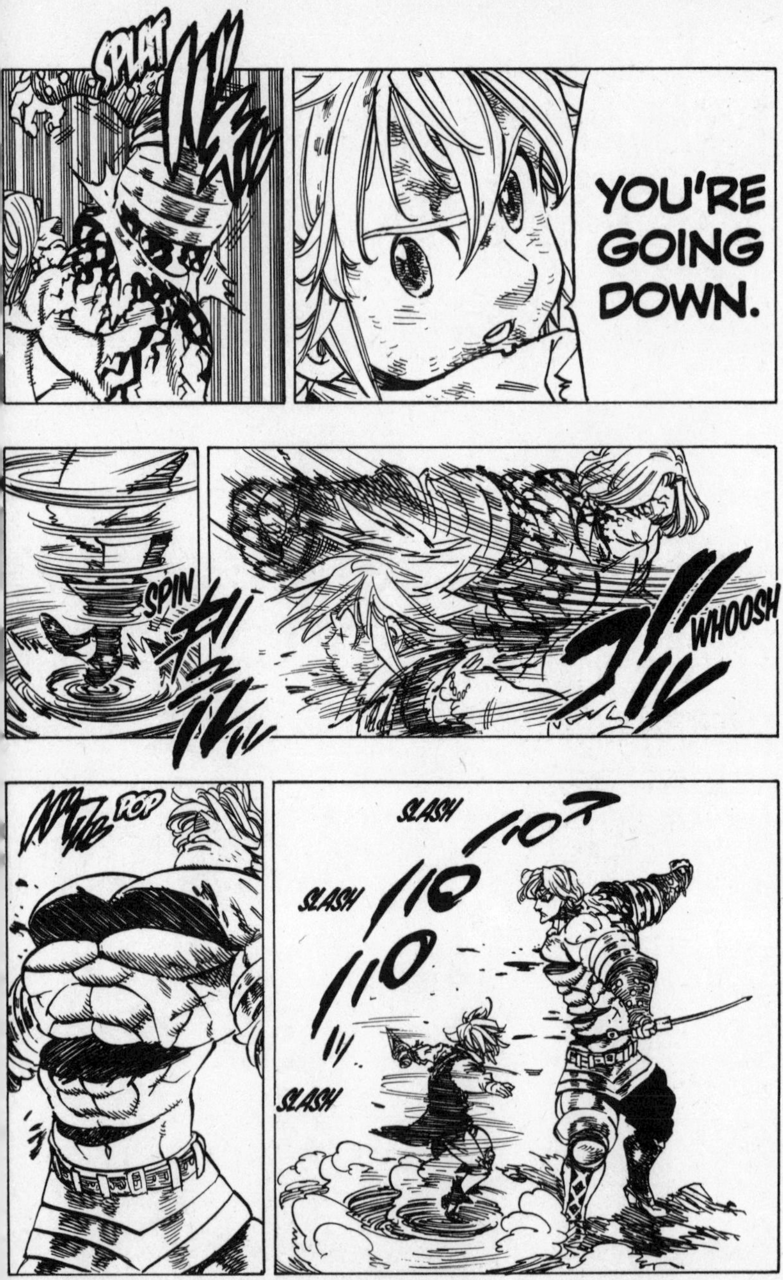
YOU'RE GOING DOWN.
SPLAT
WHOOSH
SPIN
SLASH
SLASH
SLASH
POP

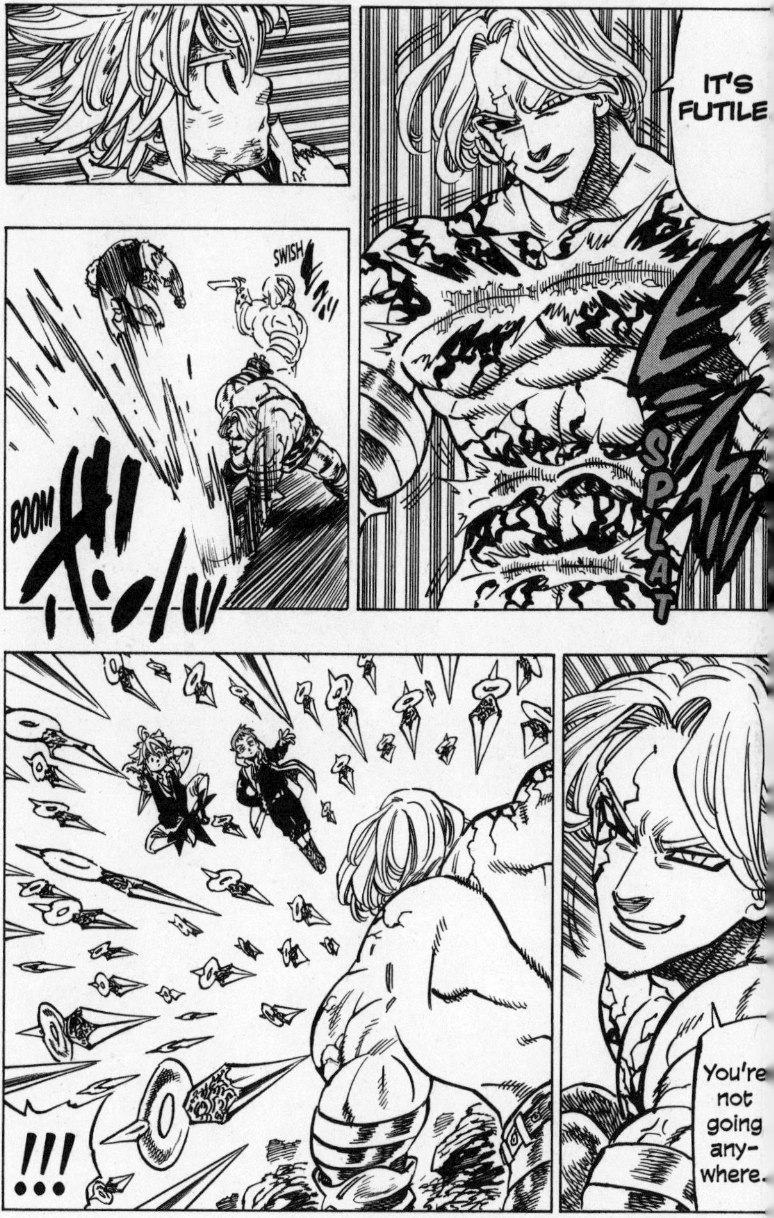
IT'S FUTILE
SPLAT
SWISH
BOOM
You're not going anywhere.
!!!

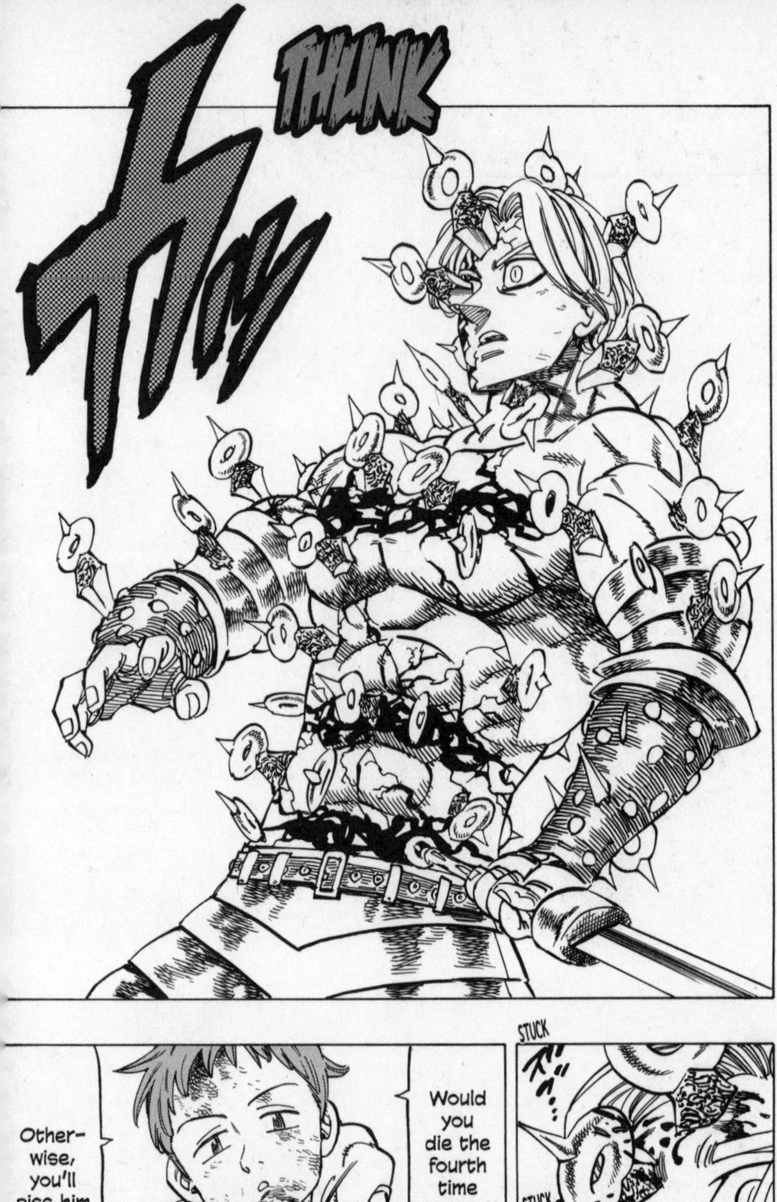
THUNK
STUCK
STUCK
Would you die the fourth time around already?
Otherwise, you'll piss him off.

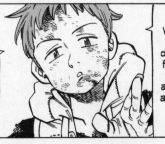

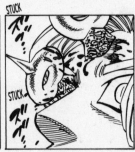

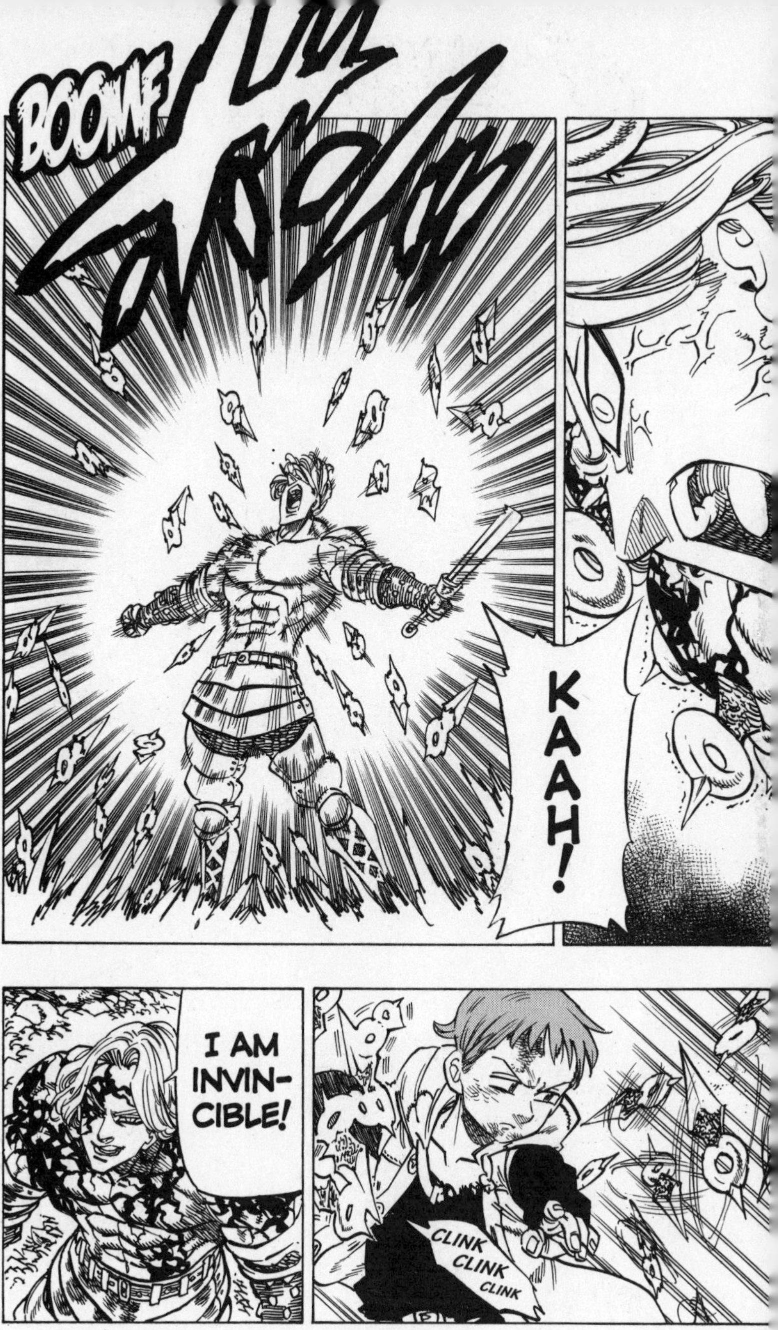
KAAH!
BOOM
CLINK
CLINK
CLINK
I AM INVINCIBLE!

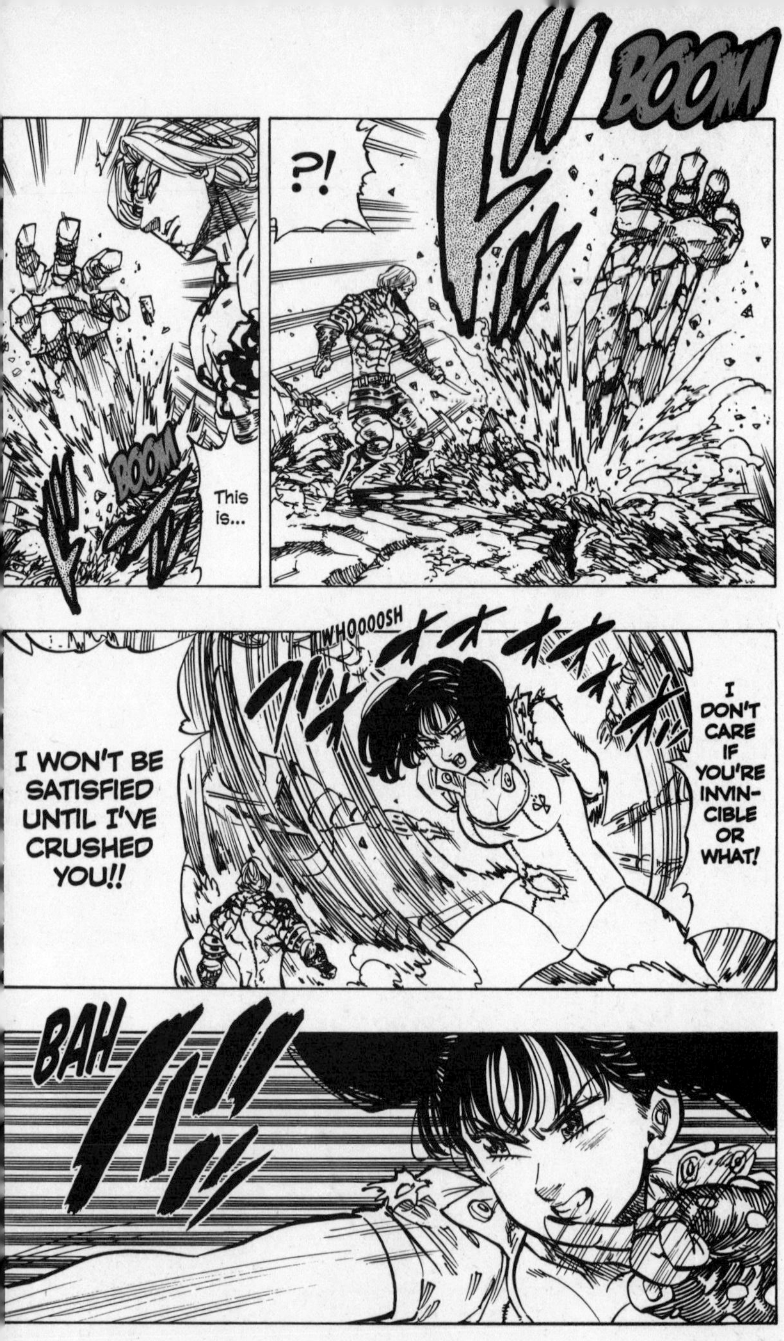
BOOM
?!
BOOM
This is...
WHOOOOSH
I DON'T CARE IF YOU'RE INVINCIBLE OR WHAT!
I WON'T BE SATISFIED UNTIL I'VE CRUSHED YOU!!
BAH

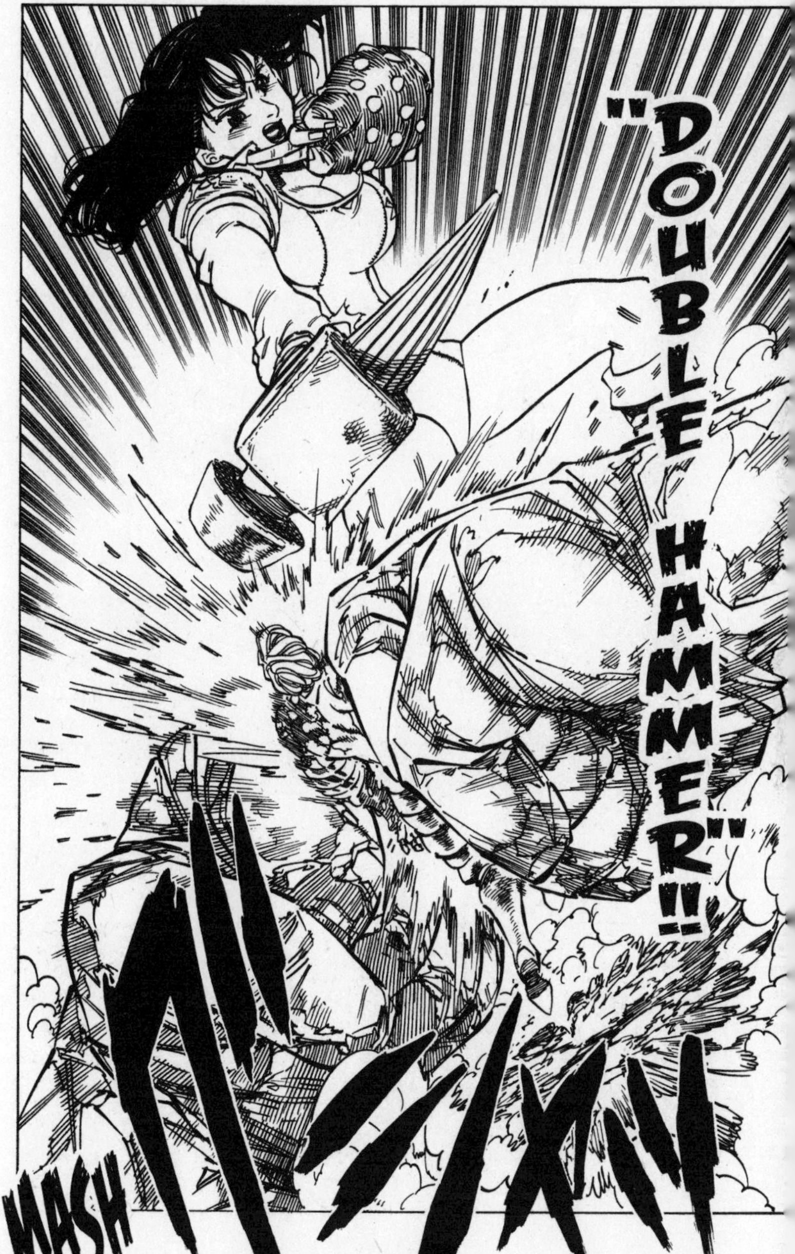
"DOUBLE HAMMER"!!
MASH

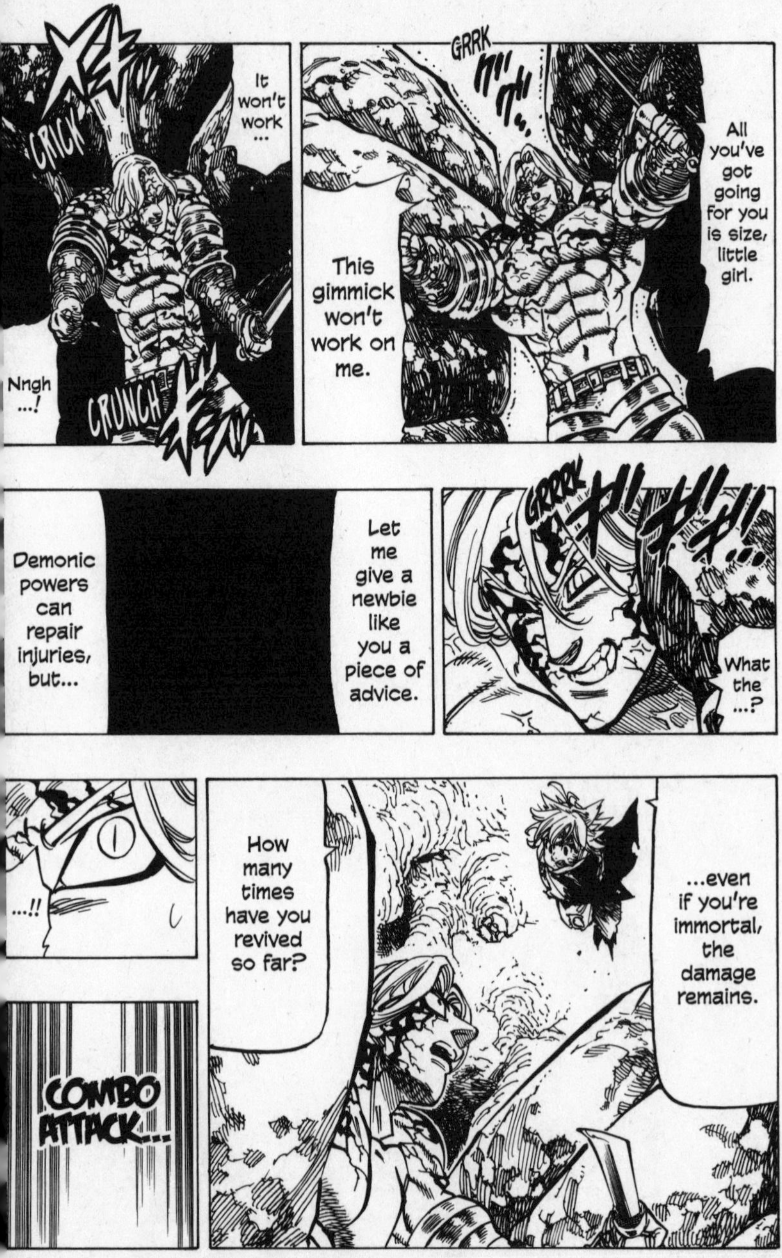
GRRK
All you've got going for you is size, little girl.
This gimmick won't work on me.
It won't work...
CRICK
CRUNCH
Nngh ...!
GRRRK
What the ...?
Let me give a newbie like you a piece of advice.
Demonic powers can repair injuries, but...
...even if you're immortal, the damage remains.
How many times have you revived so far?
...!!
COMBO ATTACK...

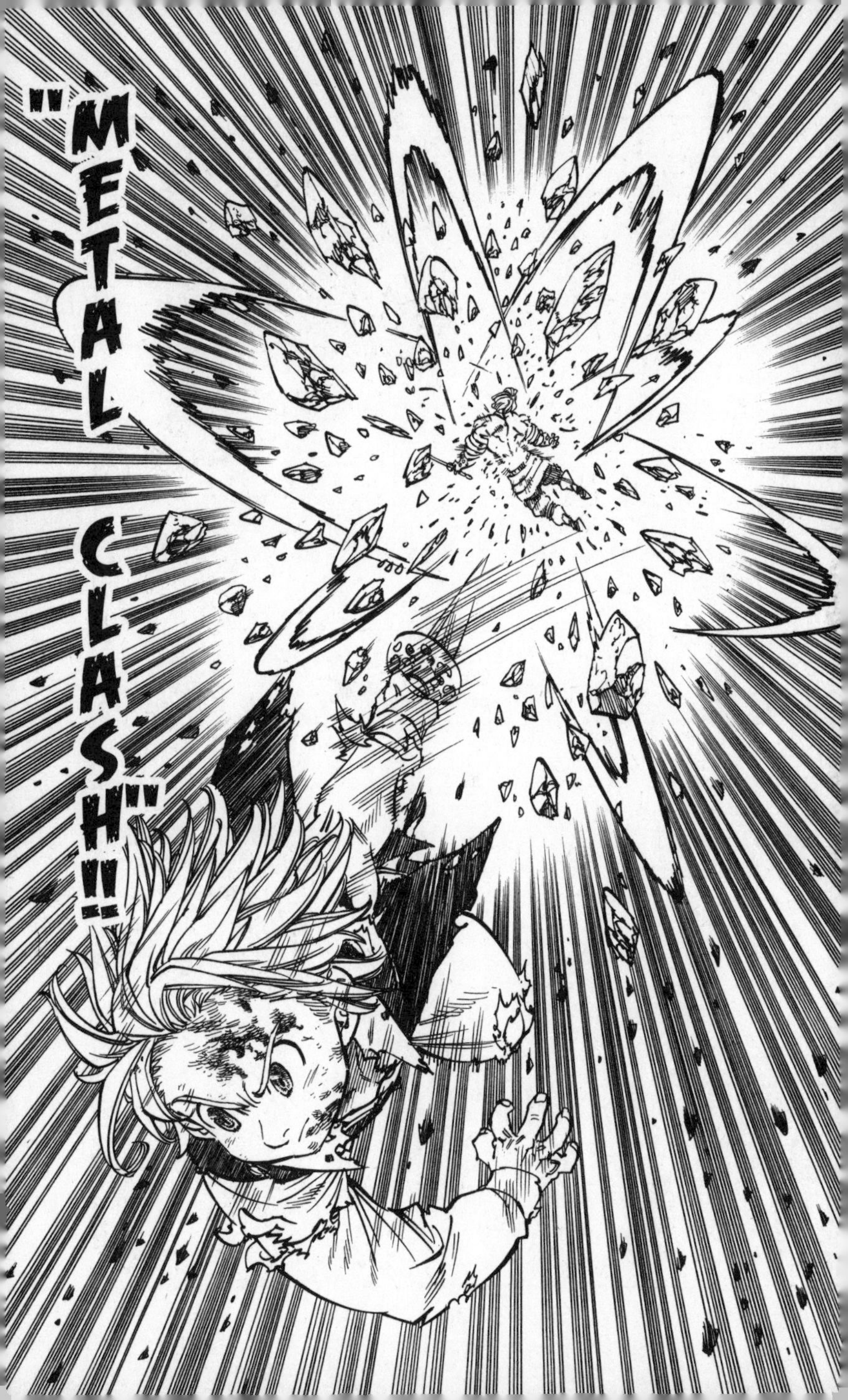
"METAL CLASH"!!

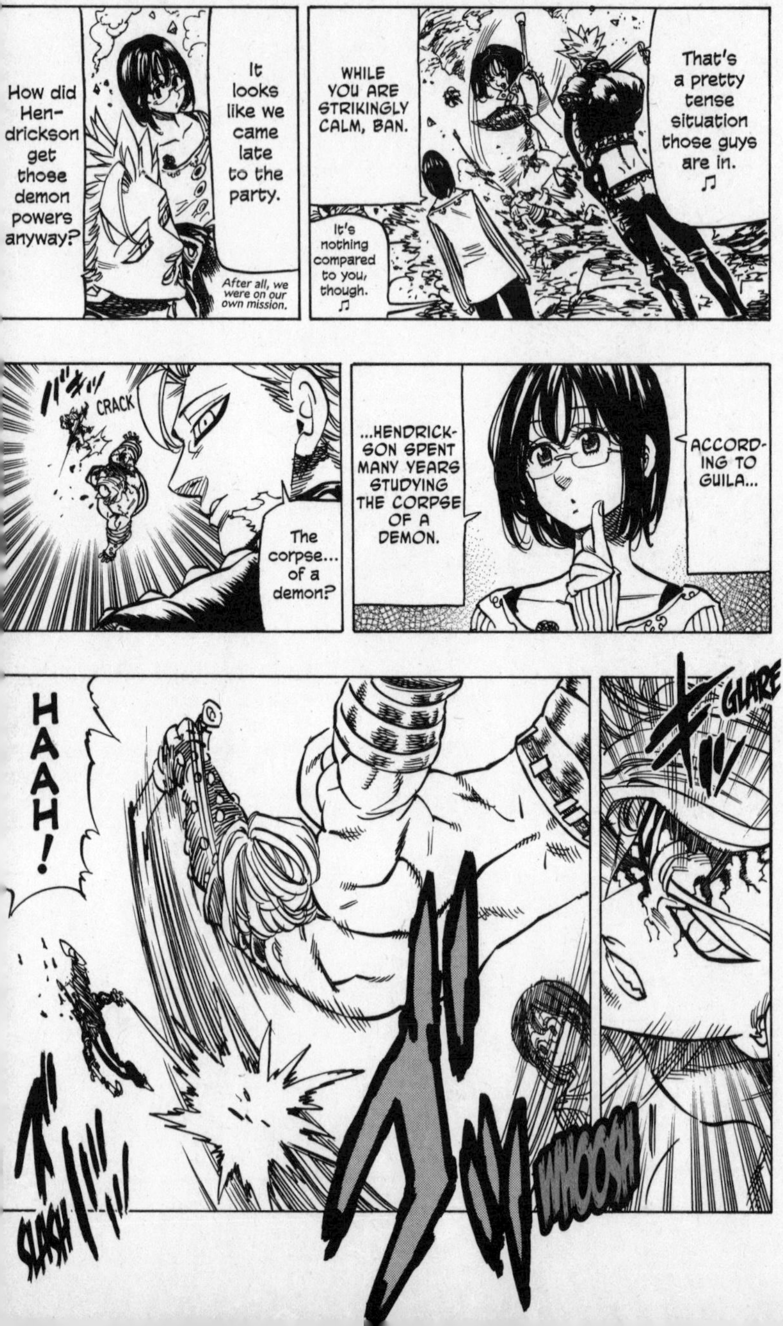
That's a pretty tense situation those guys are in. ♫
WHILE YOU ARE STRIKINGLY CALM, BAN.
It's nothing compared to you, though. ♫
It looks like we came late to the party.
After all, we were on our own mission.
How did Hen-drickson get those demon powers anyway?
ACCORD-ING TO GUILA...
...HENDRICK-SON SPENT MANY YEARS STUDYING THE CORPSE OF A DEMON.
The corpse... of a demon?
CRACK
GLARE
HAAH!
WHOOSH
SLASH

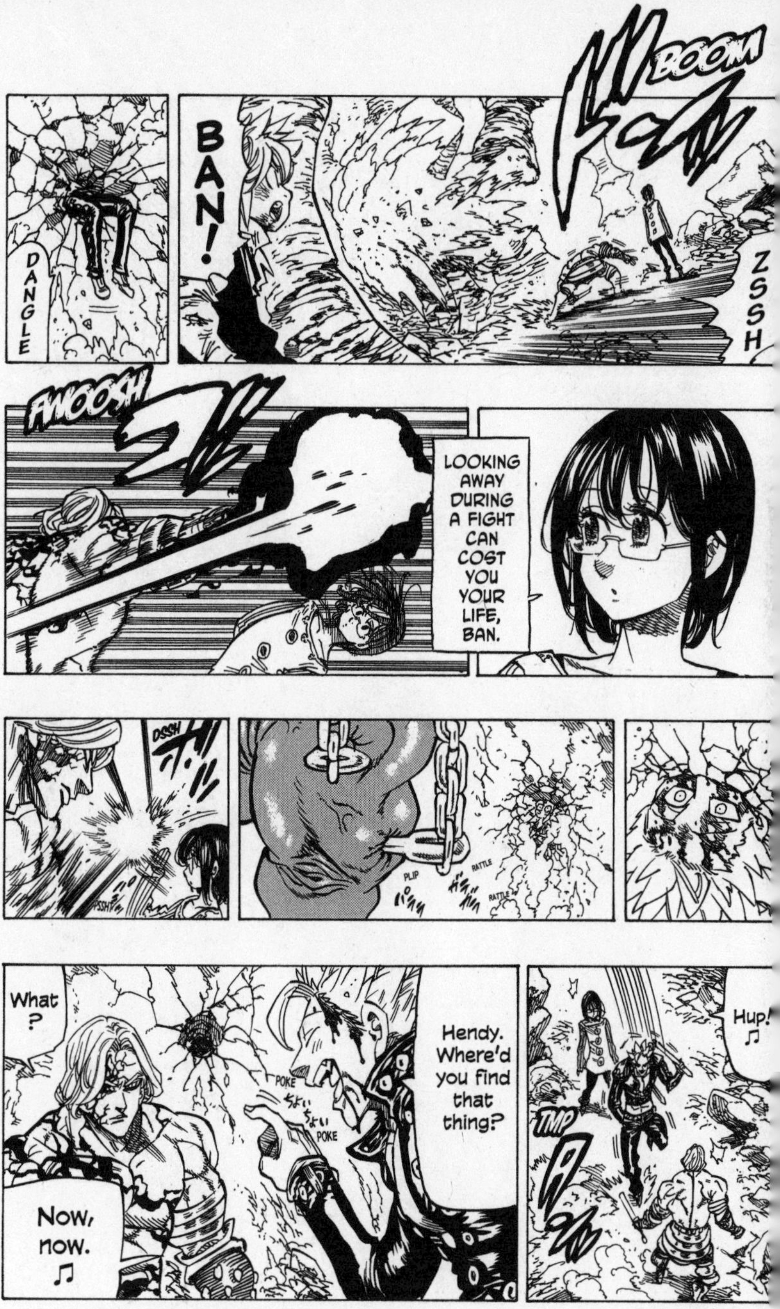
BOOM
ZSSH
BAN!
DANGLE
LOOKING AWAY DURING A FIGHT CAN COST YOU YOUR LIFE, BAN.
FWOOSH
RATTLE
RATTLE
PLIP
DSSH
Hup! ♫
TMP
Hendy. Where'd you find that thing?
POKE
ちょい
ちょい
POKE
What?
Now, now. ♫

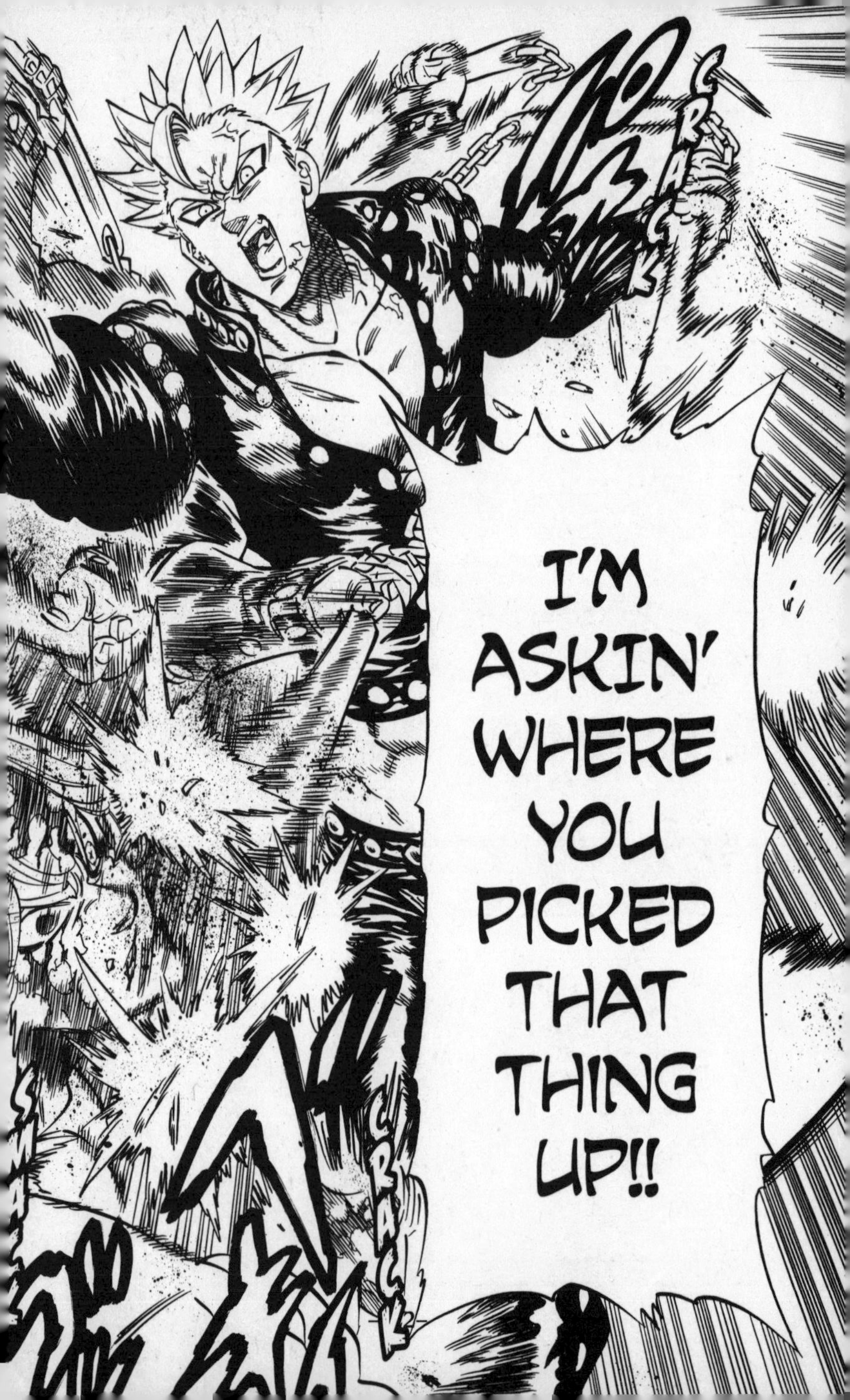
CRACK
I'M ASKIN' WHERE YOU PICKED THAT THING UP!!
CRACK

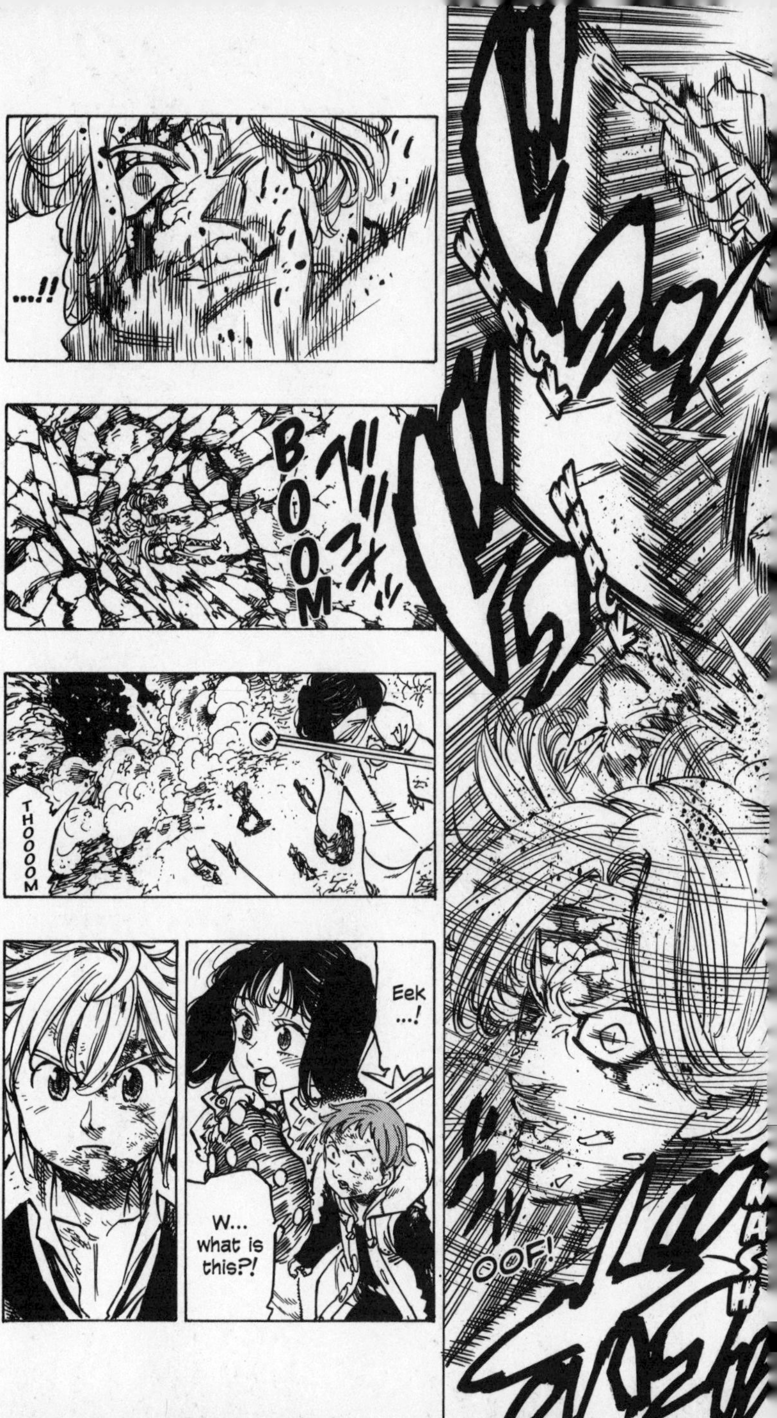
WHACK
WHACK
OOF!
NASH
...!!
BOOM
THOOOOOM
Eek ...!
W... what is this?!

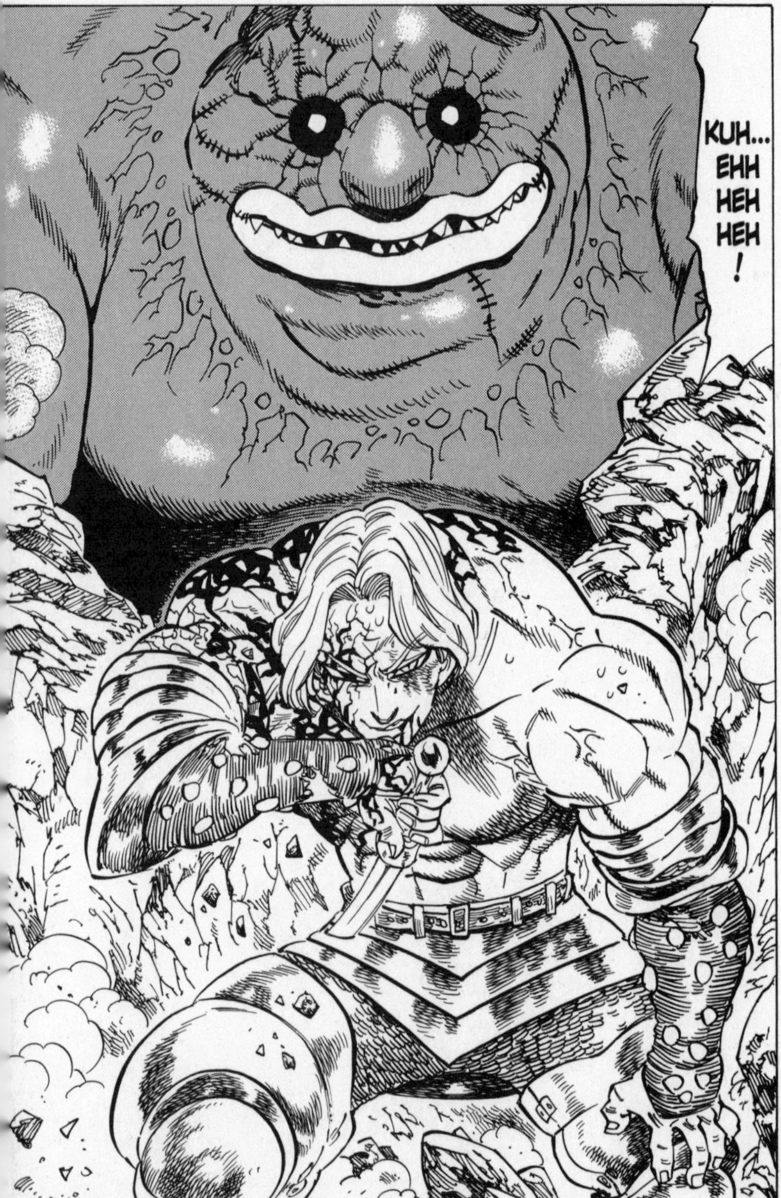
KUH... EHH HEH HEH!

Chapter 93 - Red & Ashes

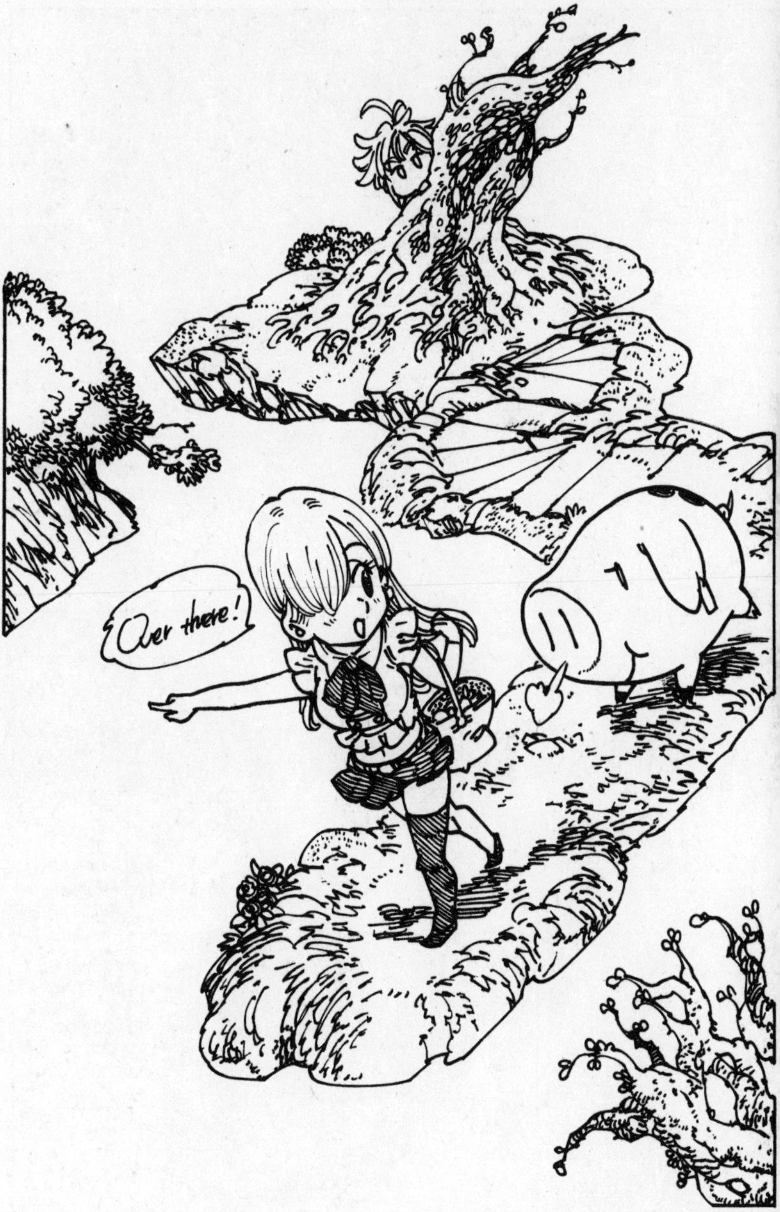
Over there!

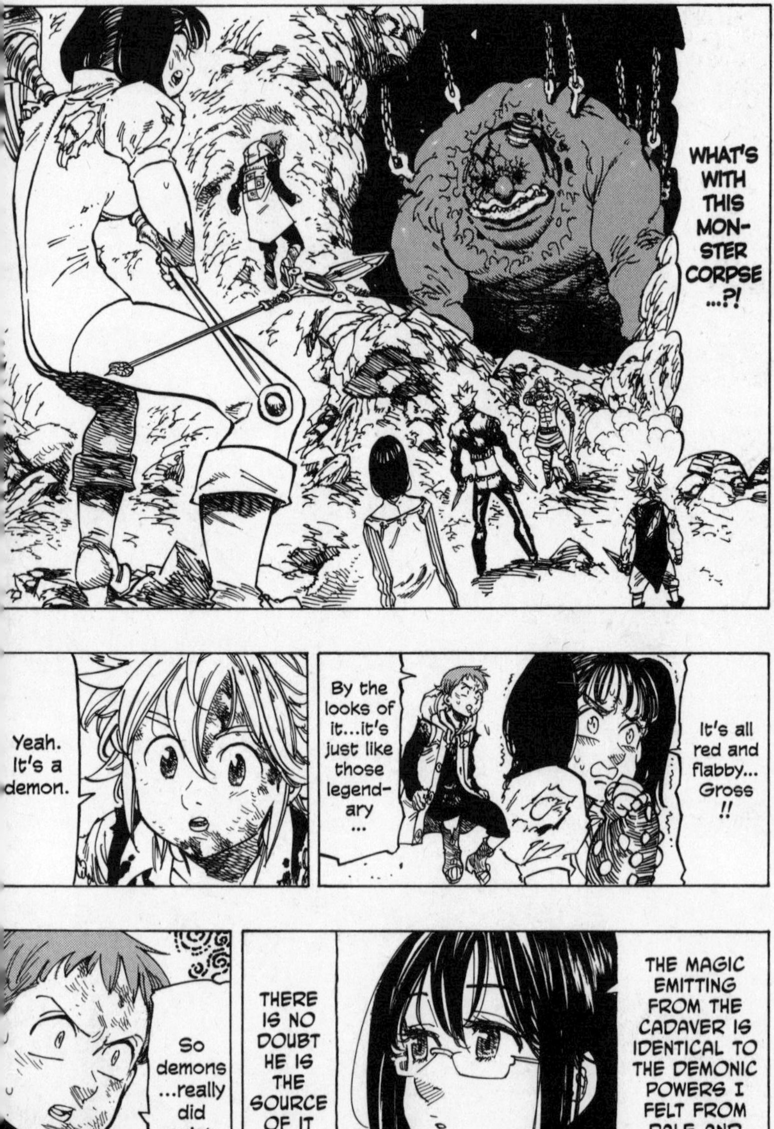
WHAT'S WITH THIS MONSTER CORPSE ...?!
It's all red and flabby... Gross!!
By the looks of it...it's just like those legendary...
Yeah. It's a demon.
THE MAGIC EMITTING FROM THE CADAVER IS IDENTICAL TO THE DEMONIC POWERS I FELT FROM DALE AND THE NEW GENERATIONS.
THERE IS NO DOUBT HE IS THE SOURCE OF IT ALL.
So demons ...really did exist ...!

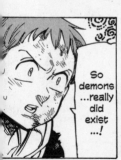

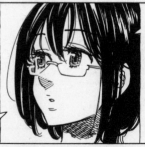

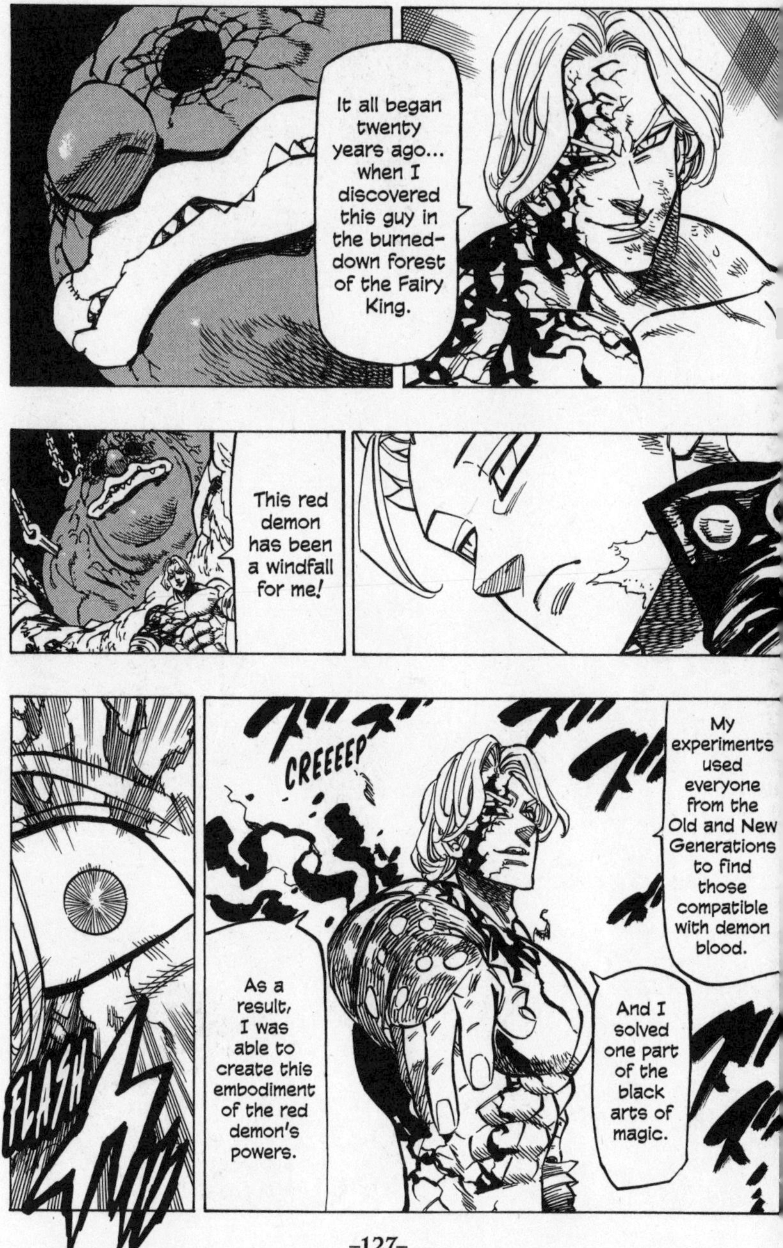
It all began twenty years ago... when I discovered this guy in the burned-down forest of the Fairy King.
This red demon has been a windfall for me!
My experiments used everyone from the Old and New Generations to find those compatible with demon blood.
CREEEEP
And I solved one part of the black arts of magic.
As a result, I was able to create this embodiment of the red demon's powers.
FLASH

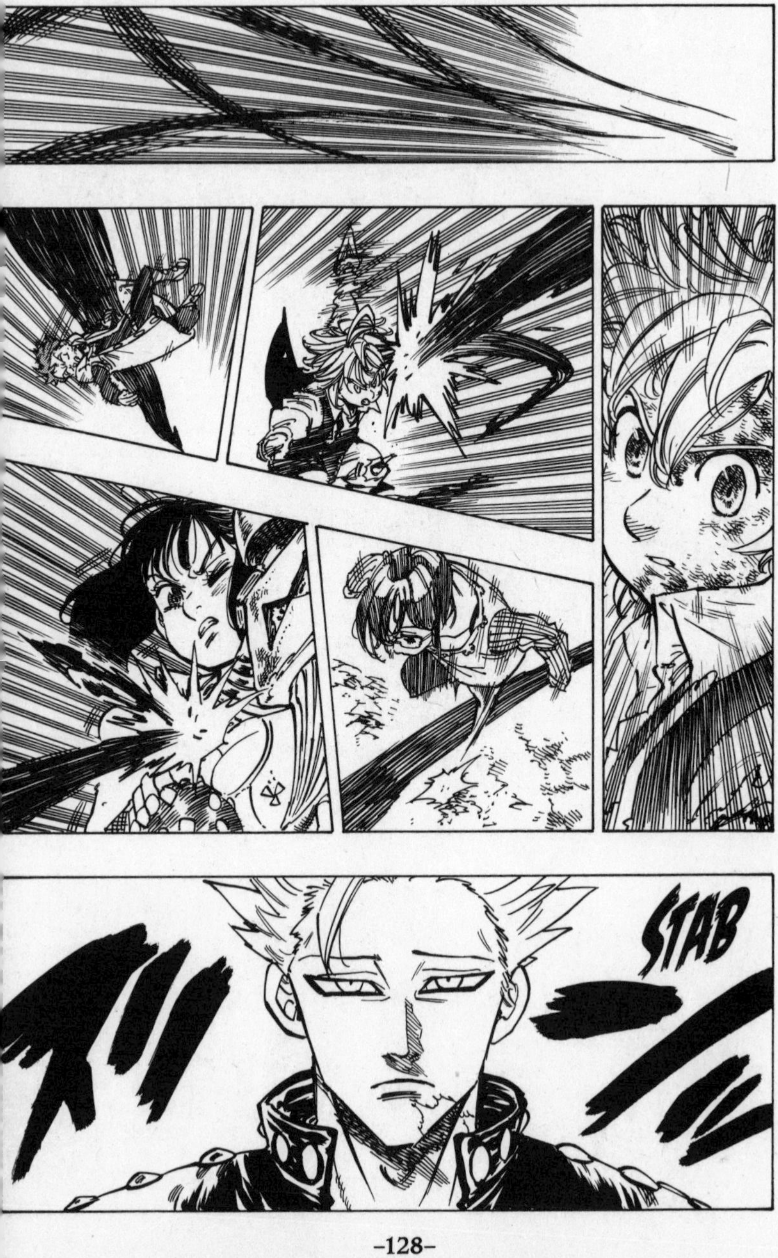
STAB

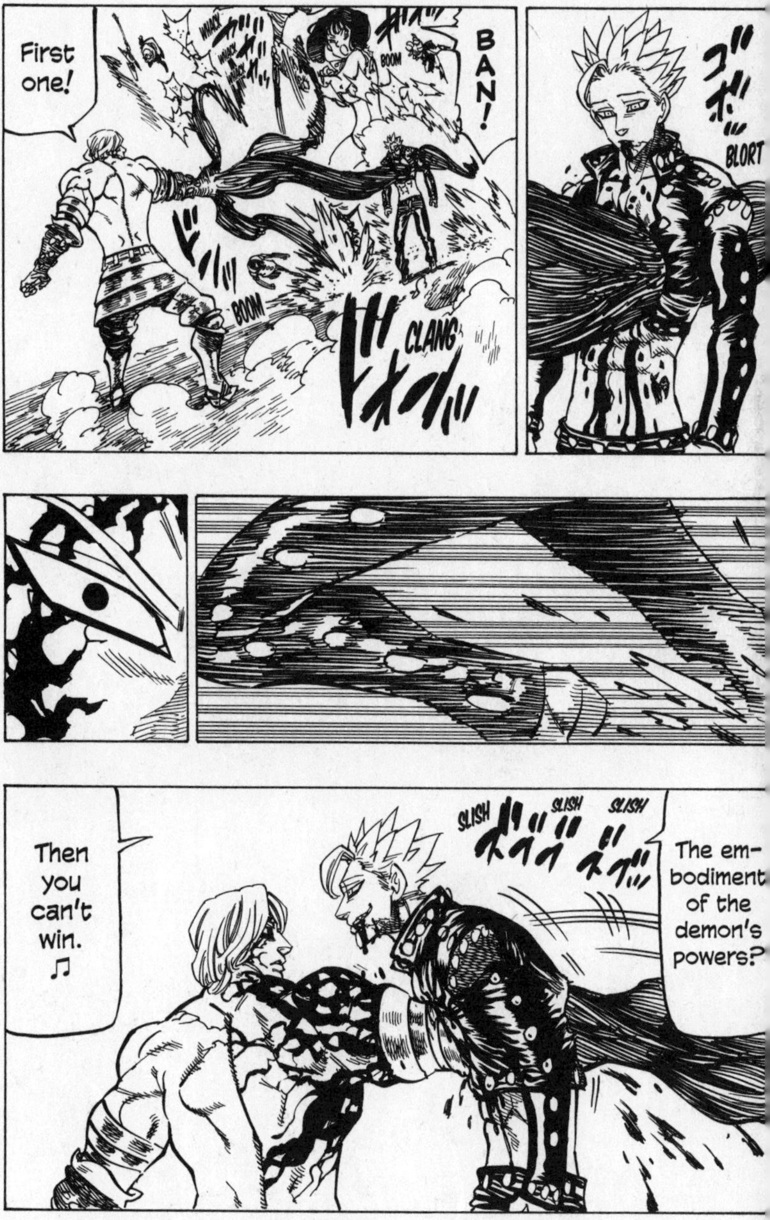
BLORT
BAN!
BOOM
WHACK
First one!
BOOM
CLANG
SLISH
SLISH
SLISH
The em-
bodiment
of the
demon's
powers?
Then
you
can't
win.
♫

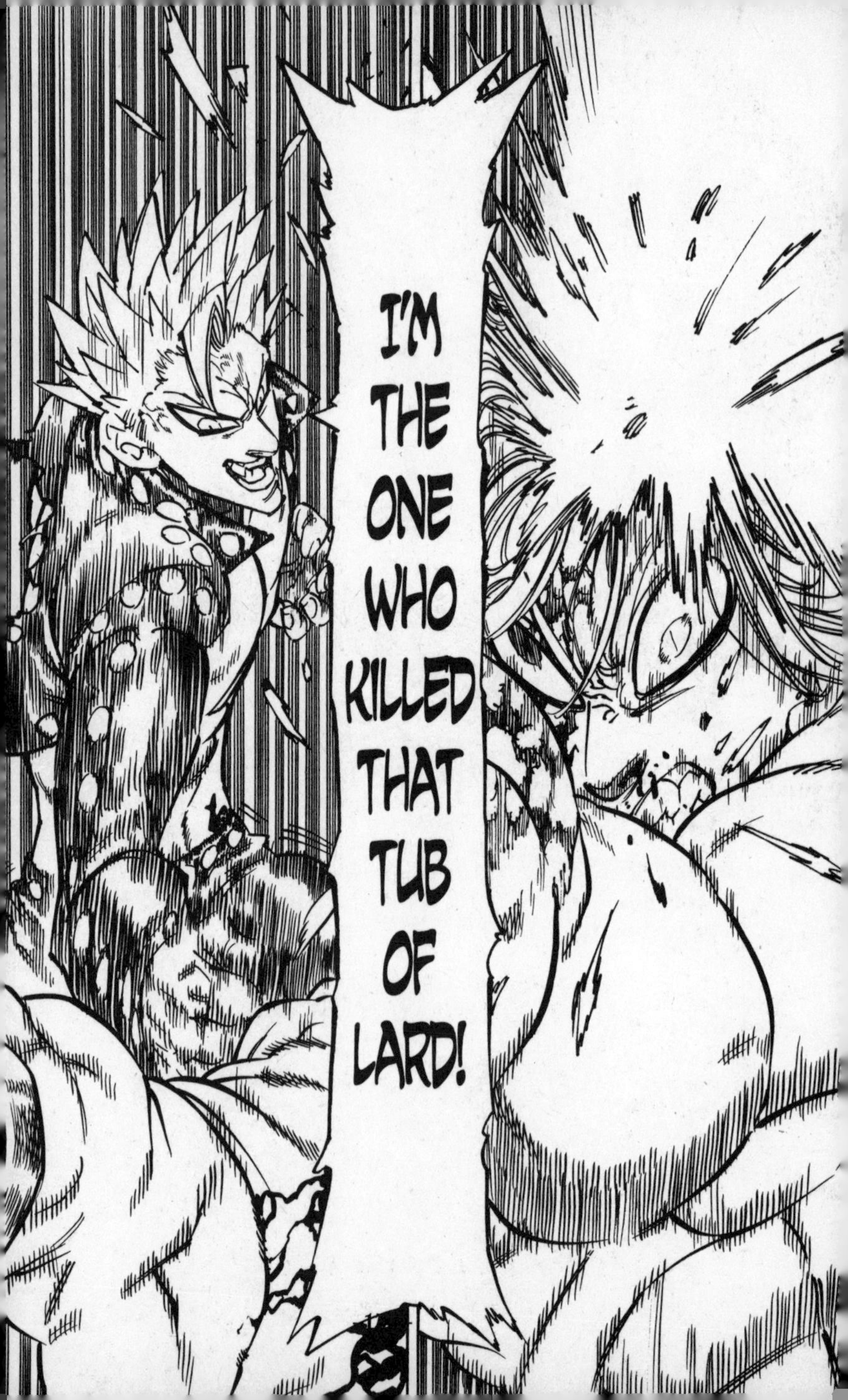
I'M THE ONE WHO KILLED THAT TUB OF LARD!

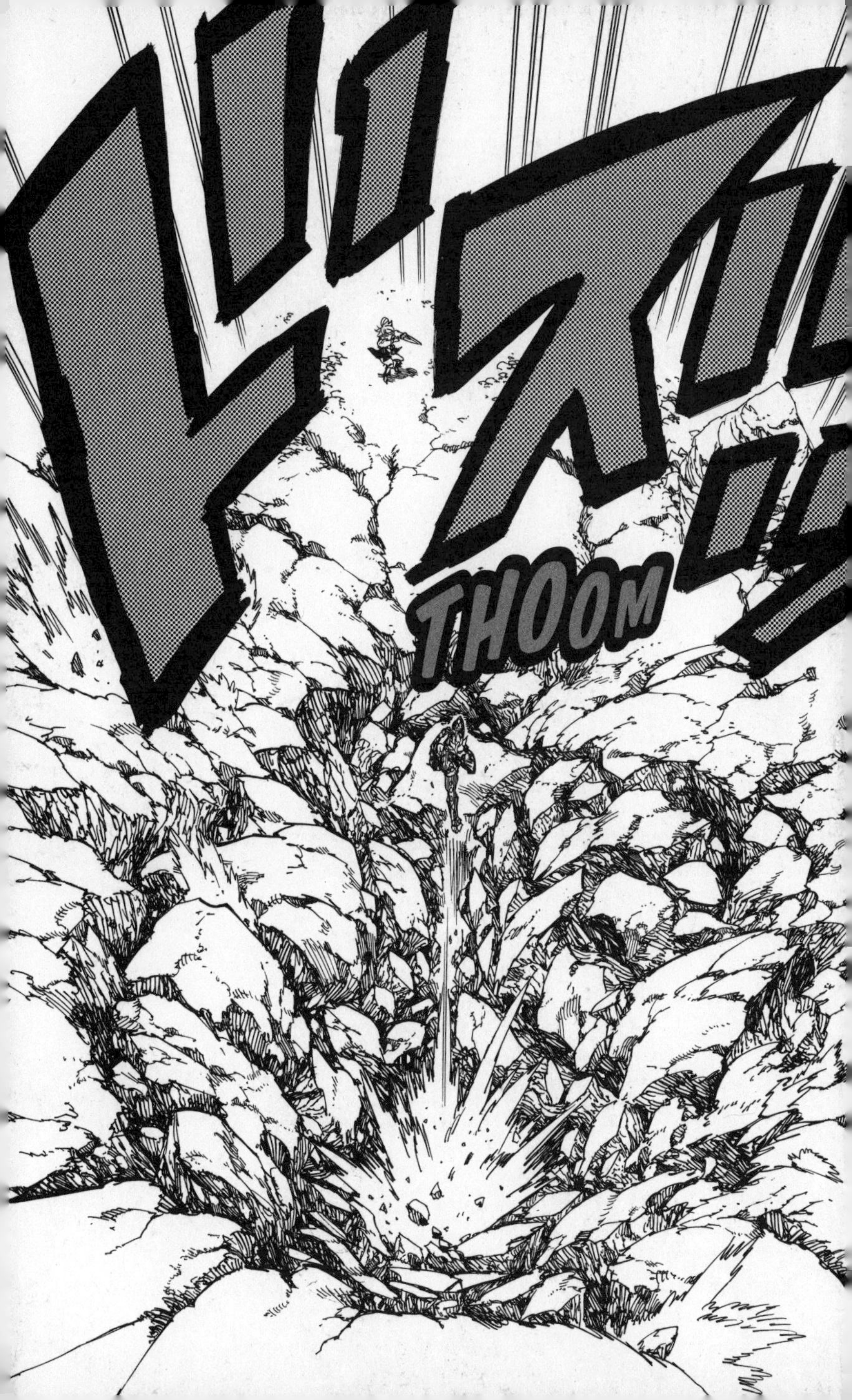
THOOM

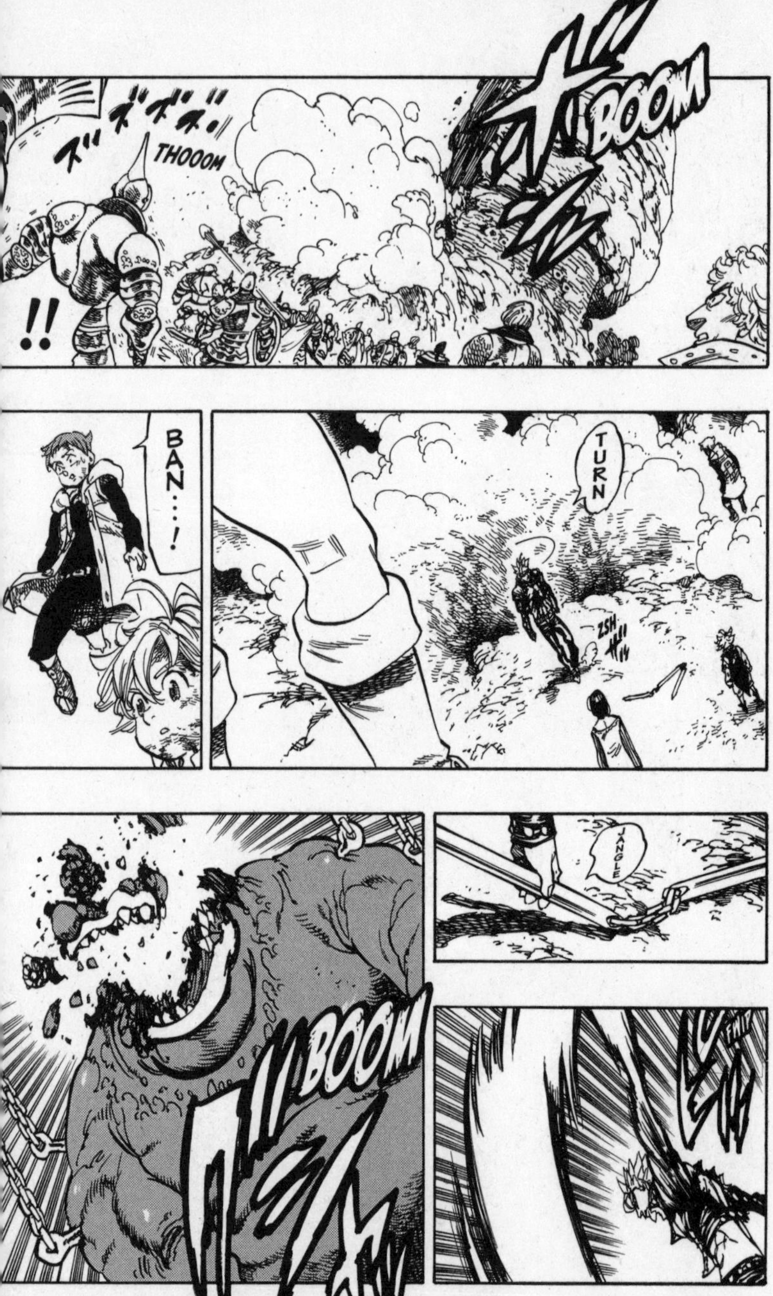

BOOM
ズズズズ
THOOOM
!!
TURN
ZSH
BAN...!
JANGLE
BOOM

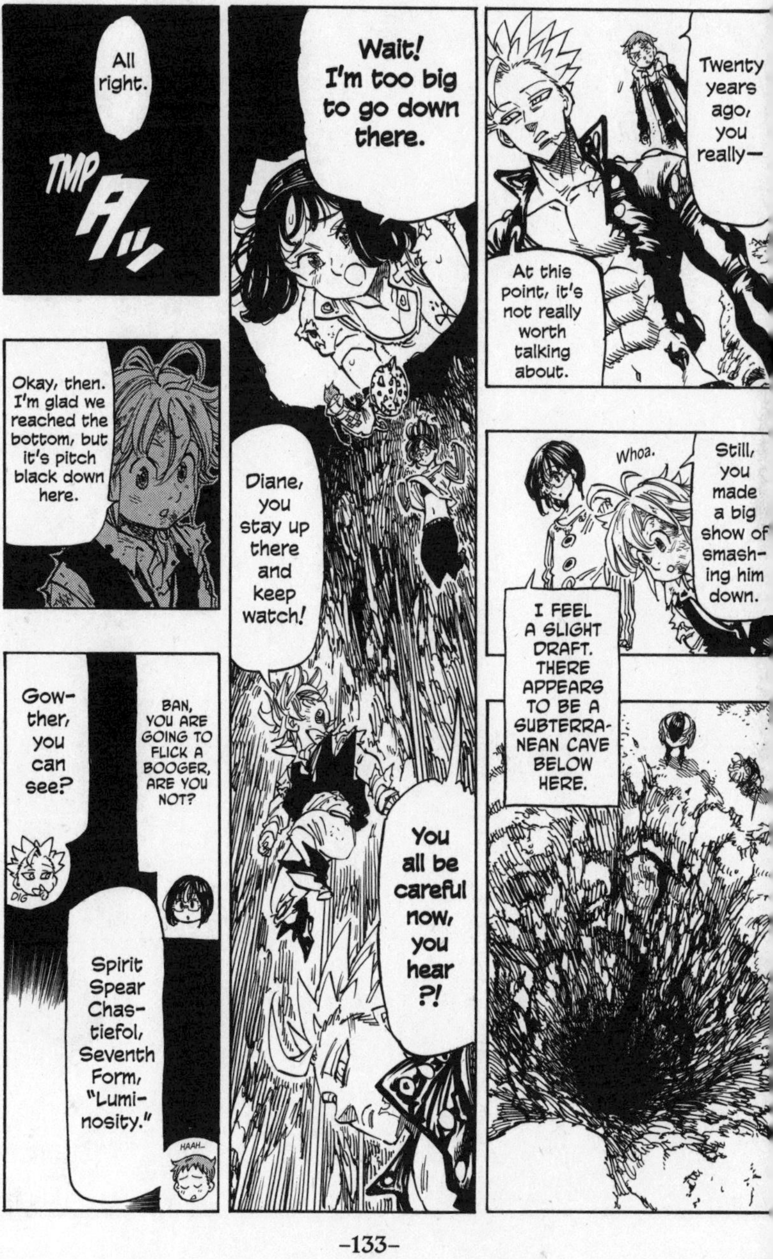
Twenty years ago, you really—
At this point, it's not really worth talking about.
Still, you made a big show of smashing him down.
Whoa.
I FEEL A SLIGHT DRAFT. THERE APPEARS TO BE A SUBTERRANEAN CAVE BELOW HERE.
Wait! I'm too big to go down there.
Diane, you stay up there and keep watch!
You all be careful now, you hear?!
All right.
TMP
Okay, then. I'm glad we reached the bottom, but it's pitch black down here.
Gowther, you can see?
BAN, YOU ARE GOING TO FLICK A BOOGER, ARE YOU NOT?
DIG
Spirit Spear Chastiefol, Seventh Form, "Luminosity."
HAAH...

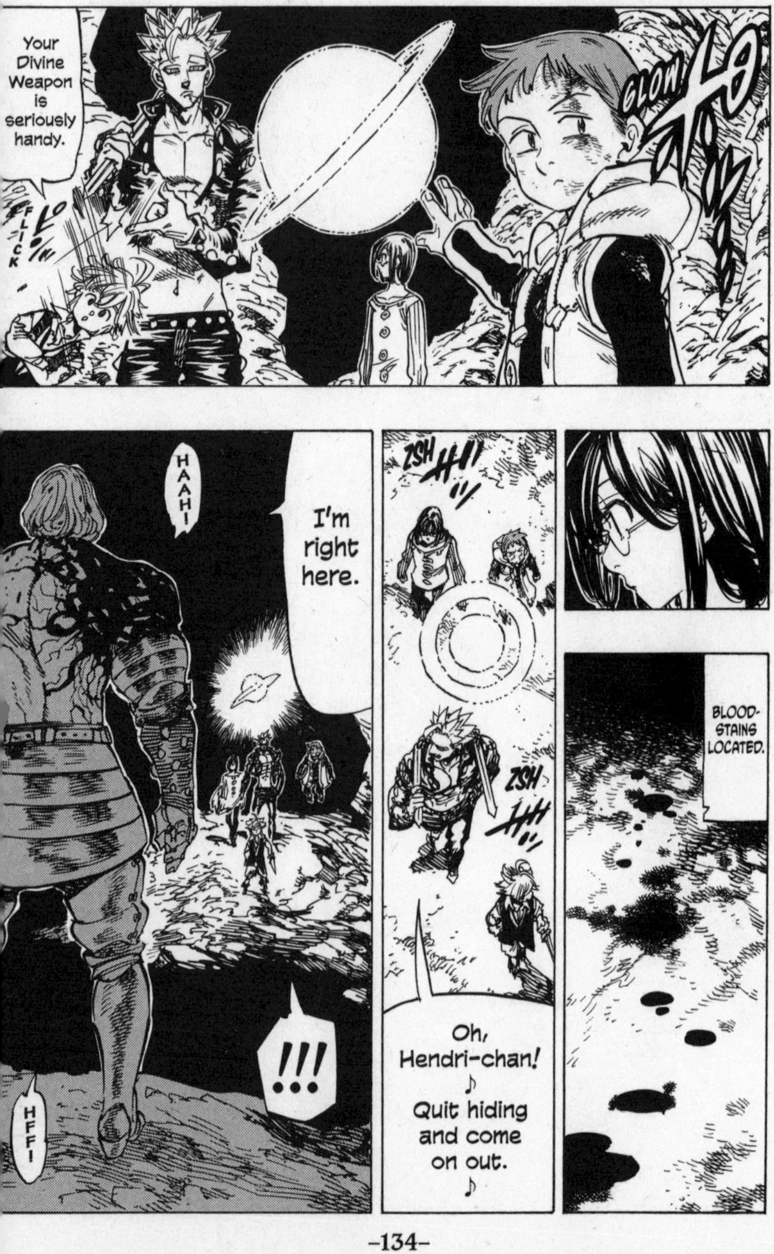
GLOW
Your Divine Weapon is seriously handy.
FLICK
BLOOD-STAINS LOCATED.
ZSH
ZSH
Oh, Hendri-chan! ♪ Quit hiding and come on out. ♪
I'm right here.
HAAH!
!!!
HFF!

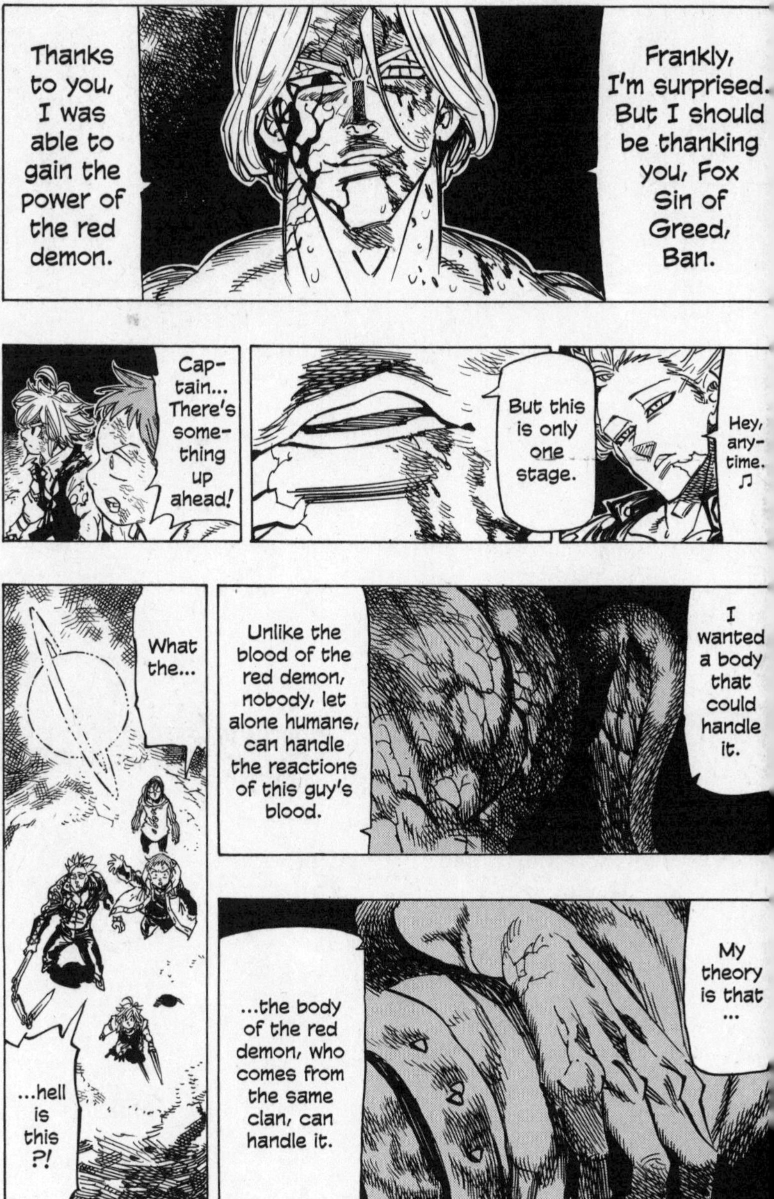
Frankly, I'm surprised. But I should be thanking you, Fox Sin of Greed, Ban.
Thanks to you, I was able to gain the power of the red demon.
Hey, anytime. ♫
But this is only one stage.
Captain... There's something up ahead!
I wanted a body that could handle it.
Unlike the blood of the red demon, nobody, let alone humans, can handle the reactions of this guy's blood.
My theory is that...
...the body of the red demon, who comes from the same clan, can handle it.
What the...
...hell is this?!

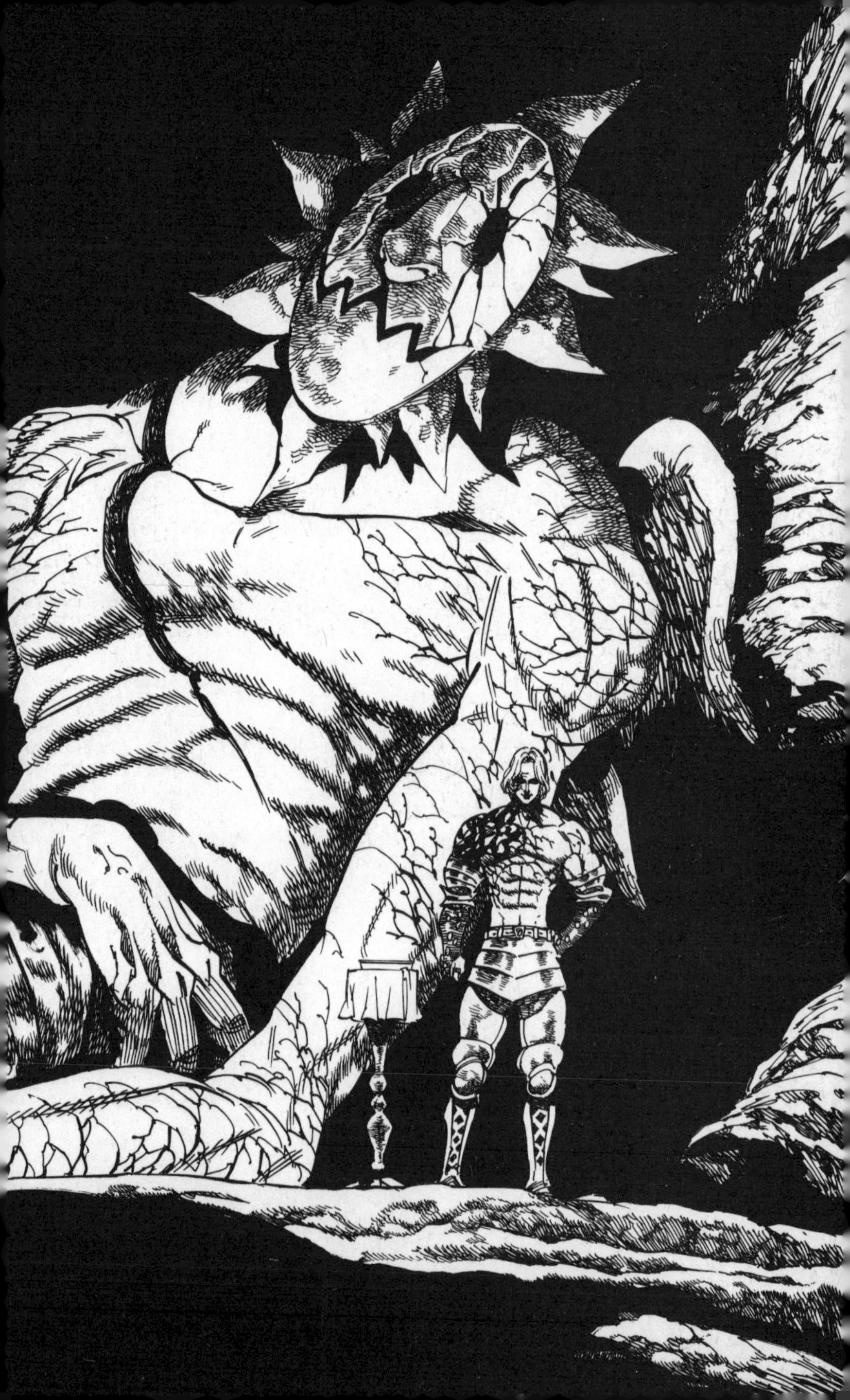

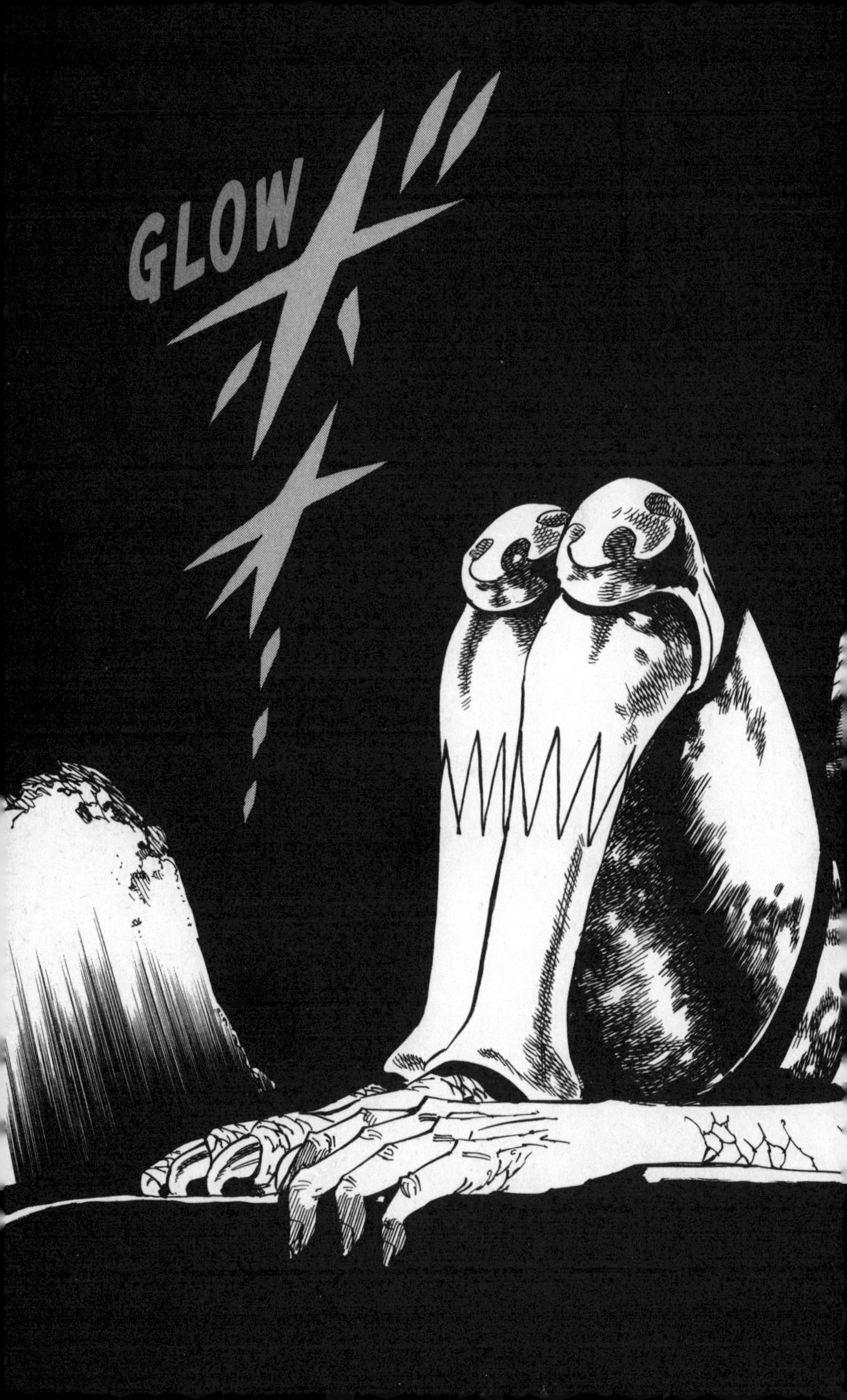
GLOW

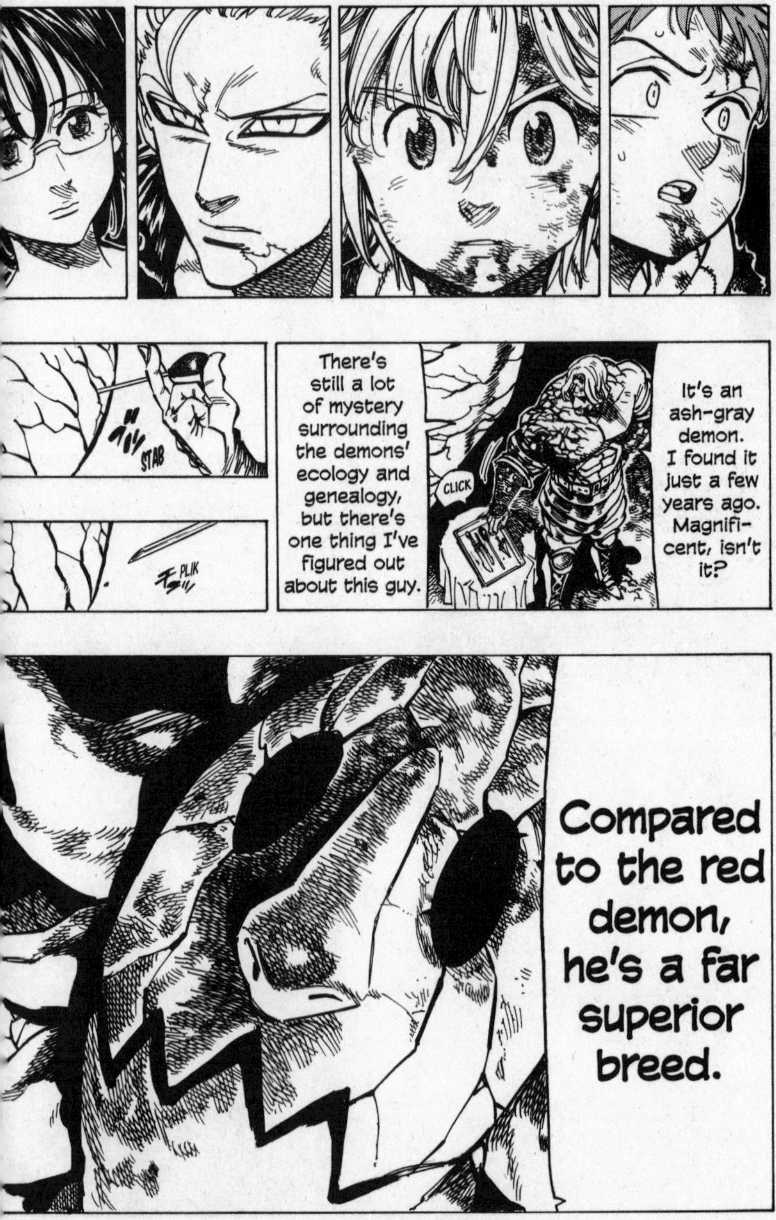
It's an ash-gray demon. I found it just a few years ago. Magnificent, isn't it?
CLICK
There's still a lot of mystery surrounding the demons' ecology and genealogy, but there's one thing I've figured out about this guy.
STAB
PLIK
Compared to the red demon, he's a far superior breed.

Are you crazy?!

What the...

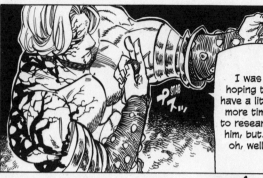

I was hoping to have a little more time to research him, but... oh, well.

GAH...!!

NNGAH!

GHH!

THADUMP!!

GLOOOW

...Haah.

Kah!

Aauh ...ah.

C... captain! What on earth ...?

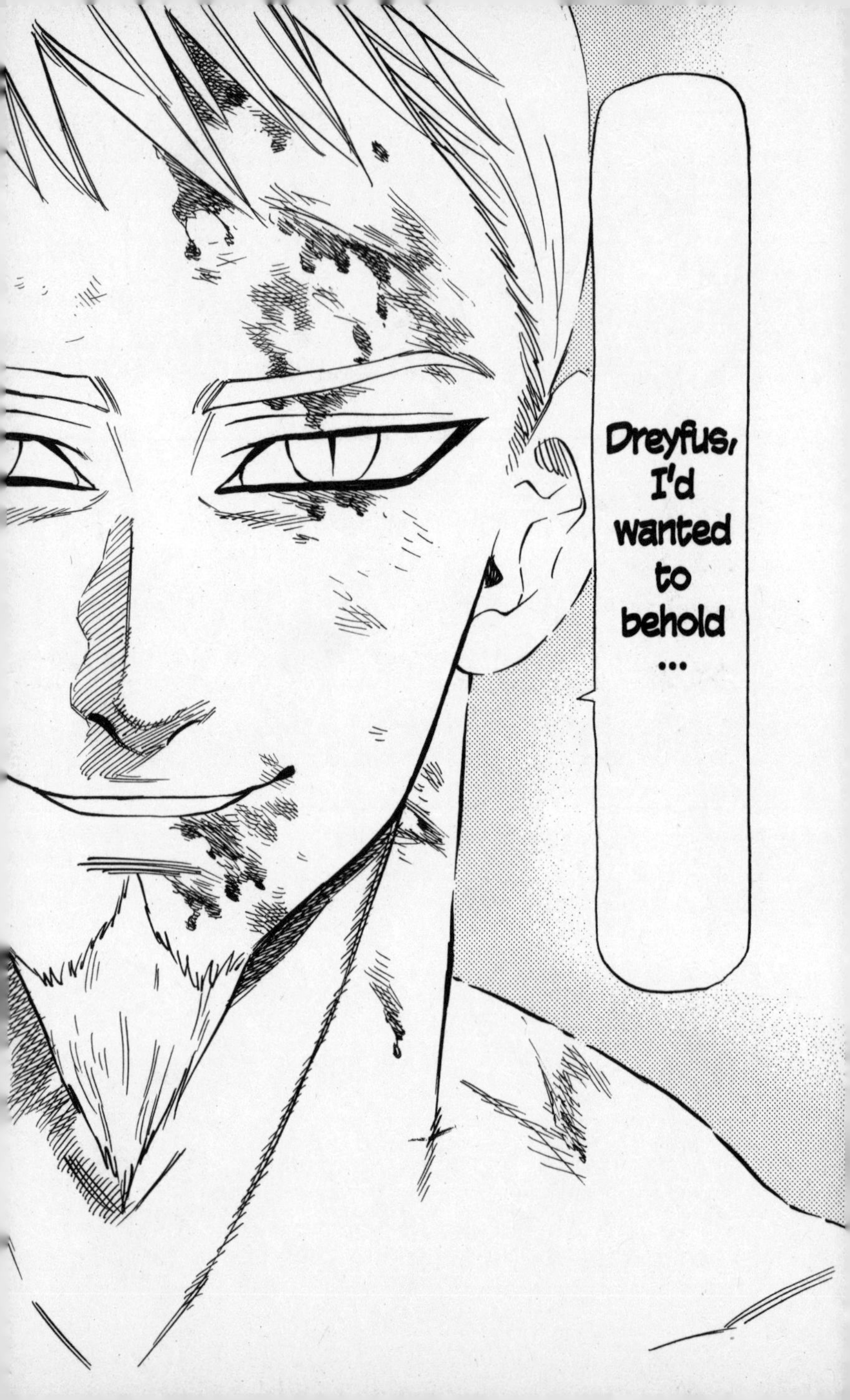
Dreyfus, I'd wanted to behold ...

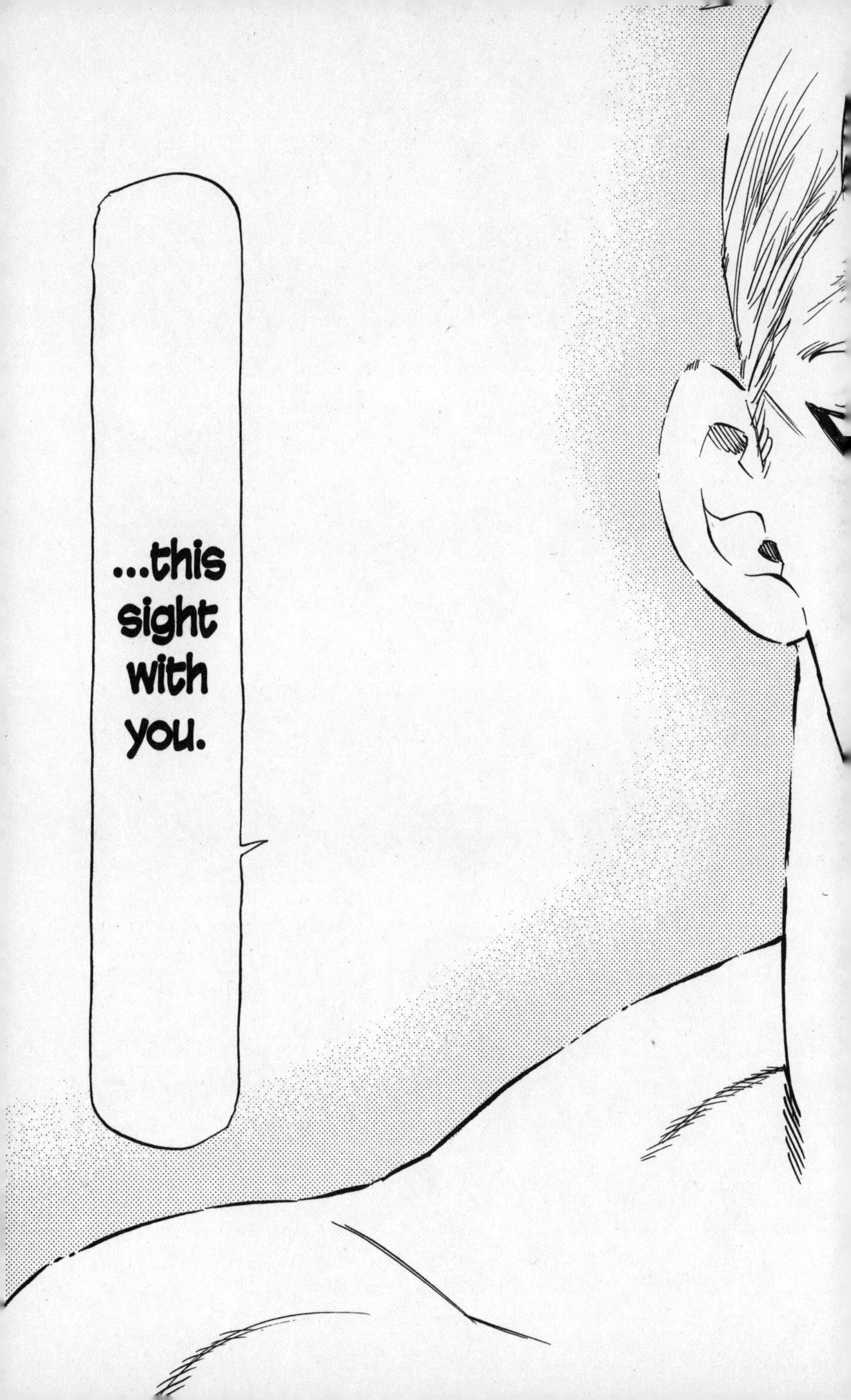
...this sight with you.

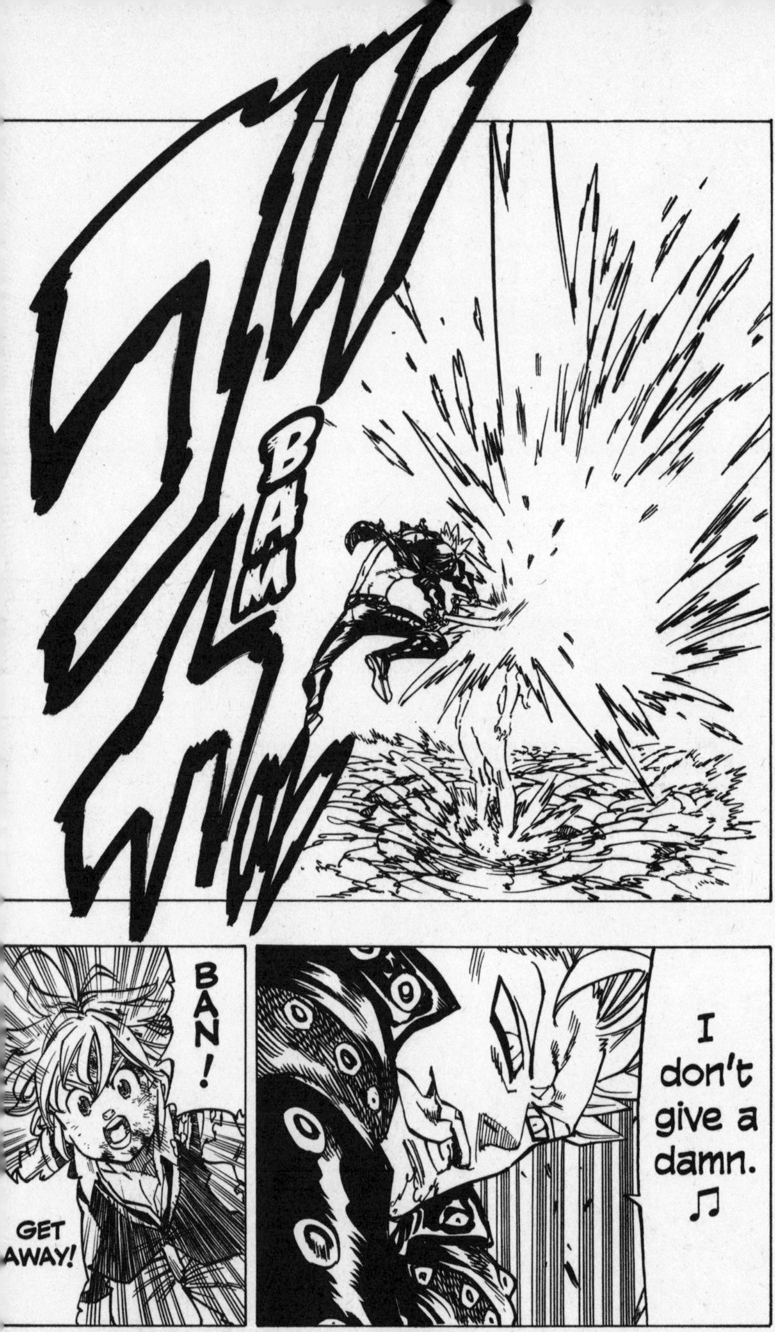
BAM
I don't give a damn. ♫
BAN!
GET AWAY!

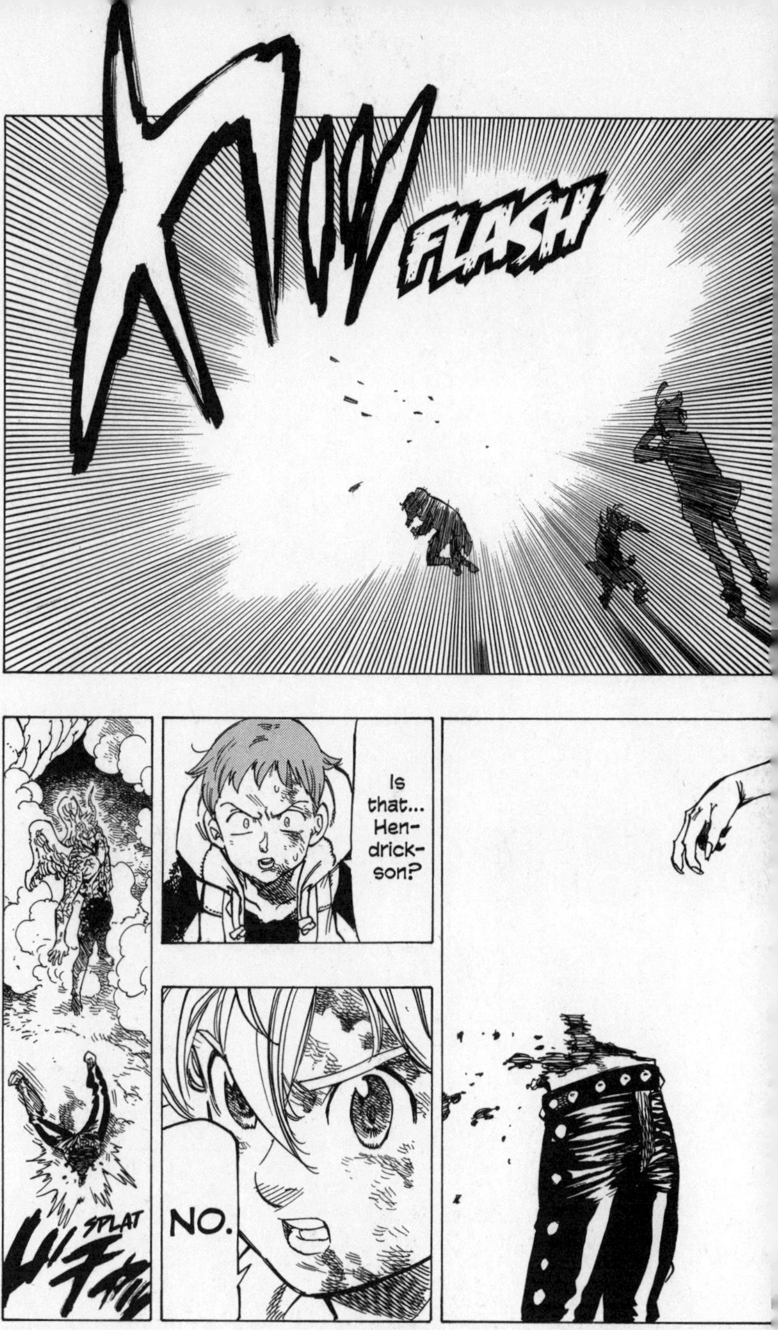
FLASH
Is that... Hen-drick-son?
NO.
SPLAT

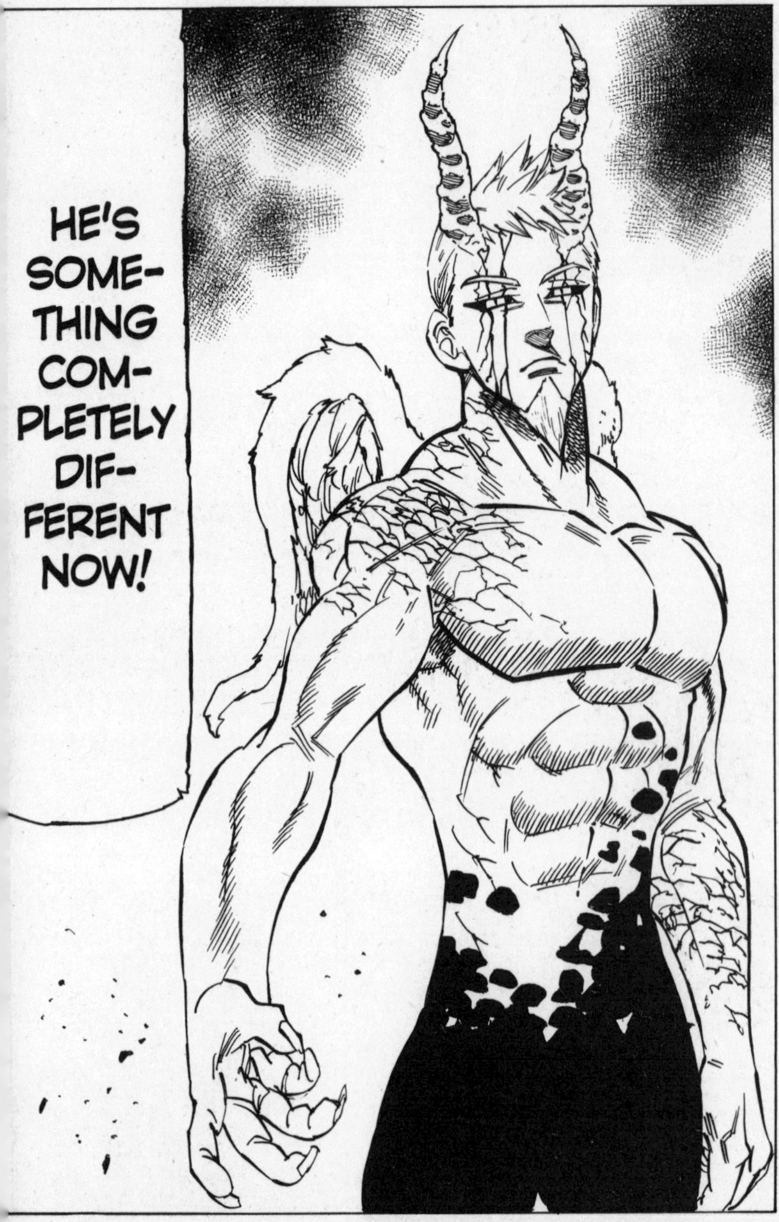
HE'S SOMETHING COMPLETELY DIFFERENT NOW!

Chapter 94 - The Advent of Despair

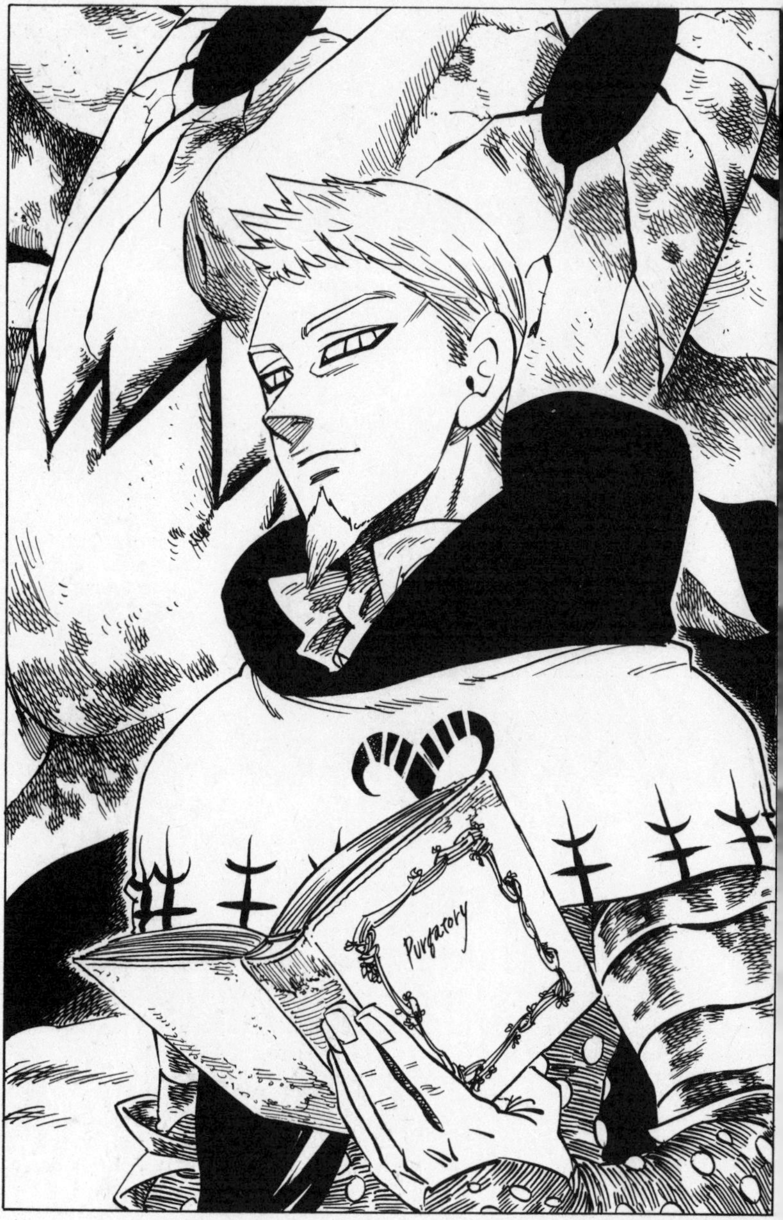
Purgatory

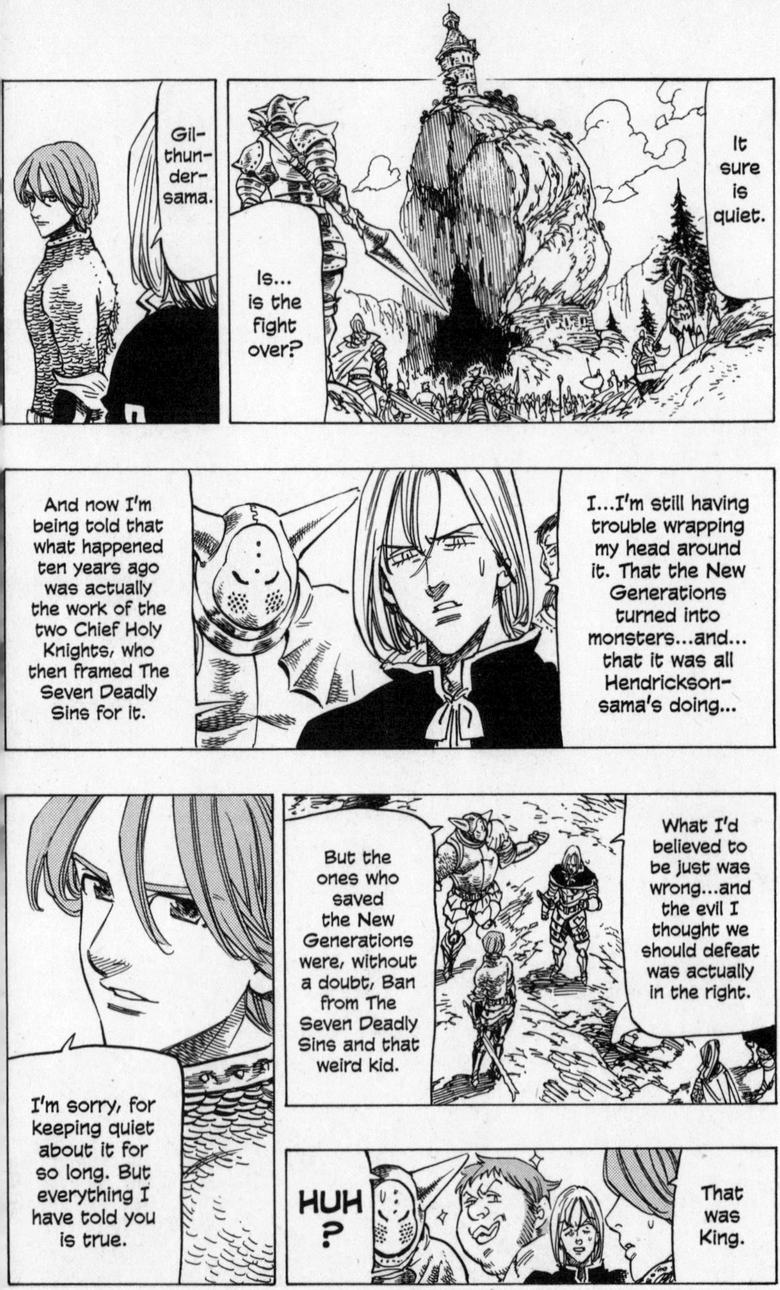
It sure is quiet.
Is... is the fight over?
Gil-thunder-sama.
I...I'm still having trouble wrapping my head around it. That the New Generations turned into monsters...and... that it was all Hendrickson-sama's doing...
And now I'm being told that what happened ten years ago was actually the work of the two Chief Holy Knights, who then framed The Seven Deadly Sins for it.
What I'd believed to be just was wrong...and the evil I thought we should defeat was actually in the right.
But the ones who saved the New Generations were, without a doubt, Ban from The Seven Deadly Sins and that weird kid.
That was King.
HUH?
I'm sorry, for keeping quiet about it for so long. But everything I have told you is true.

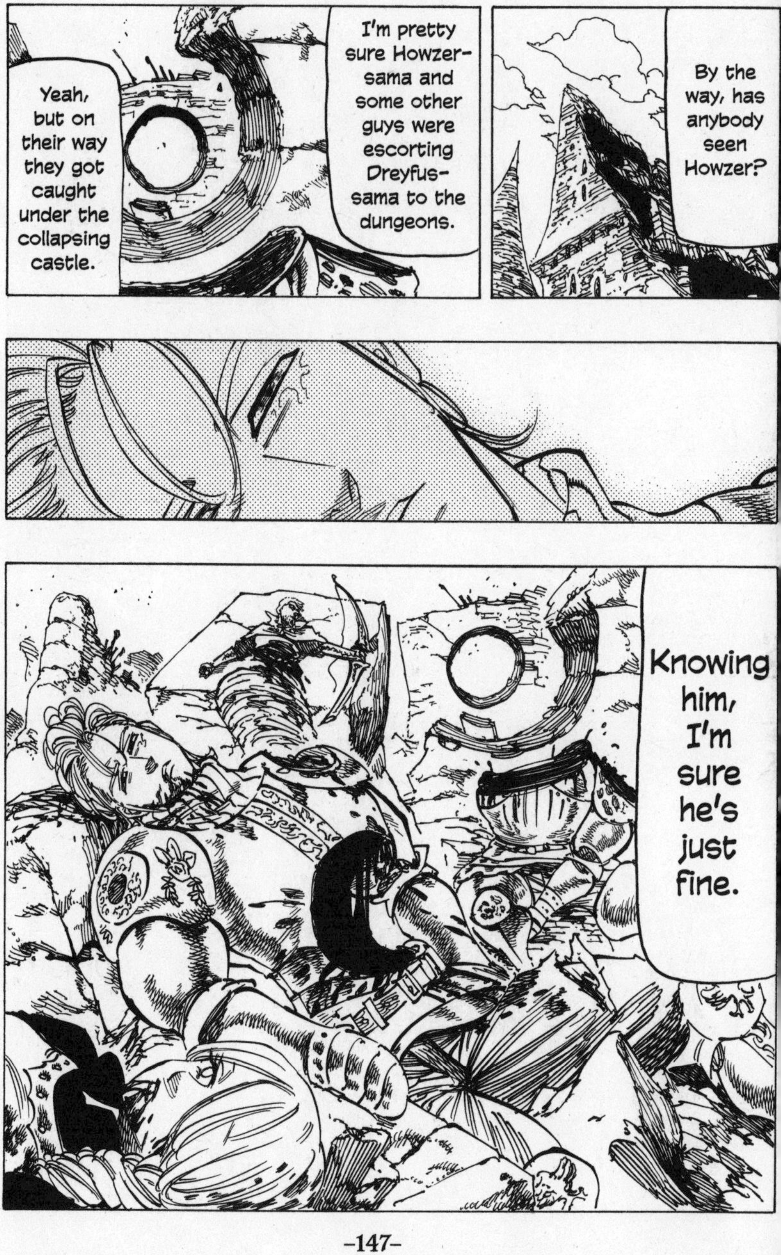
By the way, has anybody seen Howzer?
I'm pretty sure Howzer-sama and some other guys were escorting Dreyfus-sama to the dungeons.
Yeah, but on their way they got caught under the collapsing castle.
Knowing him, I'm sure he's just fine.

KABOOM

ZZ

RRRUMBLE

That
rumbling
...

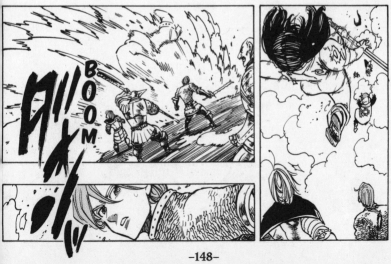

BOOM

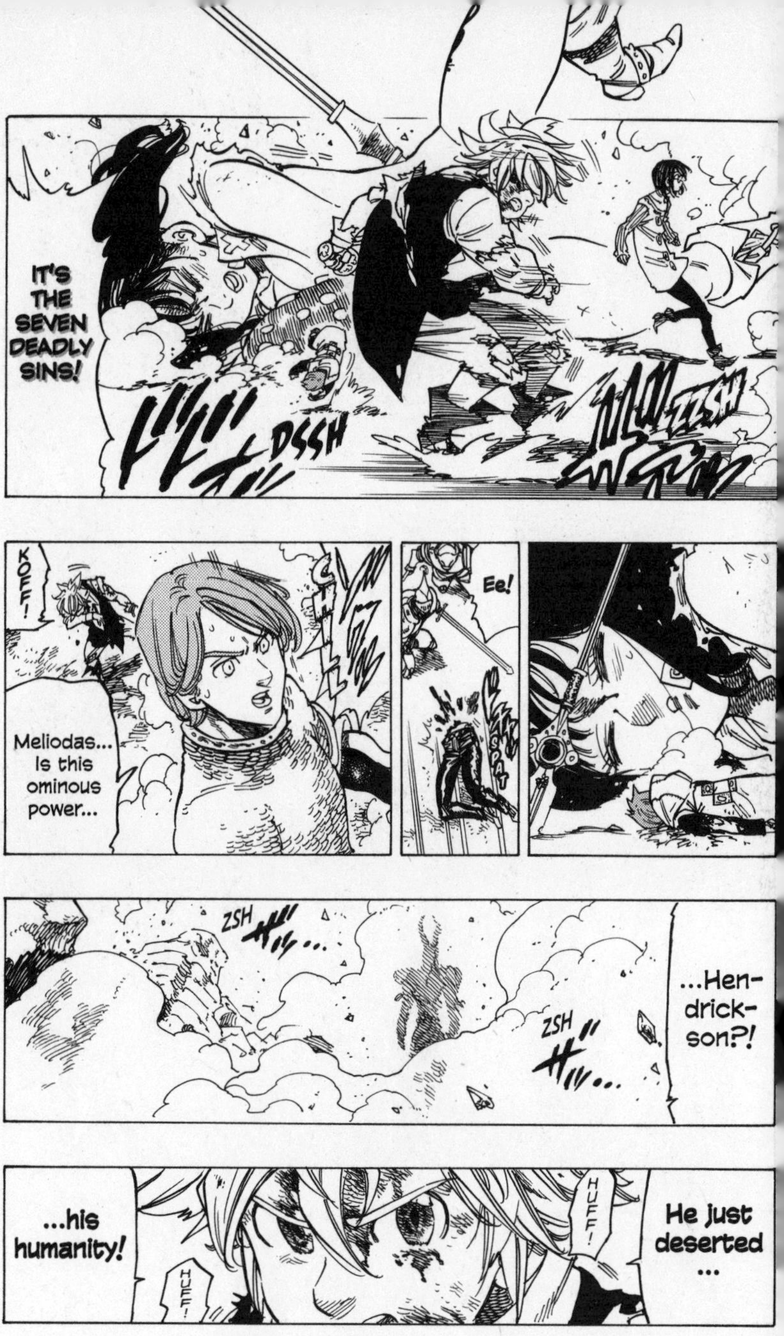
ZZSH
IT'S THE SEVEN DEADLY SINS!
DSSH
Ee!
SPAT
CHILL
KOFF!
Meliodas... Is this ominous power...
...Hen-drick-son?!
ZSH...
ZSH...
He just deserted ...
HUFF!
HUFF!
...his humanity!

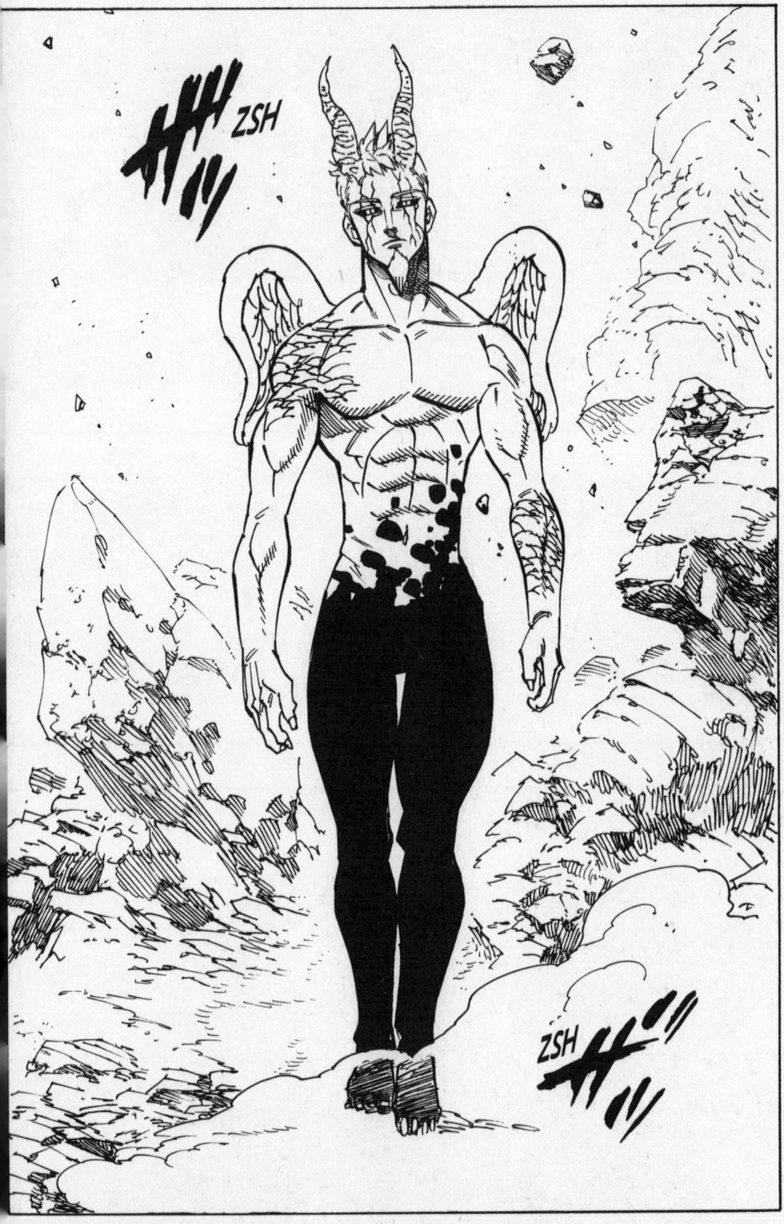
ZSH
ZSH

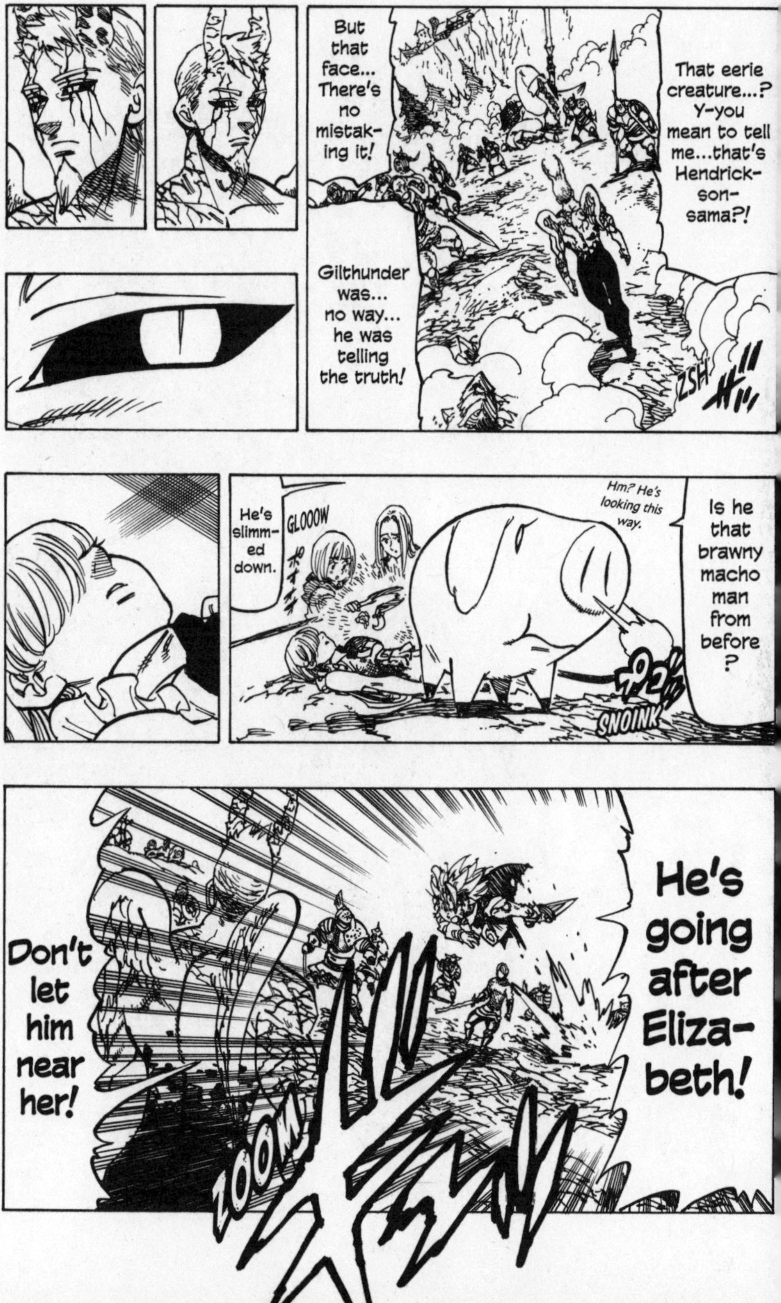
That eerie creature...? Y-you mean to tell me...that's Hendrickson-sama?!
But that face... There's no mistaking it!
Gilthunder was... no way... he was telling the truth!
ZSH
Is he that brawny macho man from before?
Hm? He's looking this way.
He's slimmed down.
GLOOOW
SNOINK
He's going after Elizabeth!
Don't let him near her!
ZOOM

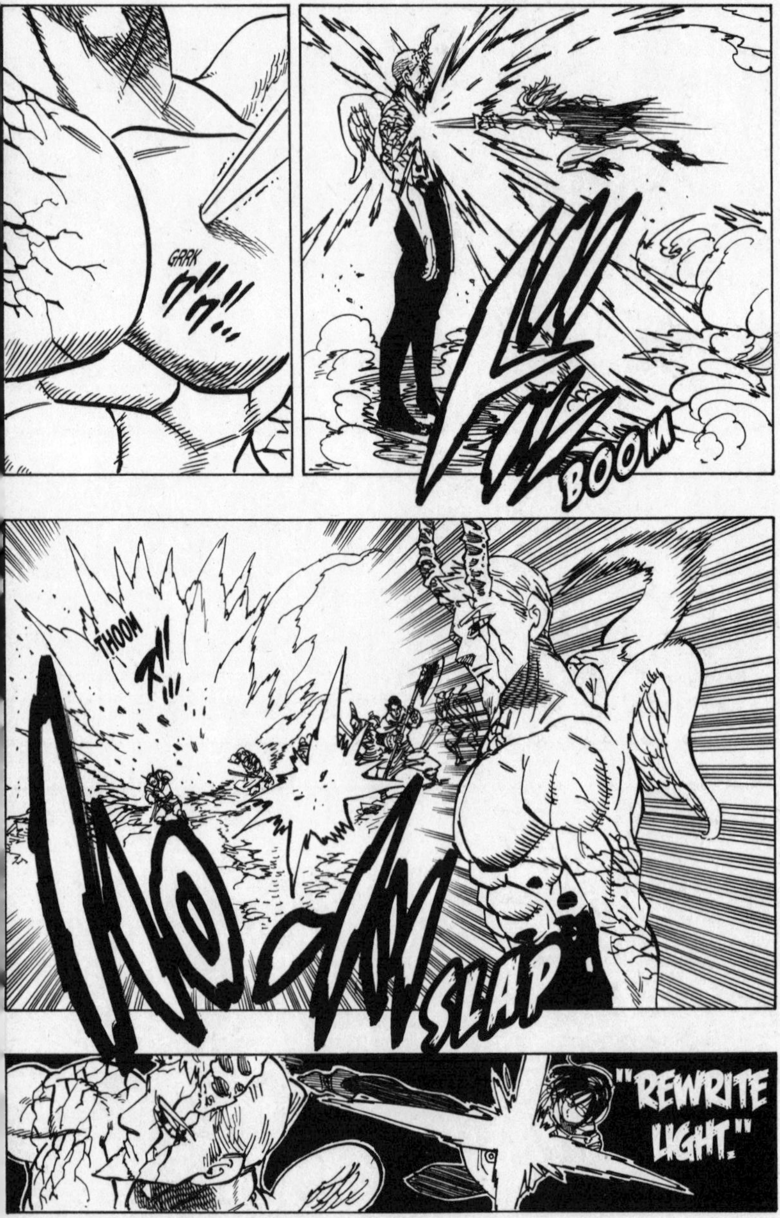
BOOM
GRRK
THOOM
SLAP
"REWRITE LIGHT."

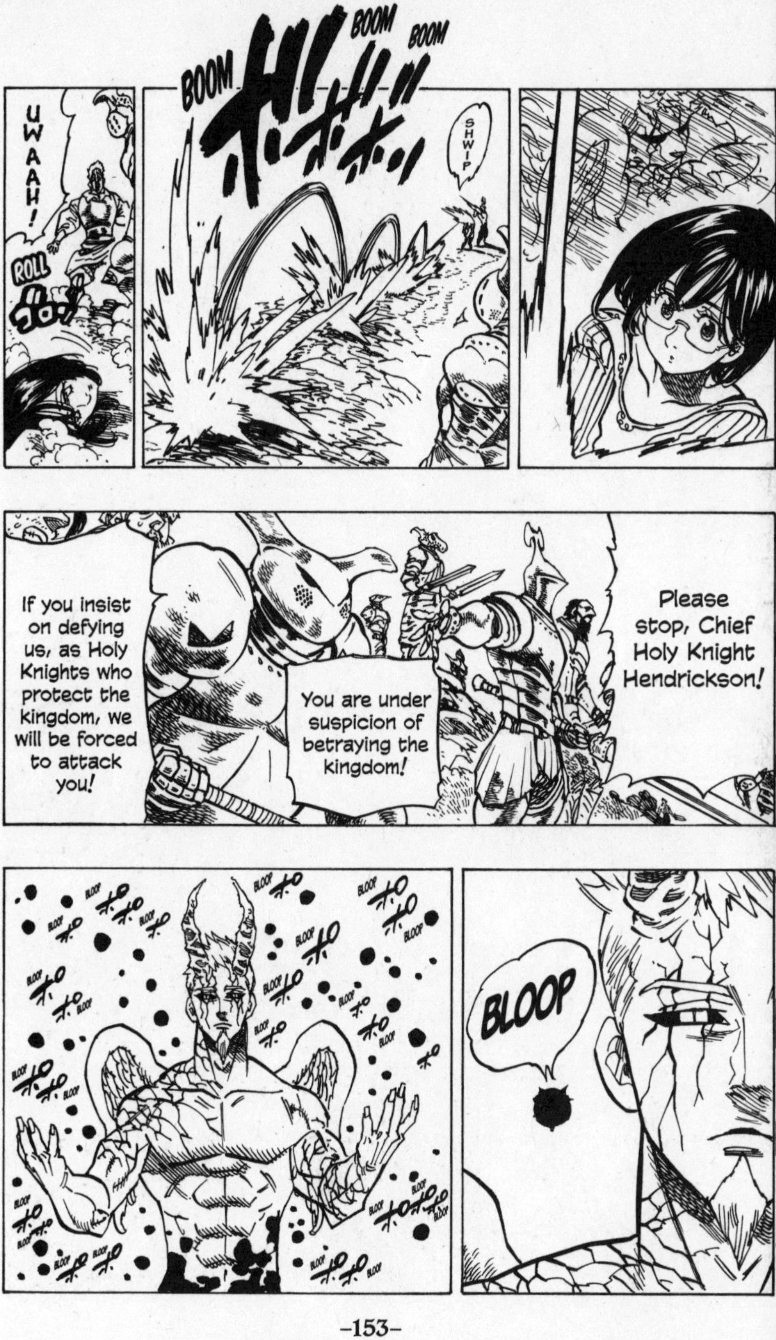
BOOM
BOOM
BOOM
SHWIP
UWAAAH!
ROLL
Please stop, Chief Holy Knight Hendrickson!
You are under suspicion of betraying the kingdom!
If you insist on defying us, as Holy Knights who protect the kingdom, we will be forced to attack you!
BLOOP
BLOOP

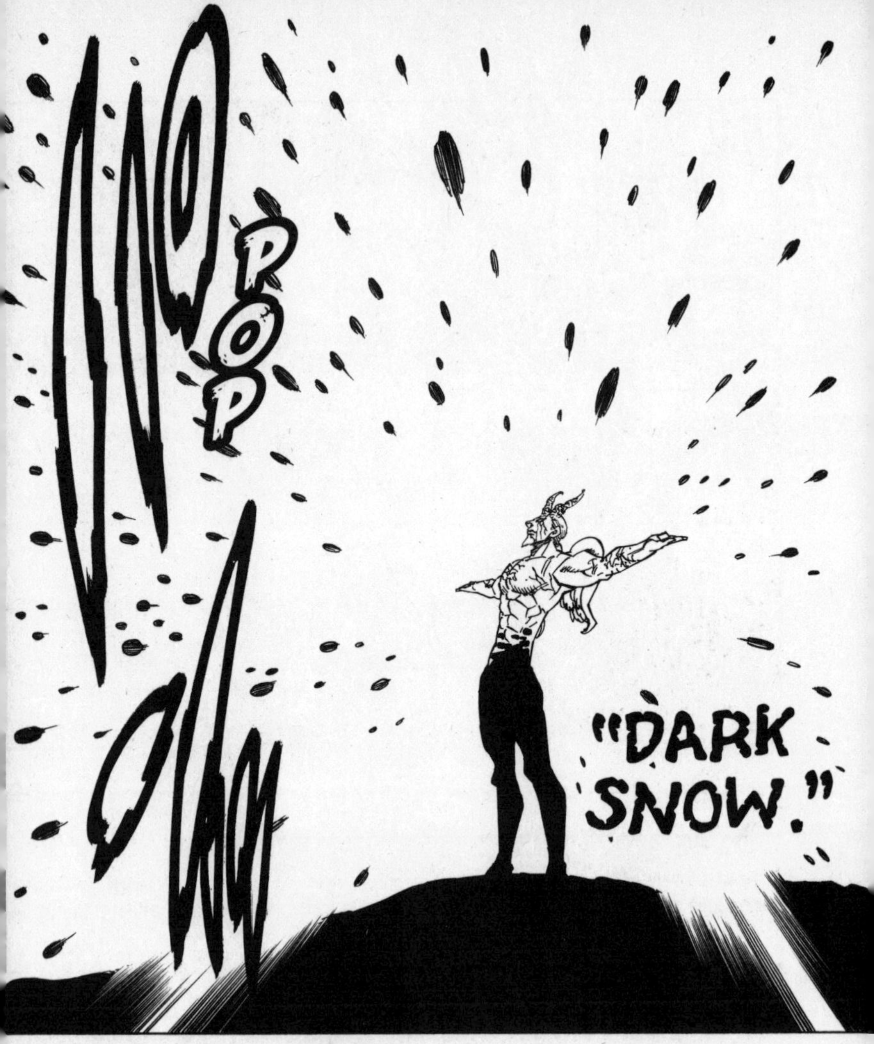
POP
"DARK SNOW."
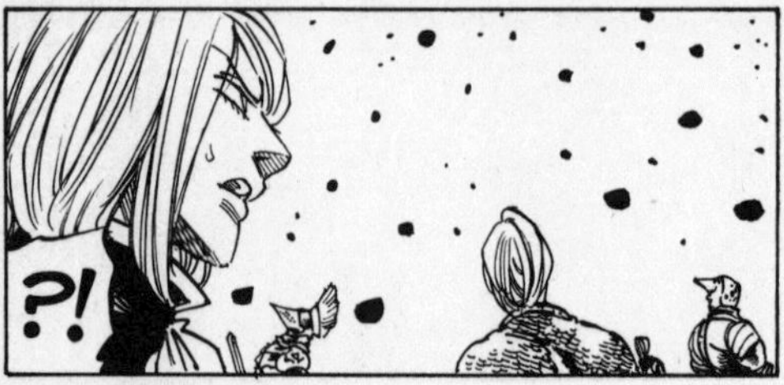
?!
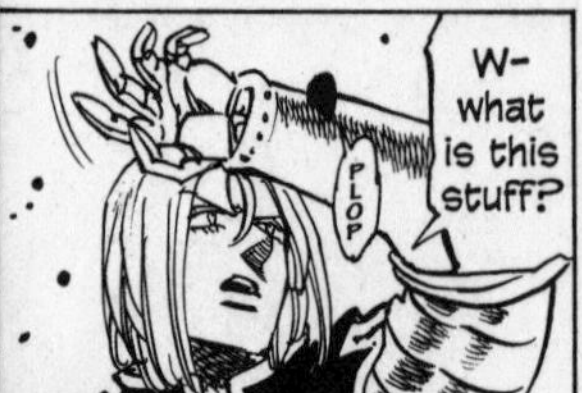
W-what is this stuff?
PLOP

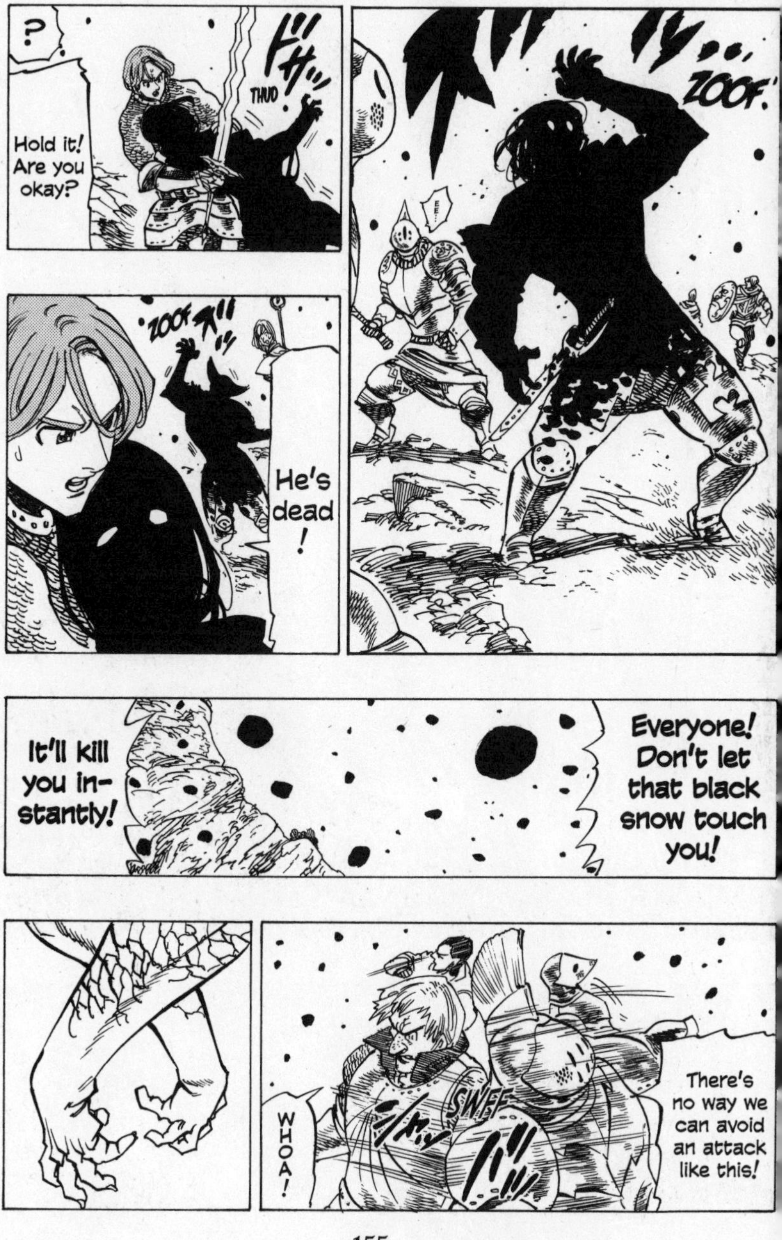
ZOOF
EE...
?
THUD
Hold it! Are you okay?
ZOOF
He's dead!
Everyone! Don't let that black snow touch you!
It'll kill you instantly!
There's no way we can avoid an attack like this!
SWFF
WHOA!

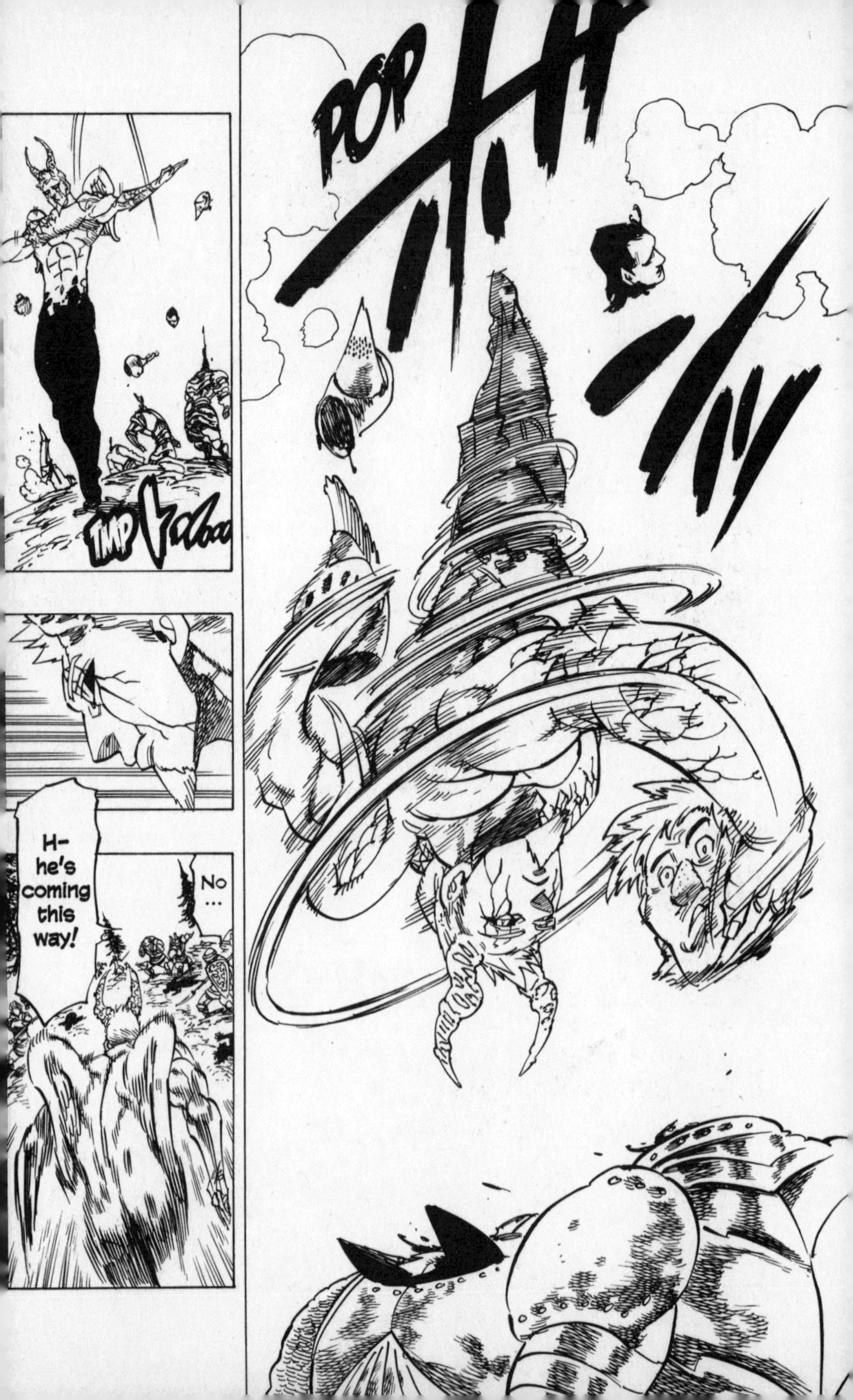
POP
TMP
H-he's coming this way!
No...

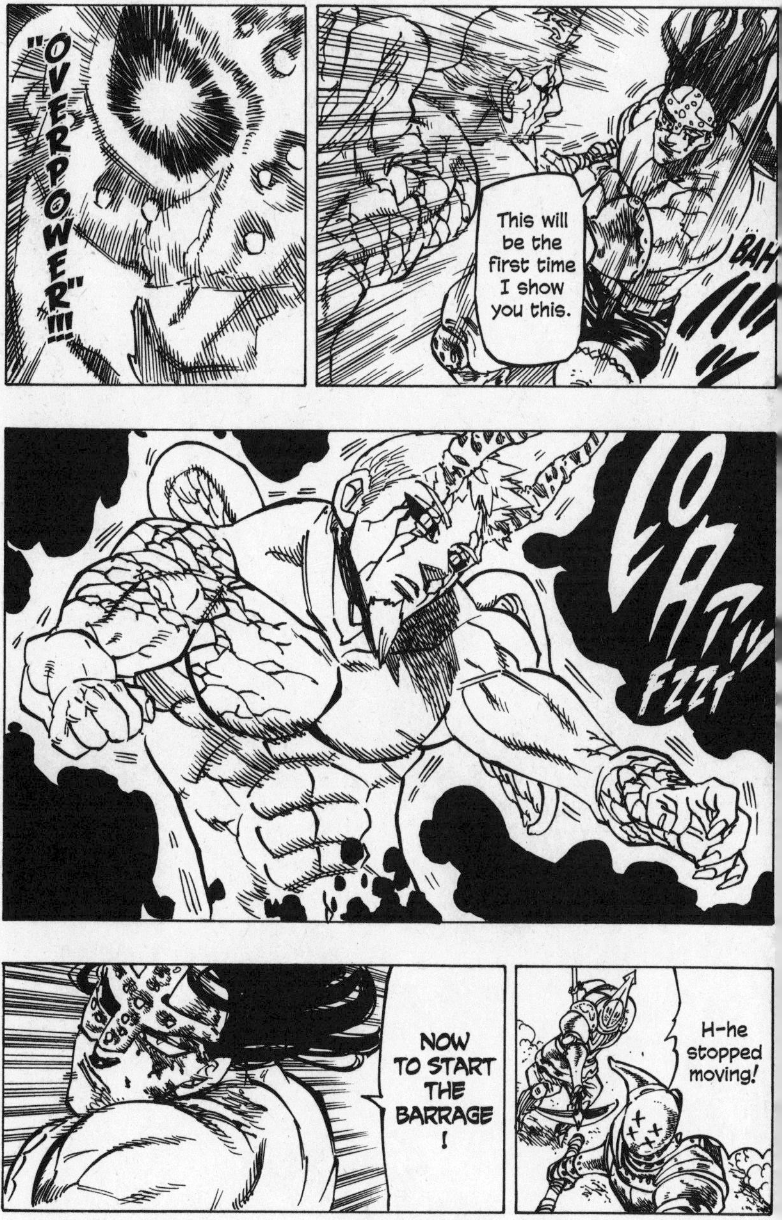
This will be the first time I show you this.
BAH
"OVERPOWER"!!!
FZZT
H-he stopped moving!
NOW TO START THE BARRAGE!

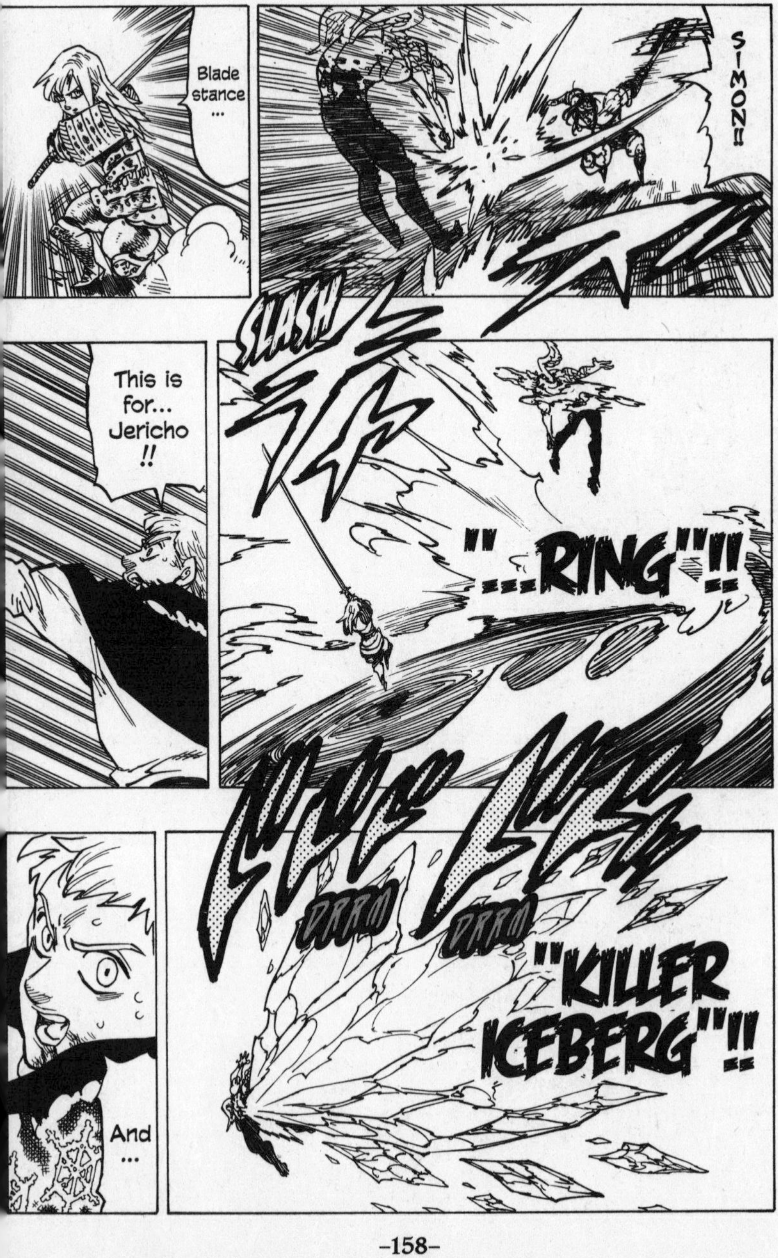
SIMON!!
Blade stance ...
SLASH
"...RING"!!
This is for... Jericho!!
DRRM
DRRM
"KILLER ICEBERG"!!
And ...

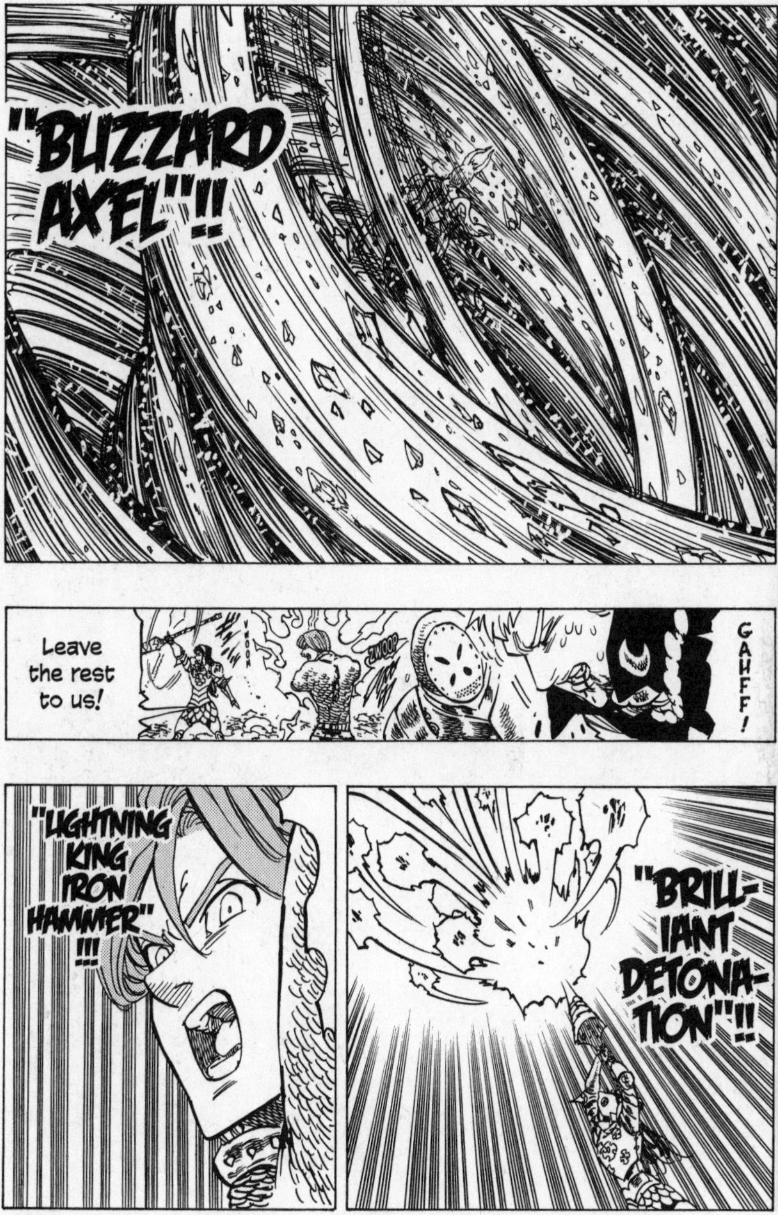
"BLIZZARD AXEL"!!
GAHFF!
ZWOOP
VWOOM
Leave the rest to us!
"BRILLIANT DETONATION"!!
"LIGHTNING KING IRON HAMMER"!!!

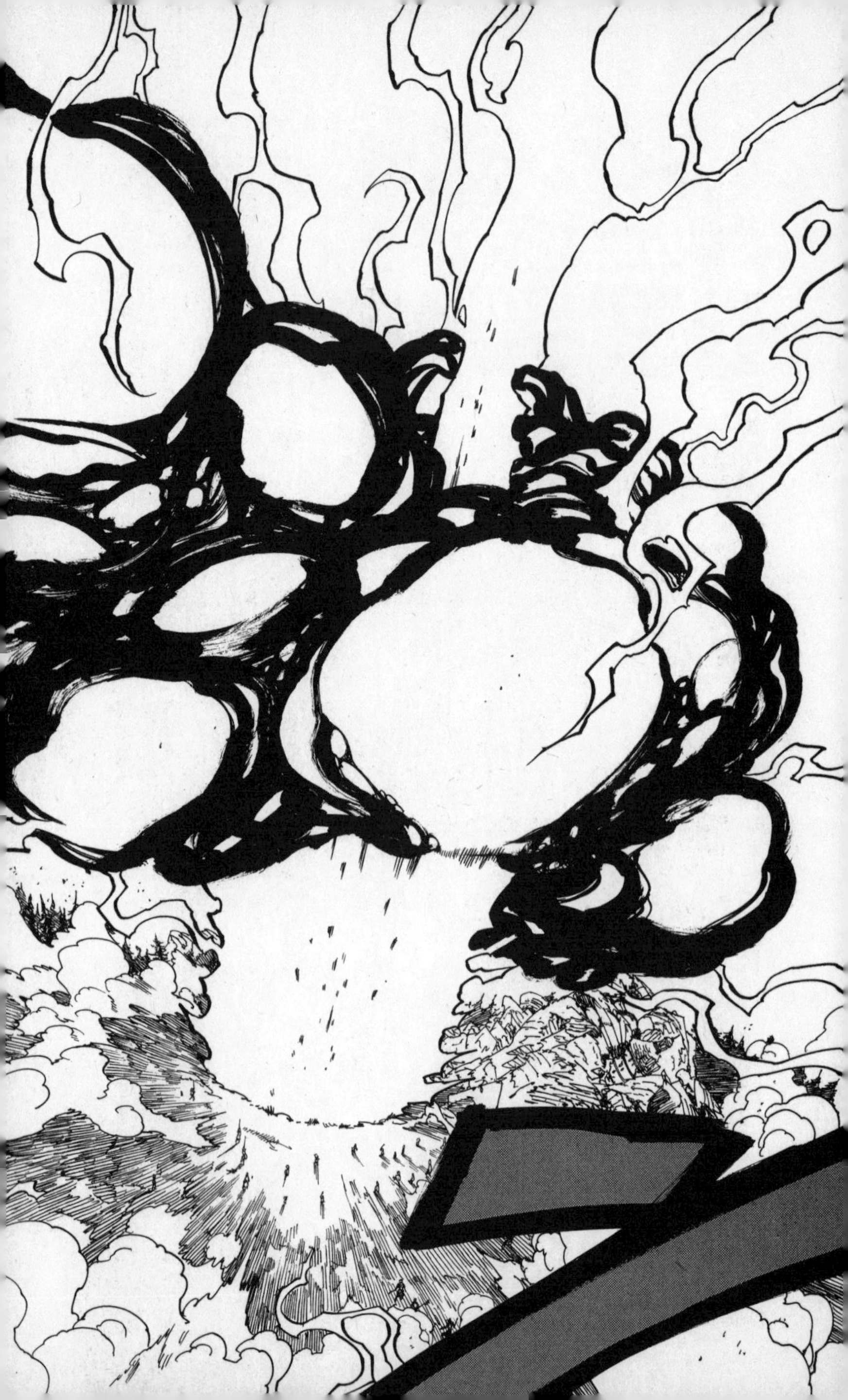

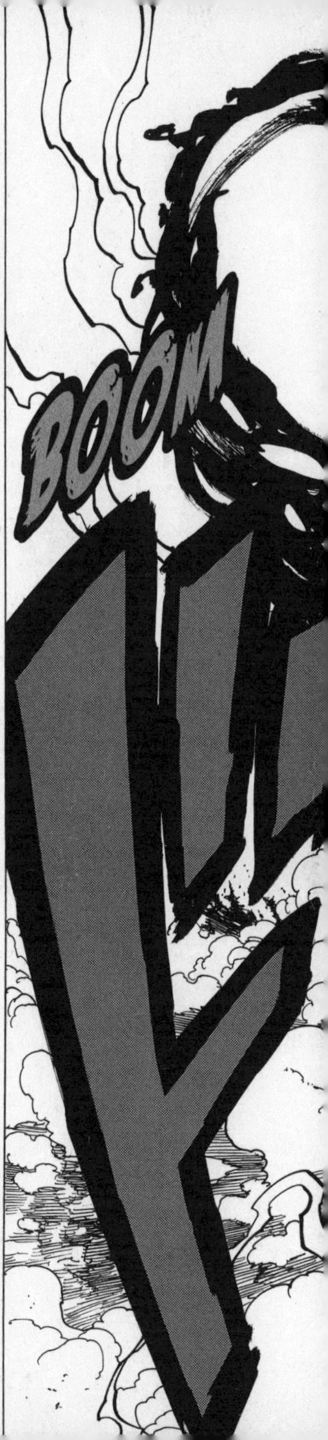
BOOM

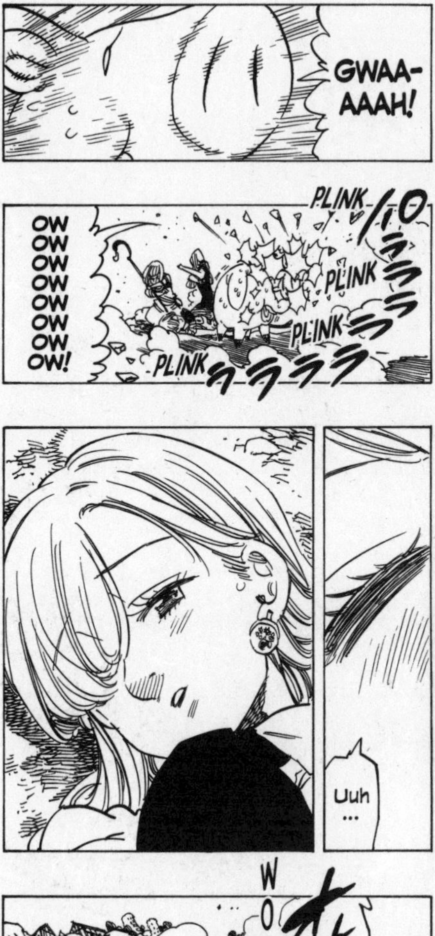
GWAA-AAAH!
PLINK
PLINK
PLINK
PLINK
OW OW OW OW OW OW OW OW!
Uuh ...
We did it!
WOOOO
Don't let your guard down. He may have taken a lot of damage, but he could still be alive!

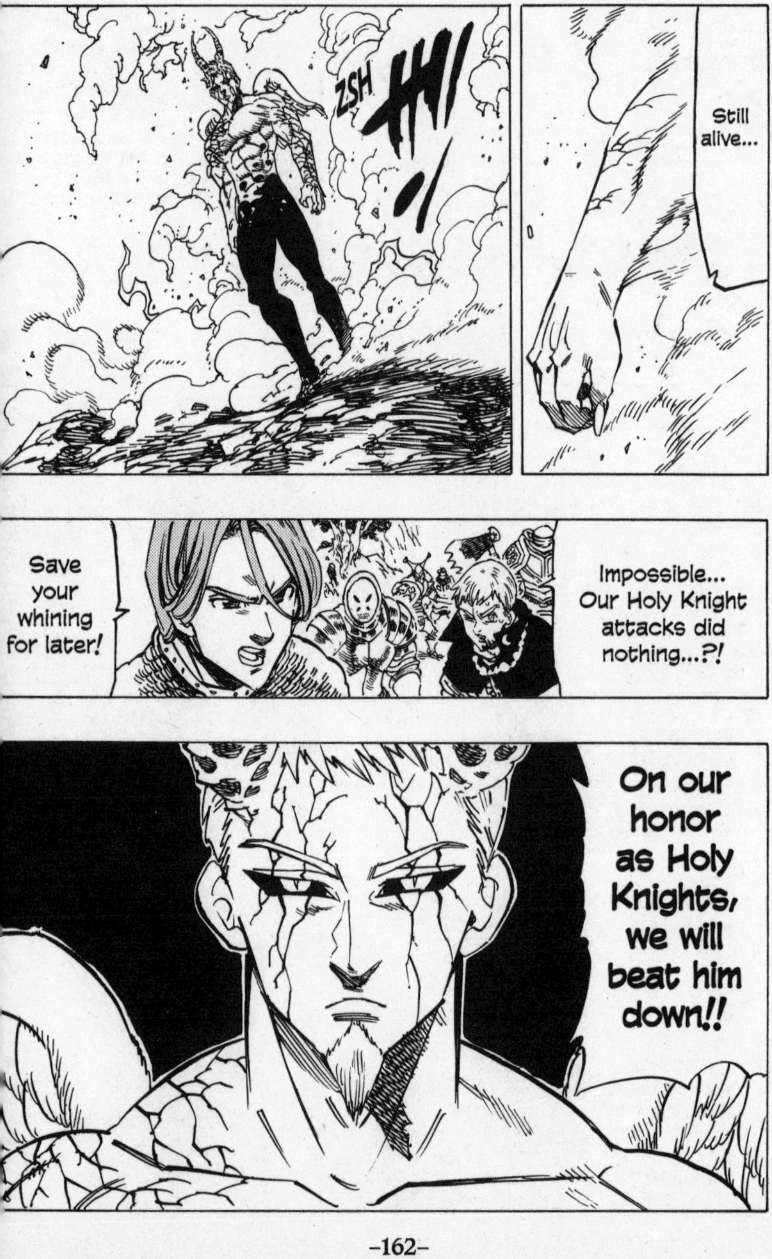
Still alive...
ZSH
Impossible... Our Holy Knight attacks did nothing...?!
Save your whining for later!
On our honor as Holy Knights, we will beat him down!!

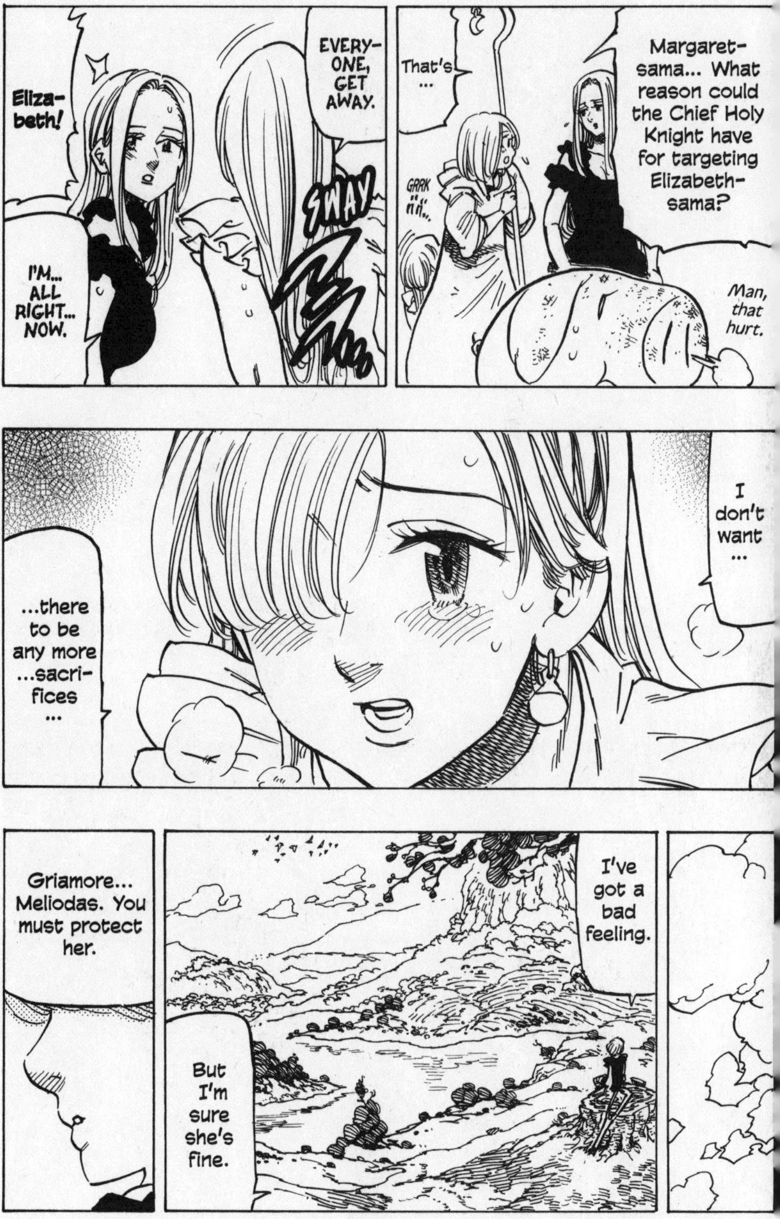

Margaret-sama... What reason could the Chief Holy Knight have for targeting Elizabeth-sama?
That's ...
Man, that hurt.
GRRK
EVERYONE, GET AWAY.
Elizabeth!
SWAY
I'M... ALL RIGHT... NOW.
I don't want ...
...there to be any more ...sacrifices ...
I've got a bad feeling.
But I'm sure she's fine.
Griamore... Meliodas. You must protect her.

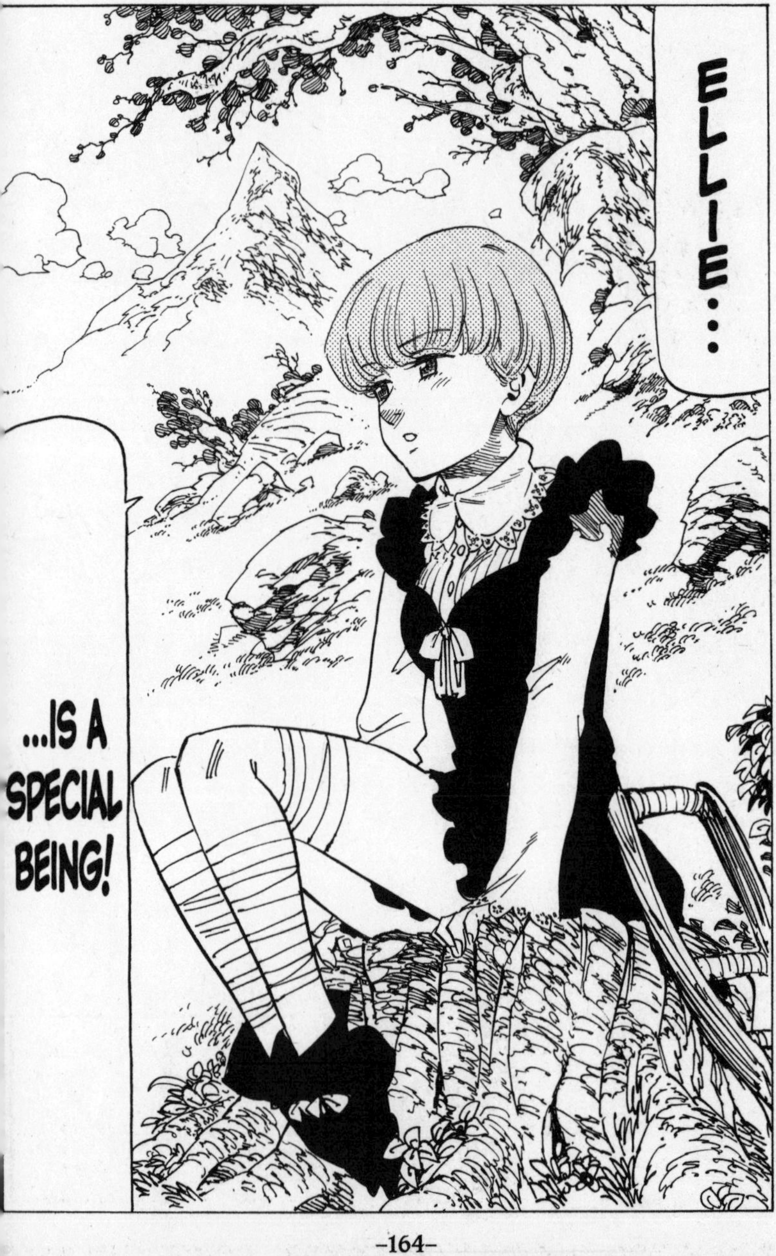
ELLIE...
...IS A SPECIAL BEING!

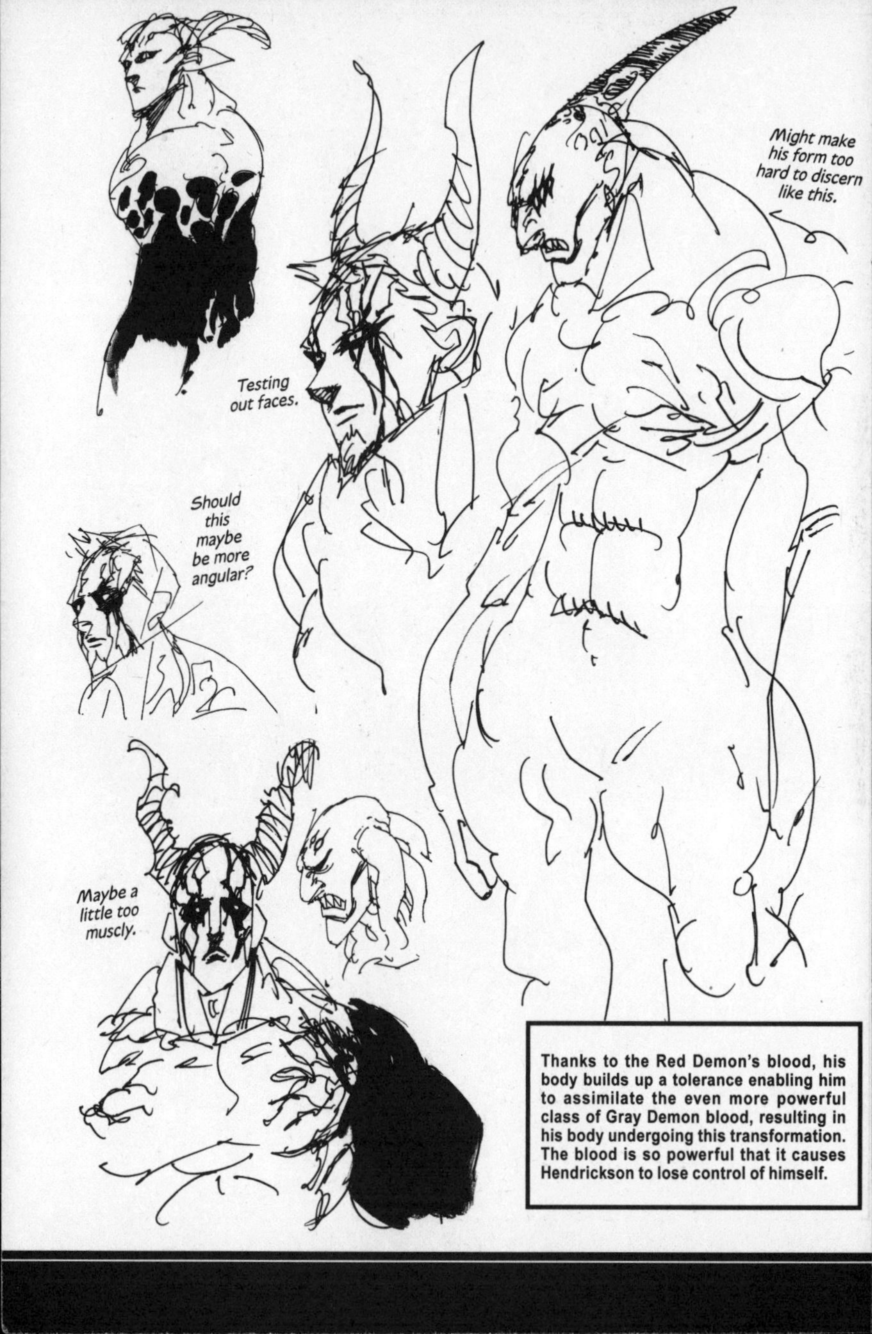
Might make his form too hard to discern like this.
Testing out faces.
Should this maybe be more angular?
Maybe a little too muscly.

Thanks to the Red Demon's blood, his body builds up a tolerance enabling him to assimilate the even more powerful class of Gray Demon blood, resulting in his body undergoing this transformation. The blood is so powerful that it causes Hendrickson to lose control of himself.

Chapter 95 - Defeated Hope

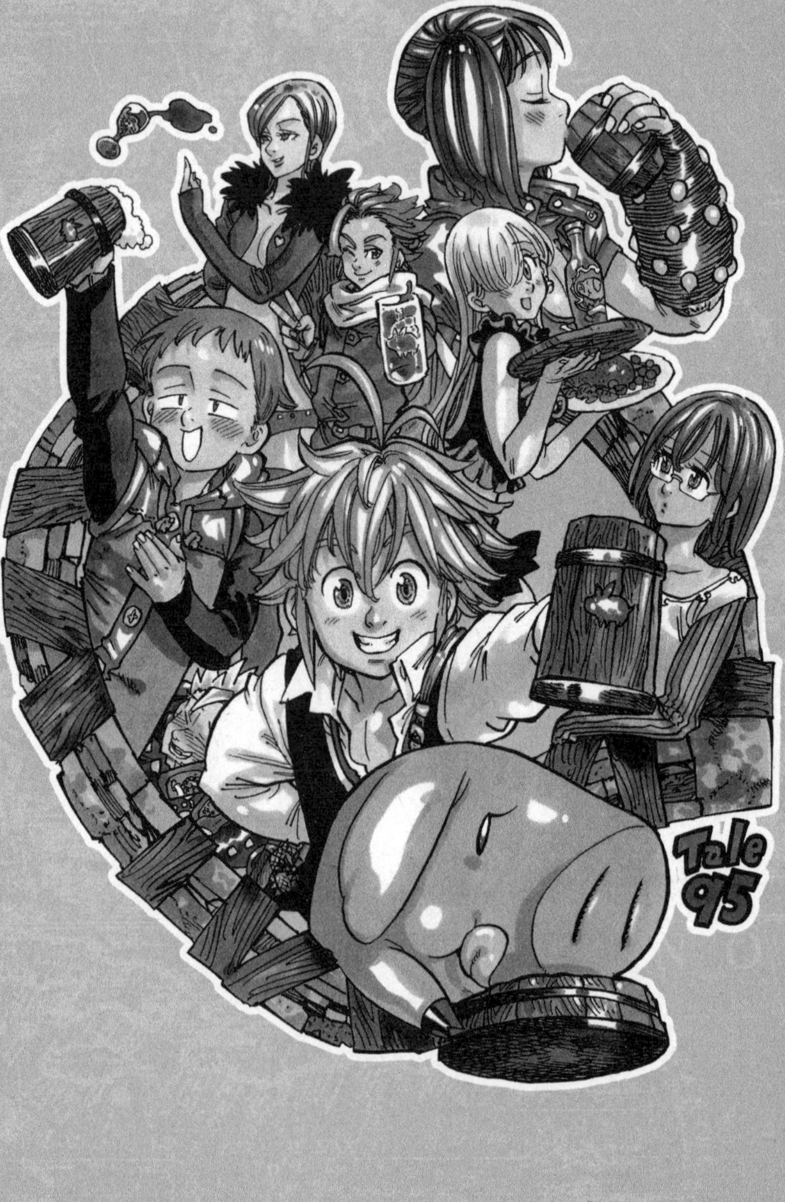
Tale 95

He's too strong! Th-this is a nightmare!

I can't believe such a monster really exists...

Who will protect the kingdom if we let fear rule us?!

People sing our praises as mighty warriors. Let's show him the pride of the kingdom's Holy Knights!

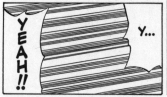

YEAH!!

Y...

ZSH

ZSH

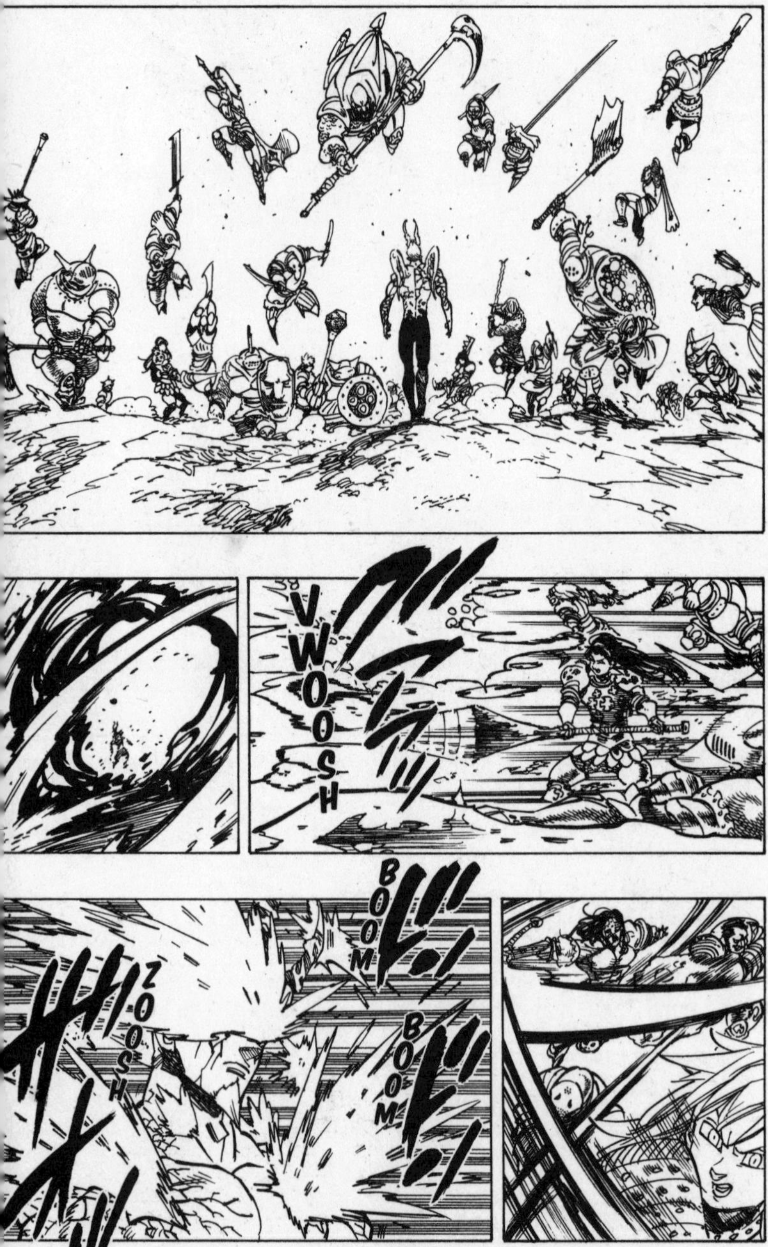
VWOOSH
BOOM
BOOM
ZOOOSH

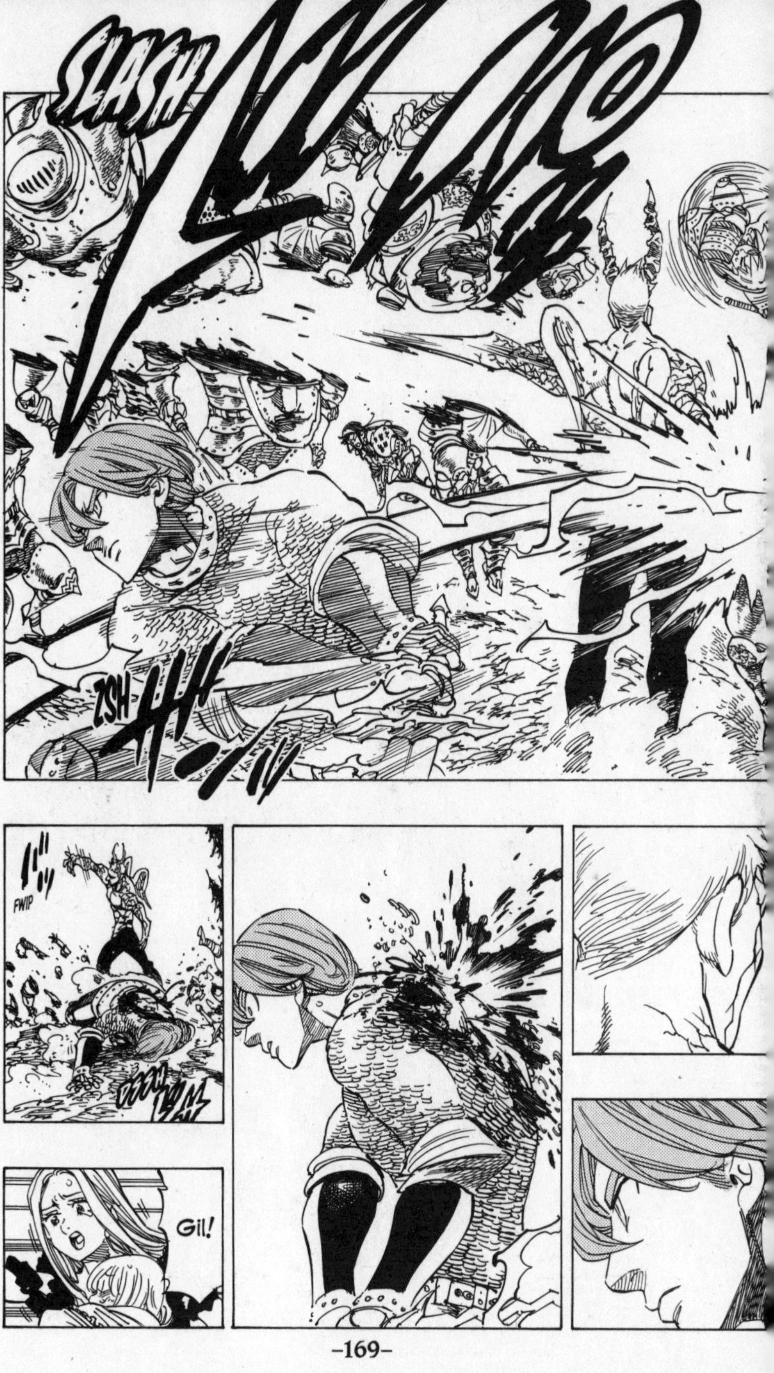
SLASH
ZSH
FWIP
Gil!

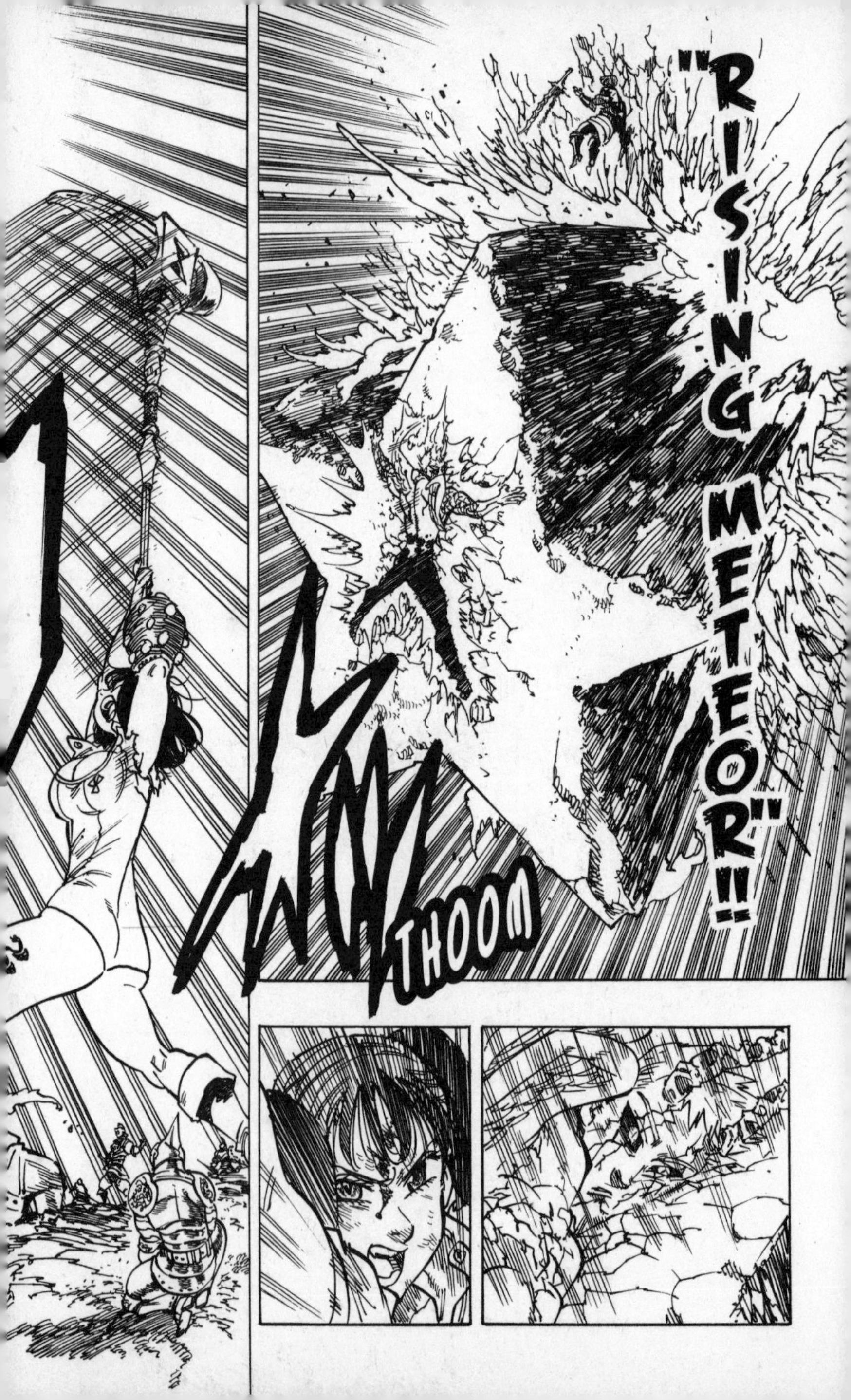
"RISING METEOR"!!
THOOM

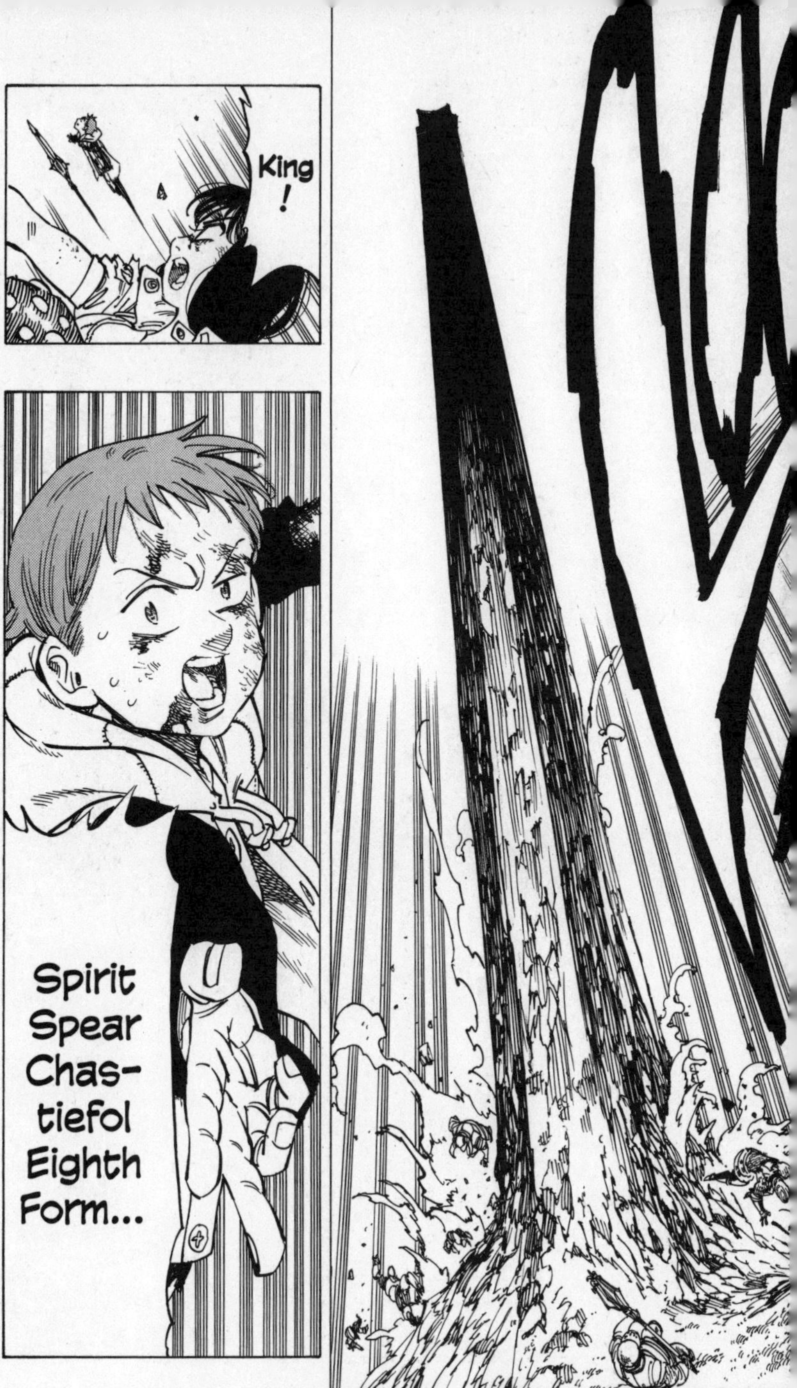
King!
Spirit Spear Chas-tiefol Eighth Form...

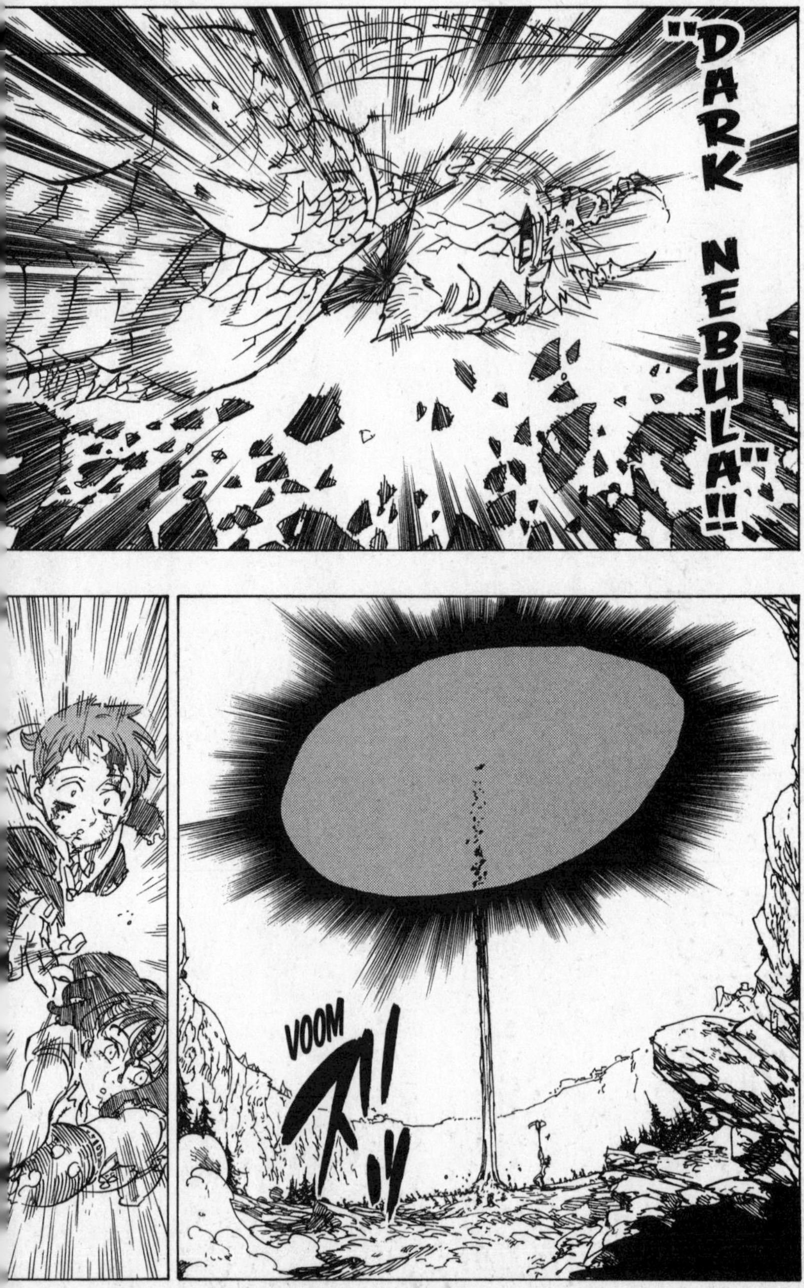
"DARK NEBULA"!!
VOOM

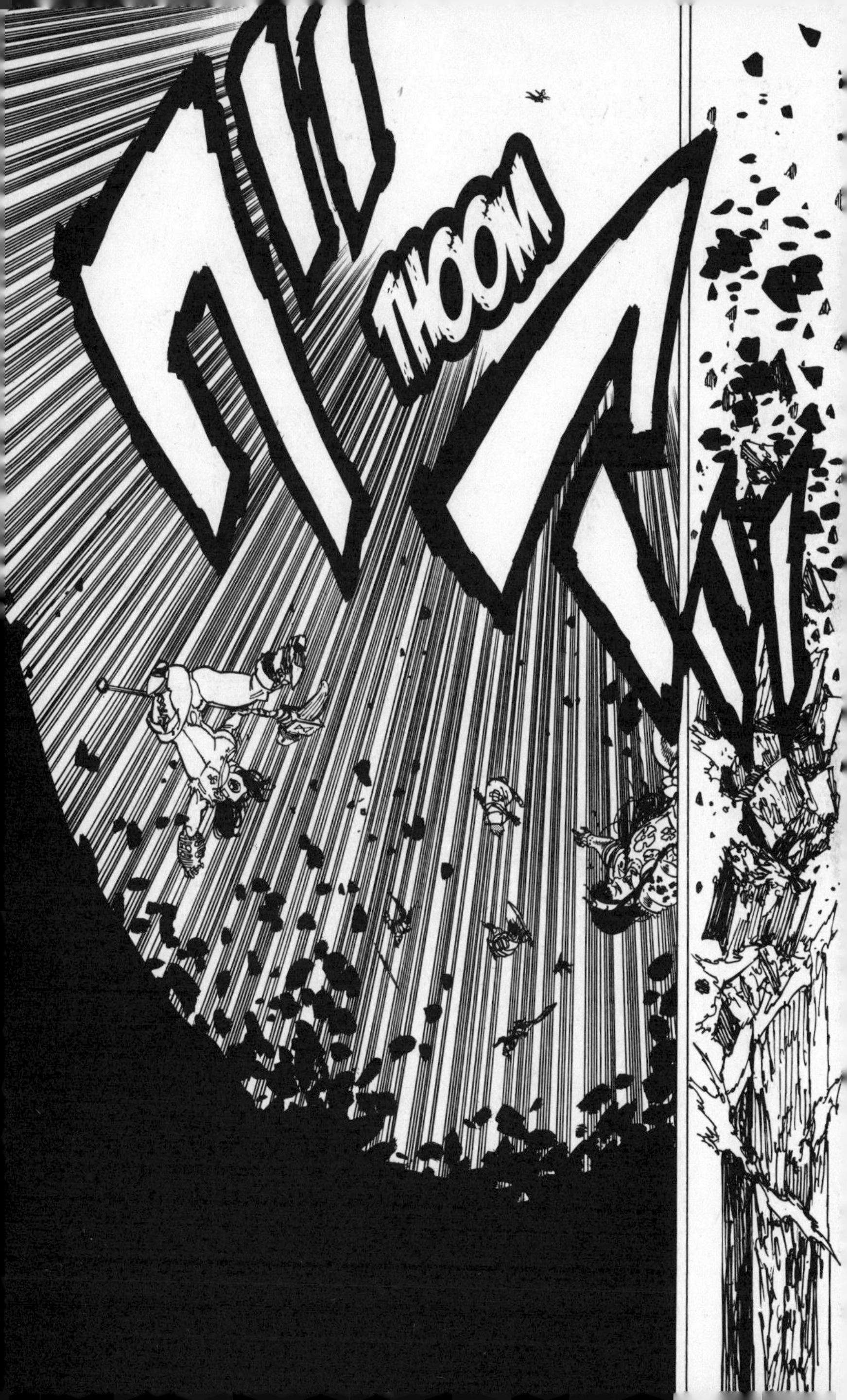
THOOM

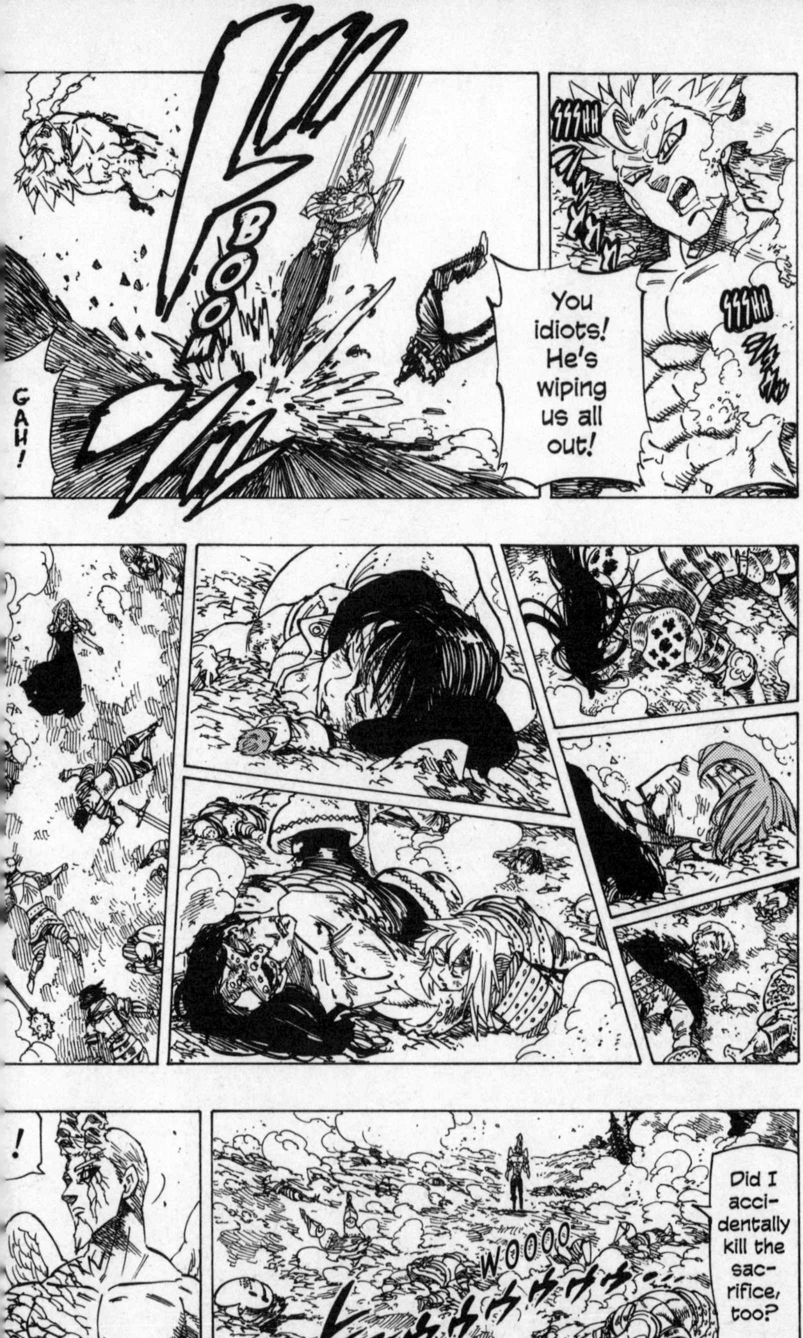
SSSHH
SSSHH
You idiots! He's wiping us all out!
BOOM
GAH!
Did I accidentally kill the sacrifice, too?
WOOOO
!

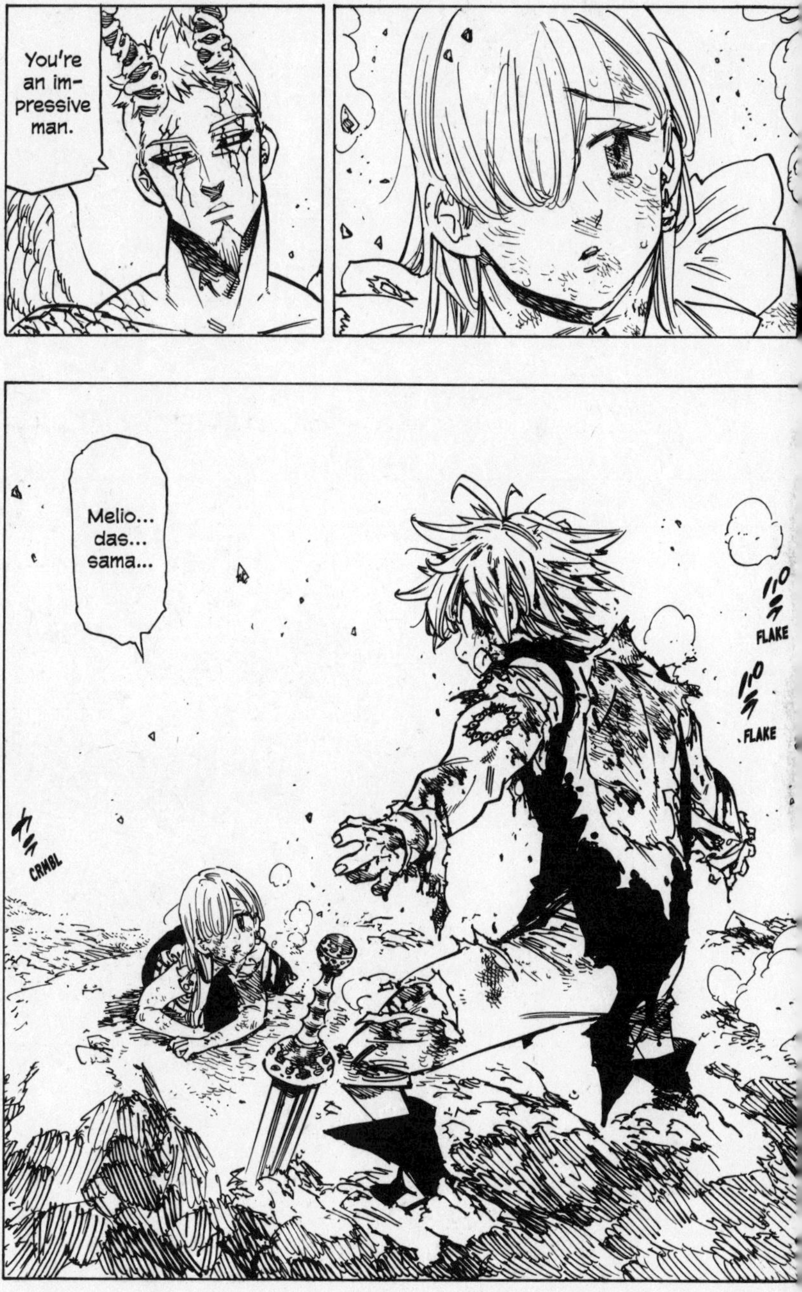
You're an impressive man.
Melio... das... sama...
FLAKE
FLAKE
CRMBL

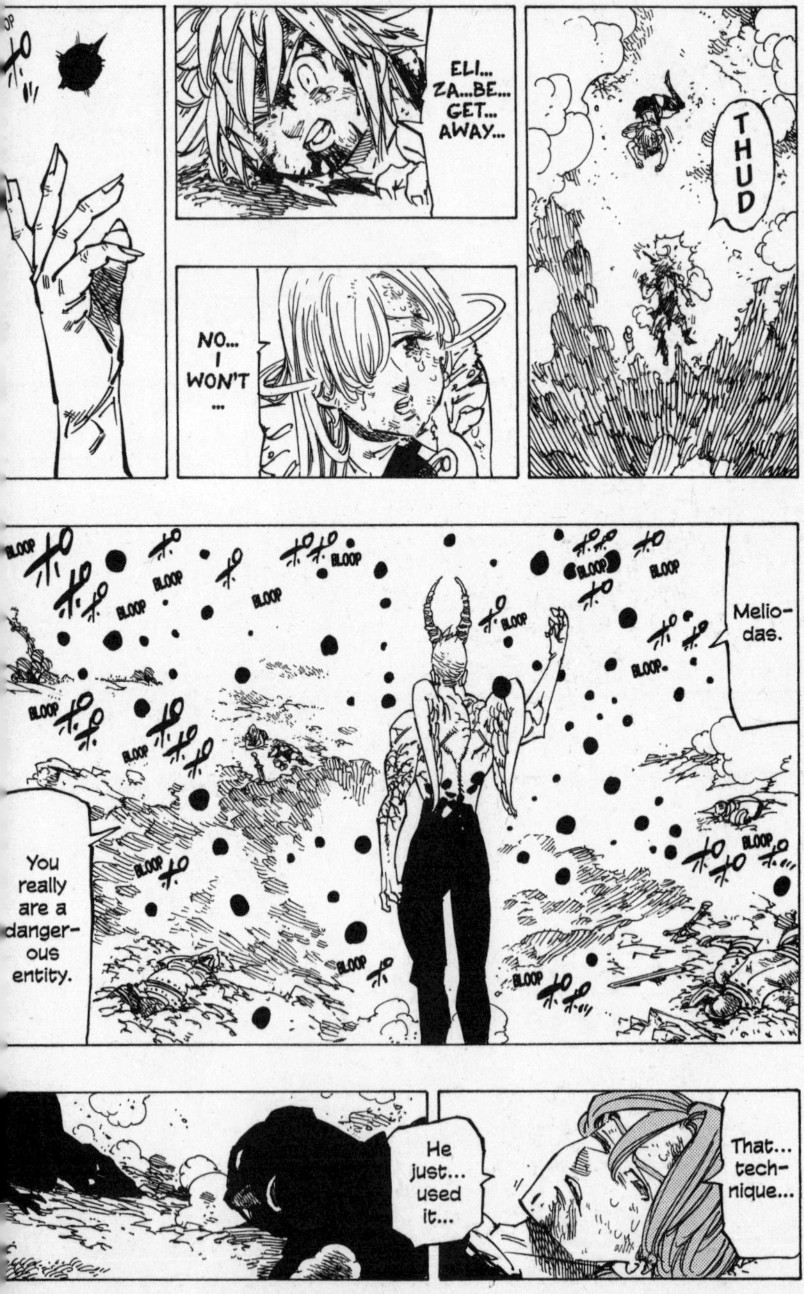
THUD
ELI... ZA...BE... GET... AWAY...
NO... I WON'T ...
OP
Melio-das.
BLOOP
BLOOP
BLOOP
BLOOP.
BLOOP
BLOOP
BLOOP
BLOOP
BLOOP
BLOOP
BLOOP
BLOOP
BLOOP
BLOOP
BLOOP
You really are a danger-ous entity.
That... tech-nique...
He just... used it...

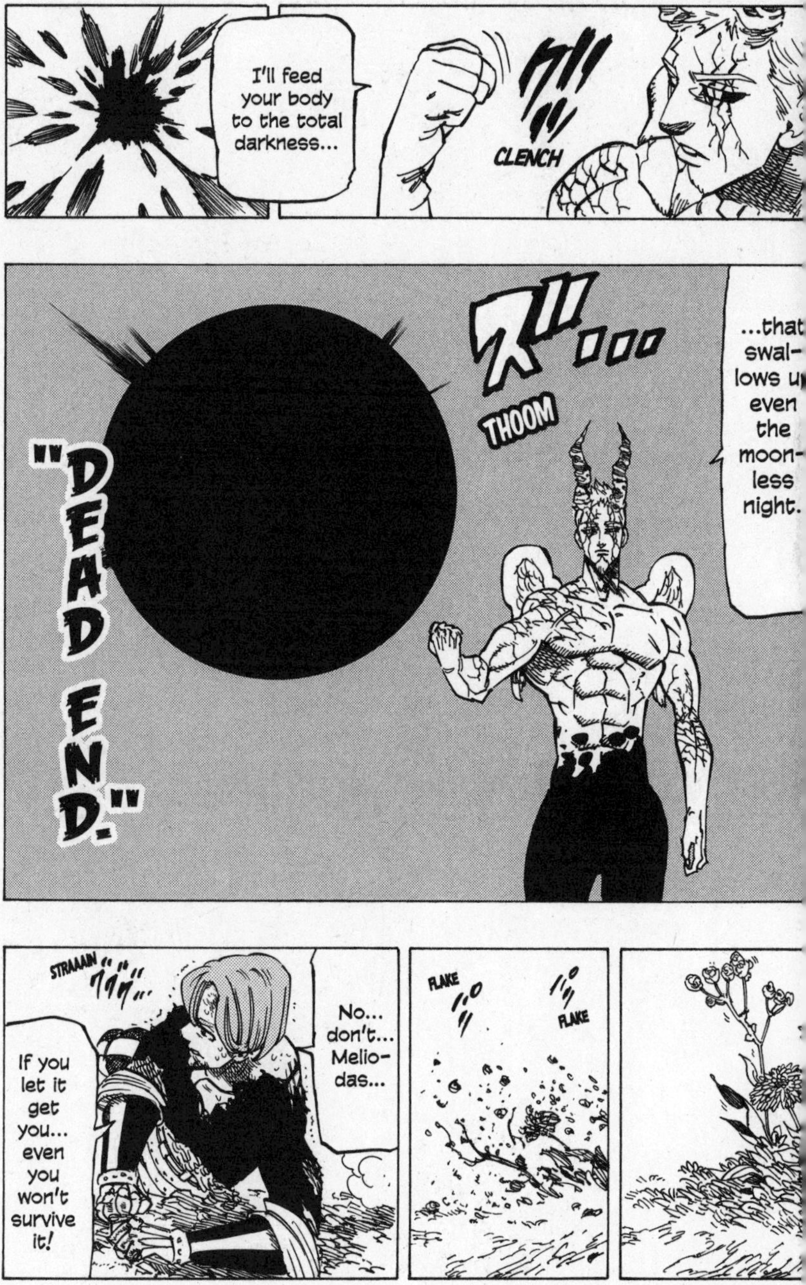
CLENCH
I'll feed your body to the total darkness...
...that swallows up even the moonless night.
THOOM
"DEAD END."
FLAKE
FLAKE
No... don't... Meliodas...
STRAAAIN
If you let it get you... even you won't survive it!

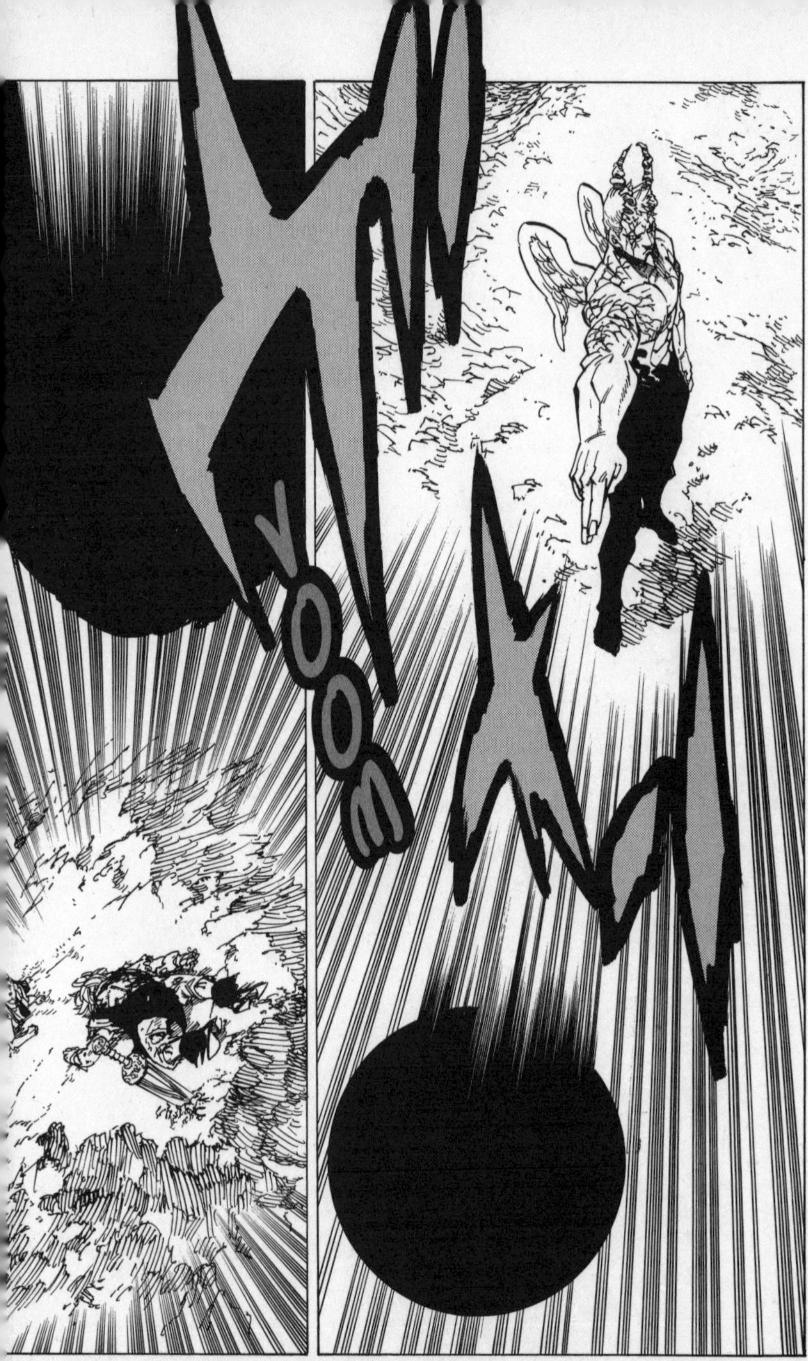
VOOM

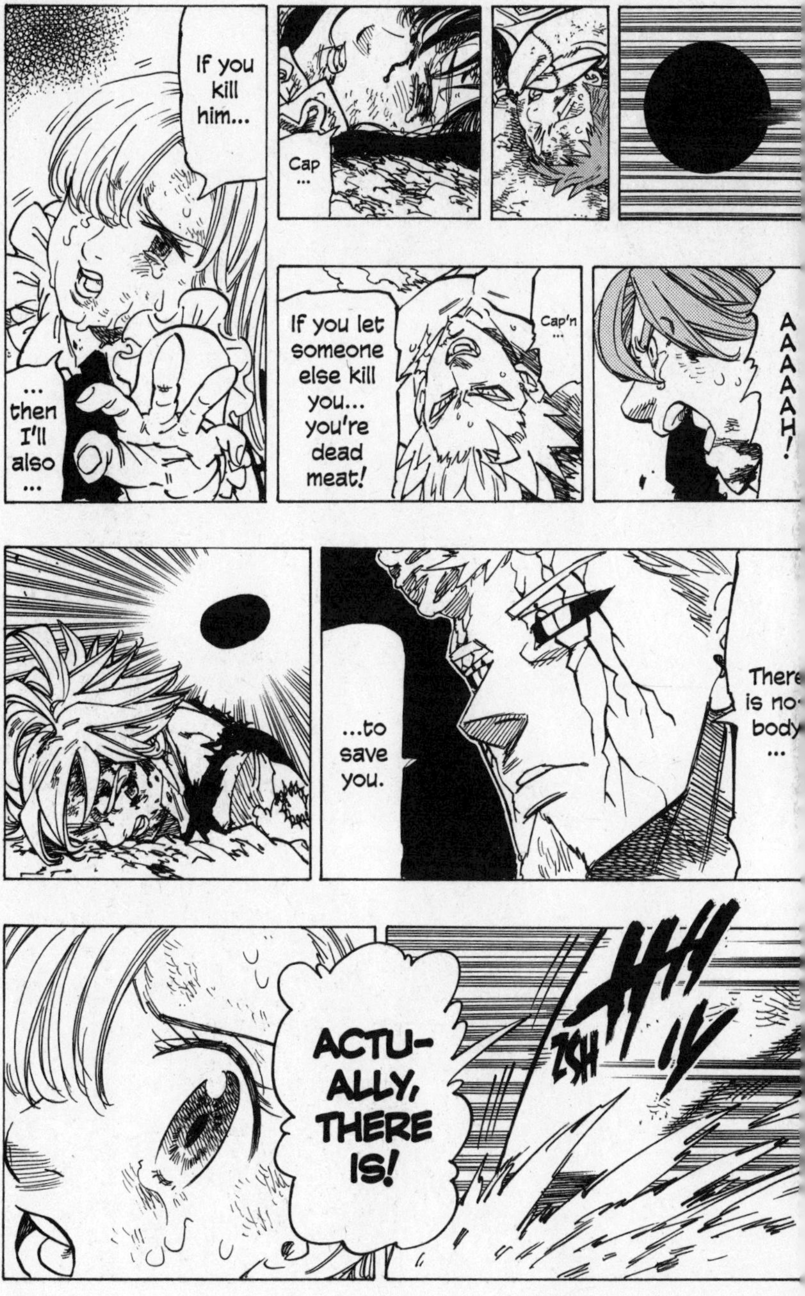
Cap
...
AAAAAH!
Cap'n
...
If you let someone else kill you... you're dead meat!
If you kill him...
...then I'll also...
There is nobody...
...to save you.
ZSH
ACTUALLY, THERE IS!

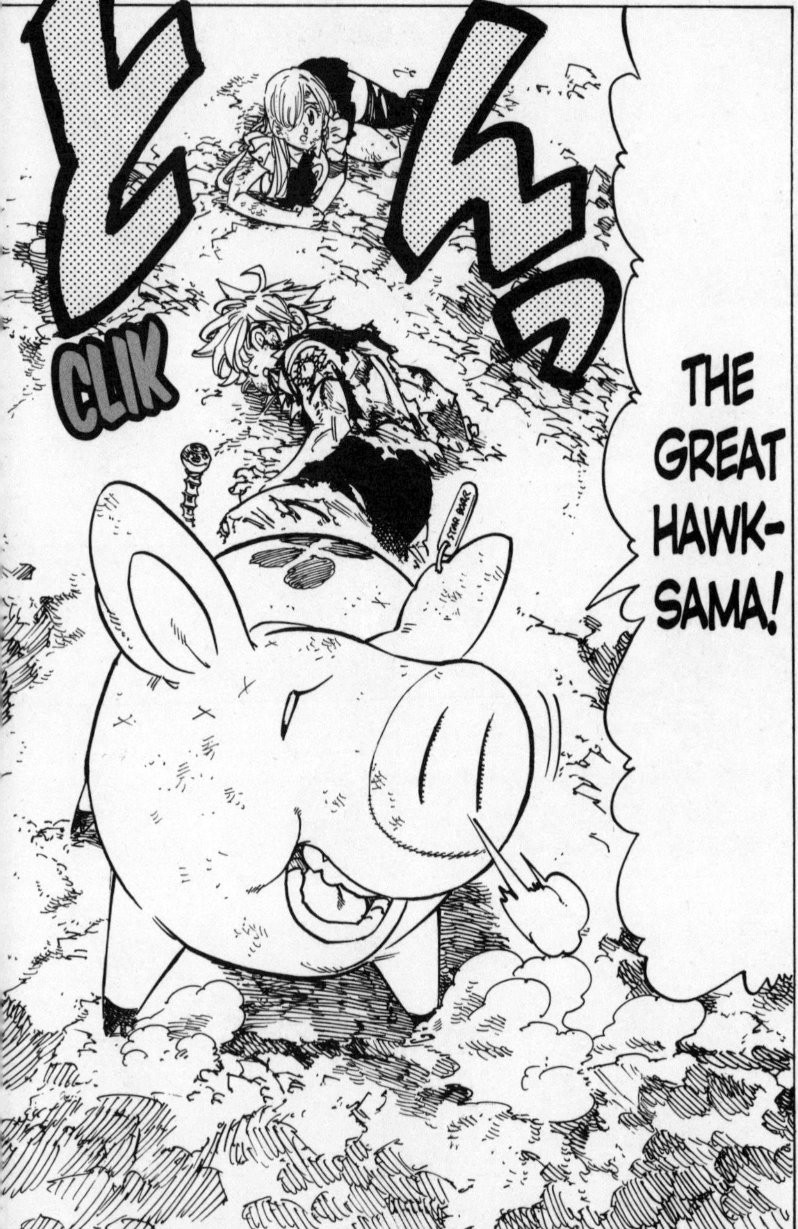
CLIK
STAR BOAR
THE GREAT HAWK-SAMA!

To Be Continued in Volume 13...

Bonus Story - Partners

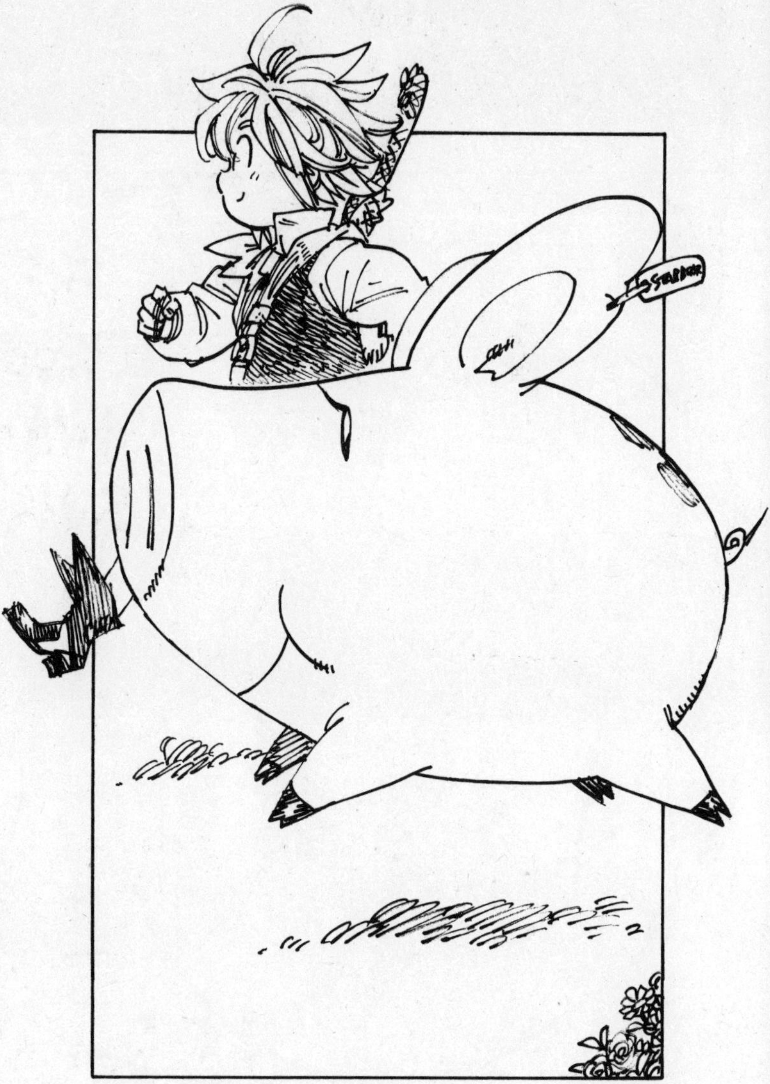

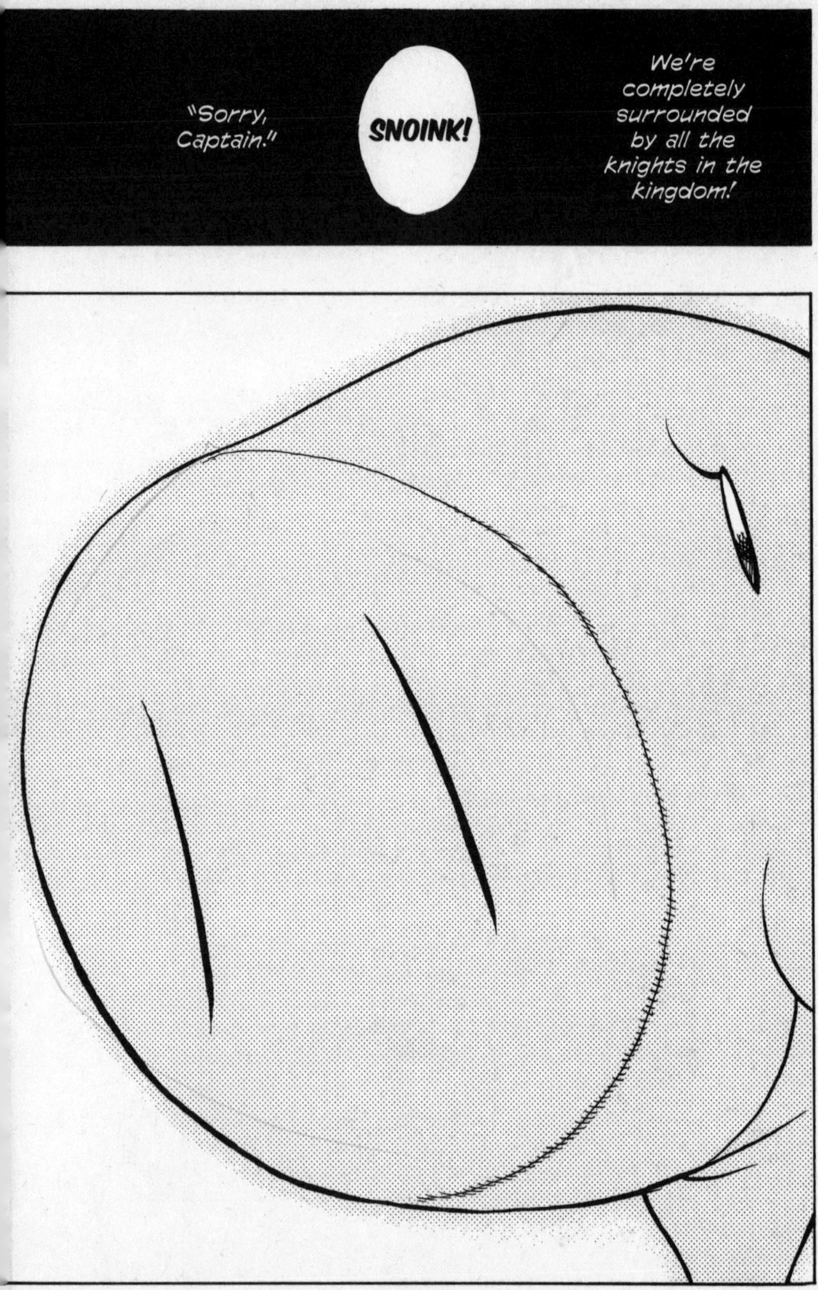
We're completely surrounded by all the knights in the kingdom!
SNOINK!
"Sorry, Captain."

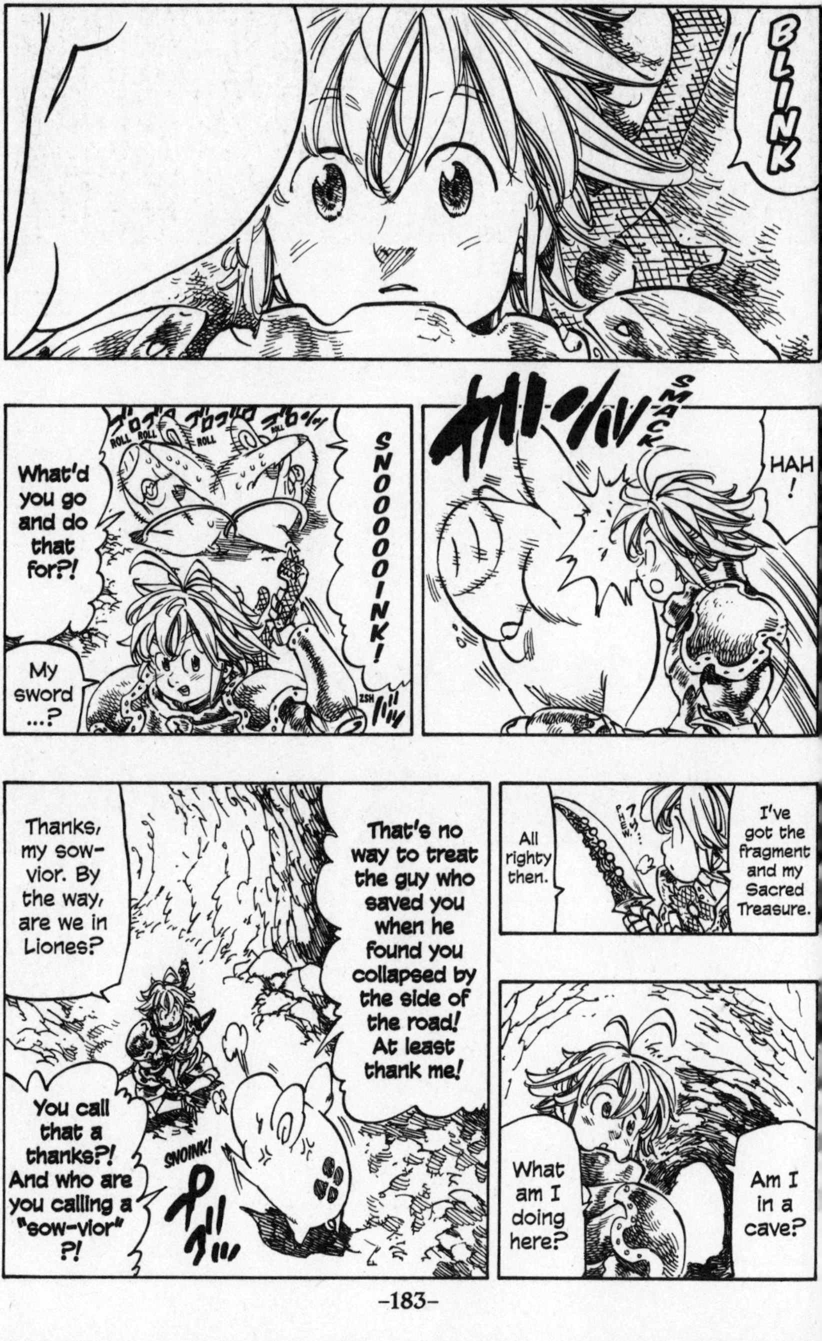
BLINK
HAH!
SMACK
SNOOOOOOINK!
ROLL ROLL ROLL
What'd you go and do that for?!
My sword ...?
ZSH
I've got the fragment and my Sacred Treasure.
PHEW...
All righty then.
Am I in a cave?
What am I doing here?
That's no way to treat the guy who saved you when he found you collapsed by the side of the road! At least thank me!
Thanks, my sow-vior. By the way, are we in Liones?
You call that a thanks?! And who are you calling a "sow-vior"?!
SNOINK!

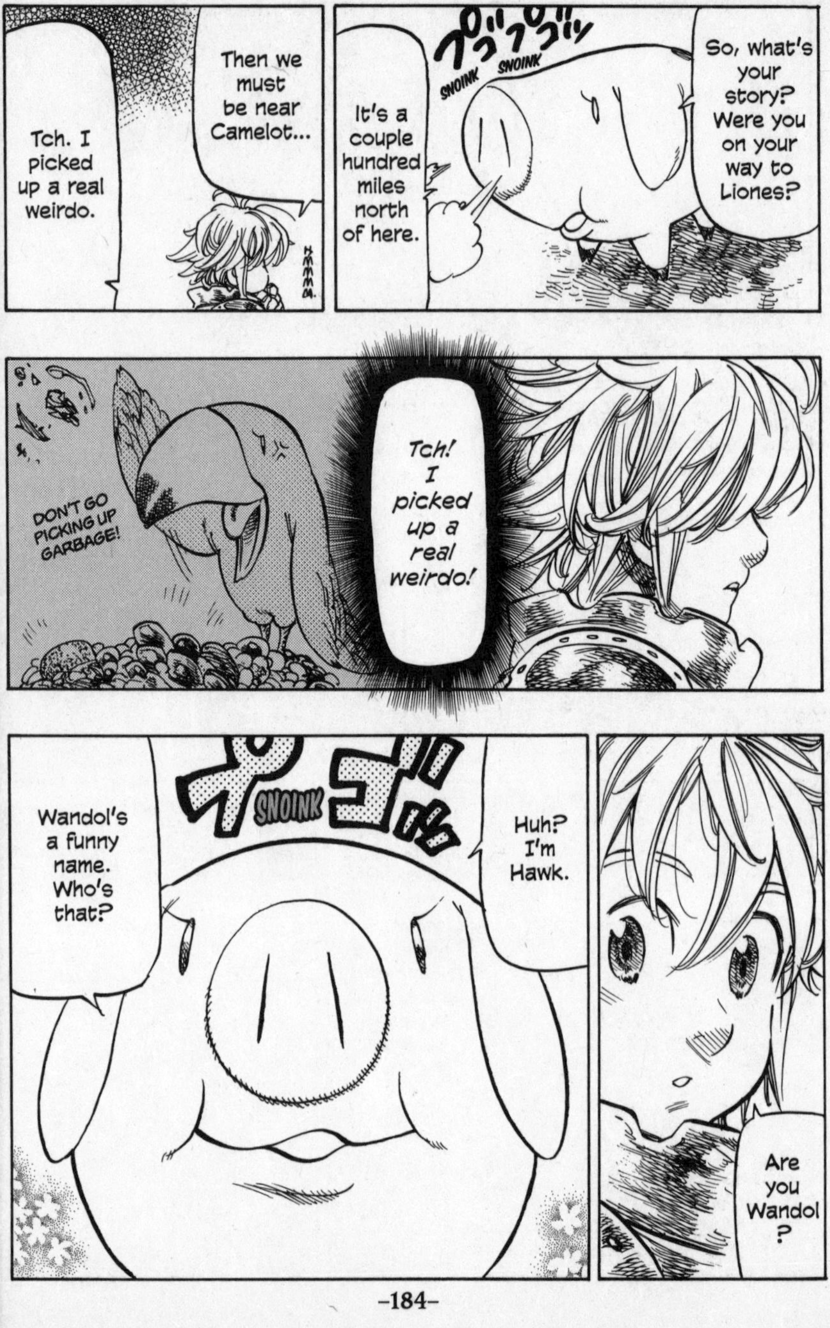
So, what's your story? Were you on your way to Liones?
SNOINK SNOINK
It's a couple hundred miles north of here.
Then we must be near Camelot...
Tch. I picked up a real weirdo.
Tch! I picked up a real weirdo!
DON'T GO PICKING UP GARBAGE!
Are you Wandol?
Huh? I'm Hawk.
SNOINK
Wandol's a funny name. Who's that?

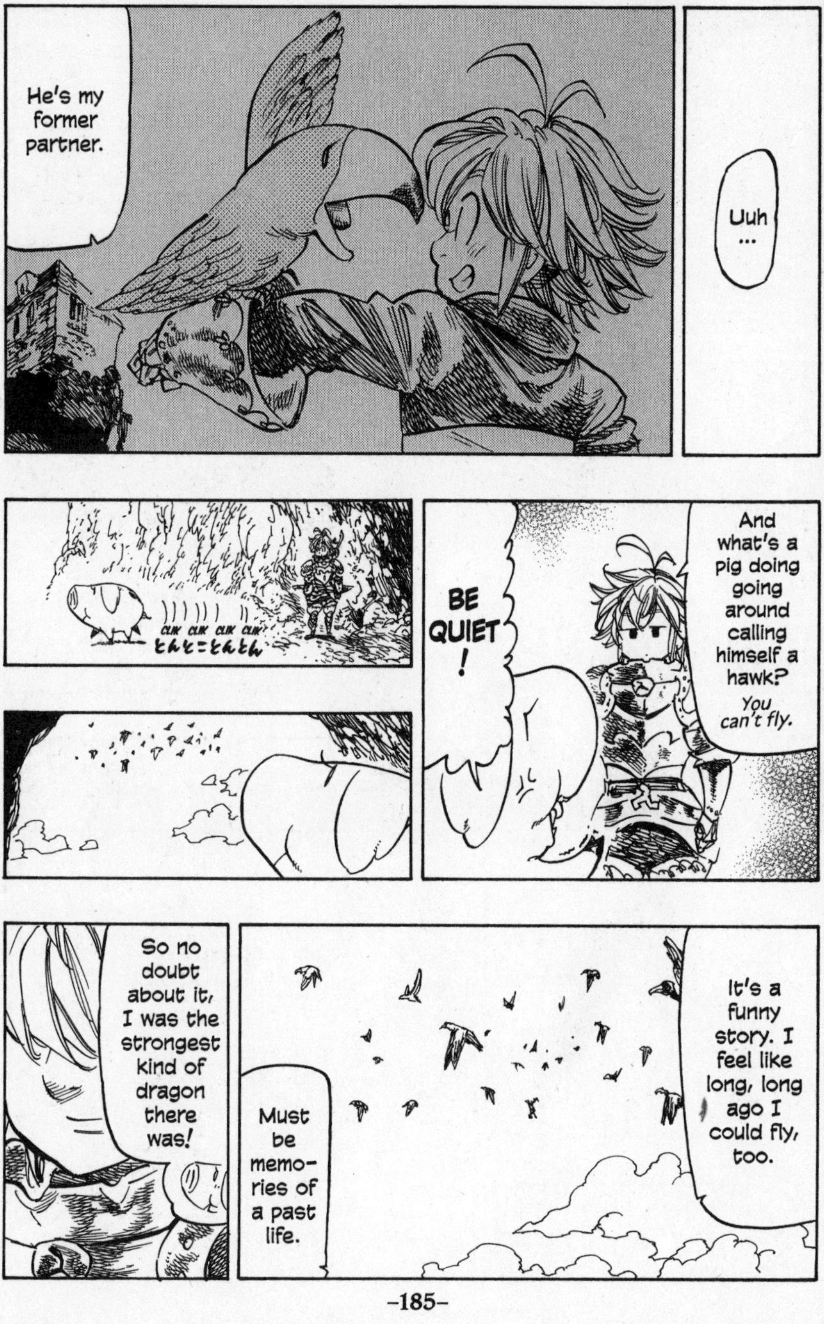
Uuh ...
He's my former partner.
And what's a pig doing going around calling himself a hawk? You can't fly.
BE QUIET!
CLIK CLIK CLIK CLIK
とんとことんとん
It's a funny story. I feel like long, long ago I could fly, too.
Must be memories of a past life.
So no doubt about it, I was the strongest kind of dragon there was!

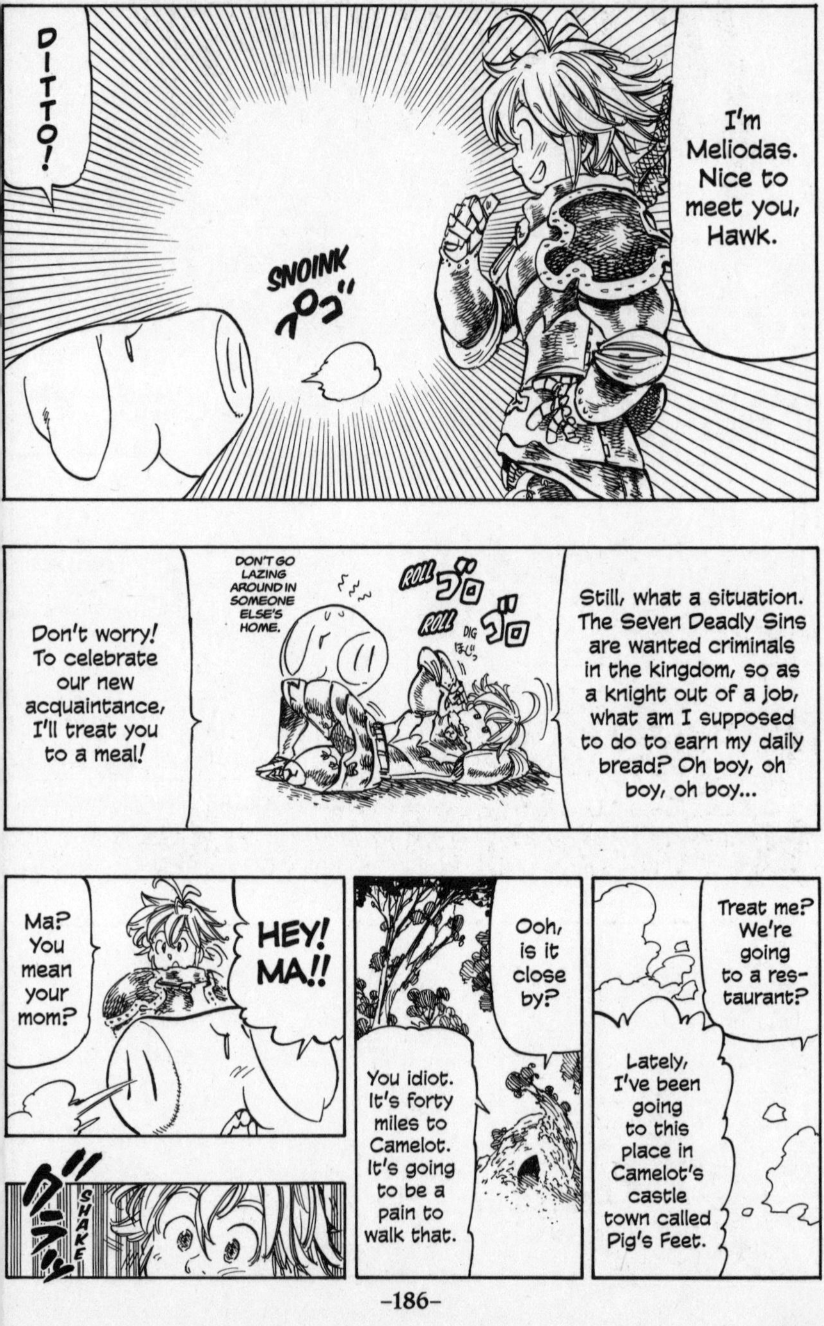
I'm Meliodas. Nice to meet you, Hawk.
SNOINK
DITTO!
Still, what a situation. The Seven Deadly Sins are wanted criminals in the kingdom, so as a knight out of a job, what am I supposed to do to earn my daily bread? Oh boy, oh boy, oh boy...
ROLL
ROLL
DIG
DON'T GO LAZING AROUND IN SOMEONE ELSE'S HOME.
Don't worry! To celebrate our new acquaintance, I'll treat you to a meal!
Treat me? We're going to a restaurant?
Lately, I've been going to this place in Camelot's castle town called Pig's Feet.
Ooh, is it close by?
You idiot. It's forty miles to Camelot. It's going to be a pain to walk that.
HEY! MA!!
Ma? You mean your mom?
SHAKE

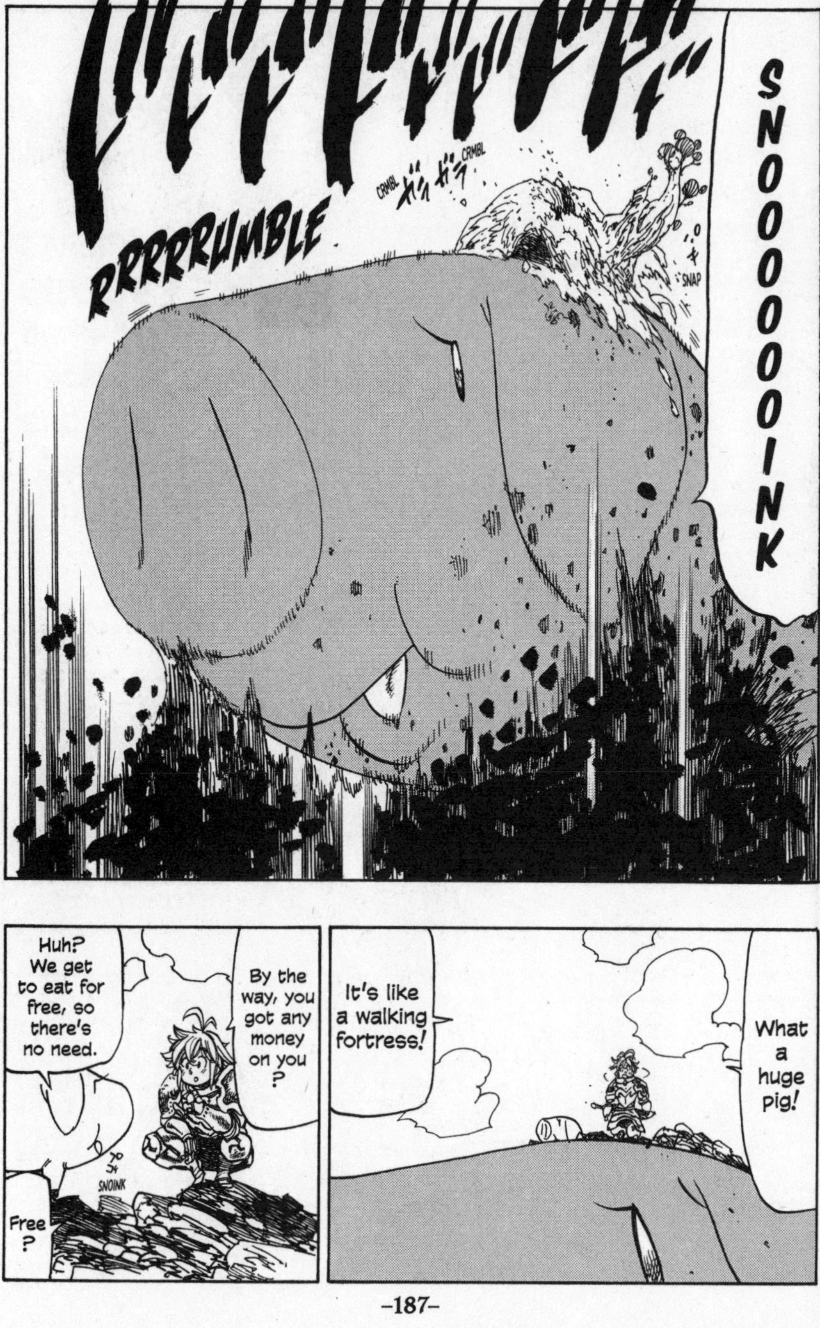
SNOOOOOOOINK
SNAP
CRMBL
CRMBL
RRRRRUMBLE
What a huge pig!
It's like a walking fortress!
By the way, you got any money on you?
Huh? We get to eat for free, so there's no need.
SNOINK
Free?

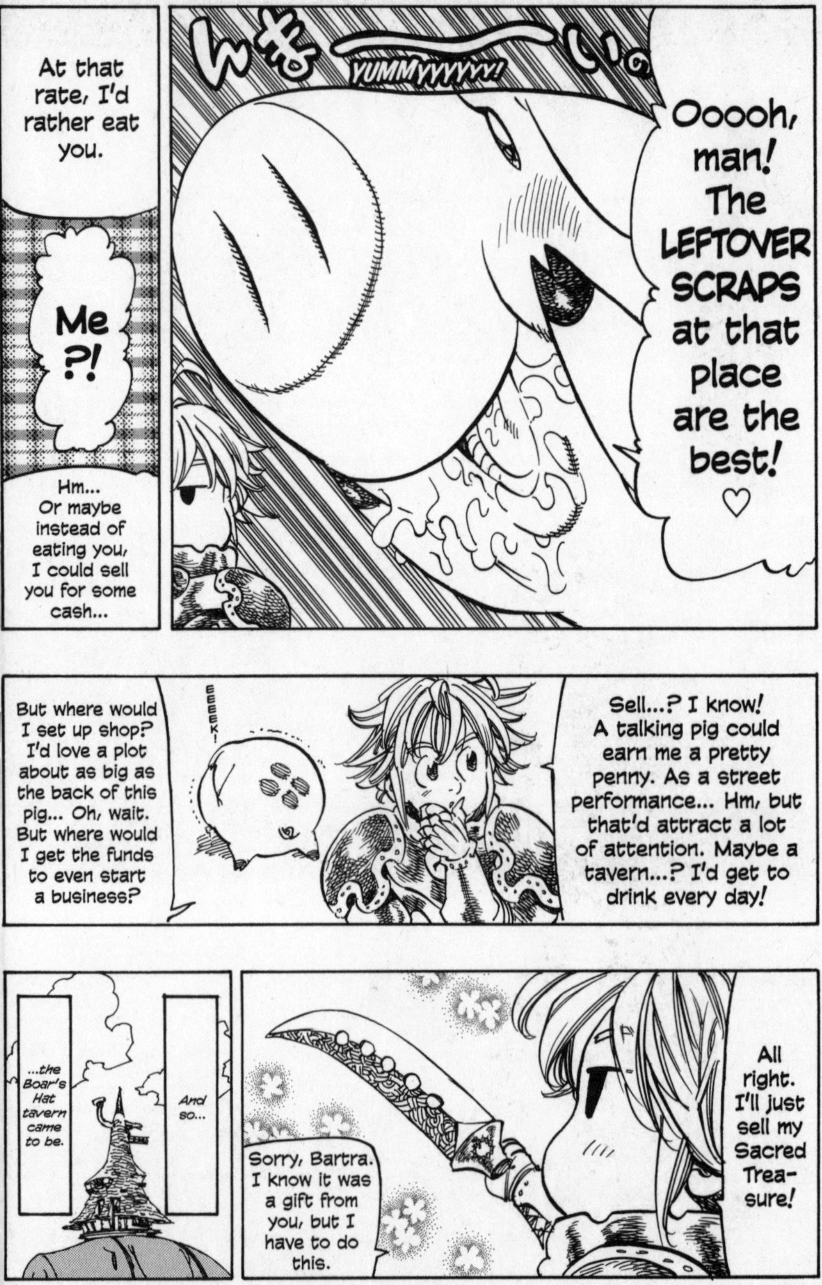
んまーーーい。
YUMMYYYYYY!
Ooooh, man! The LEFTOVER SCRAPS at that place are the best! ♡
At that rate, I'd rather eat you.
Me?!
Hm... Or maybe instead of eating you, I could sell you for some cash...
Sell...? I know! A talking pig could earn me a pretty penny. As a street performance... Hm, but that'd attract a lot of attention. Maybe a tavern...? I'd get to drink every day!
EEEEK!
But where would I set up shop? I'd love a plot about as big as the back of this pig... Oh, wait. But where would I get the funds to even start a business?
All right. I'll just sell my Sacred Treasure!
Sorry, Bartra. I know it was a gift from you, but I have to do this.
And so...
...the Boar's Hat tavern came to be.

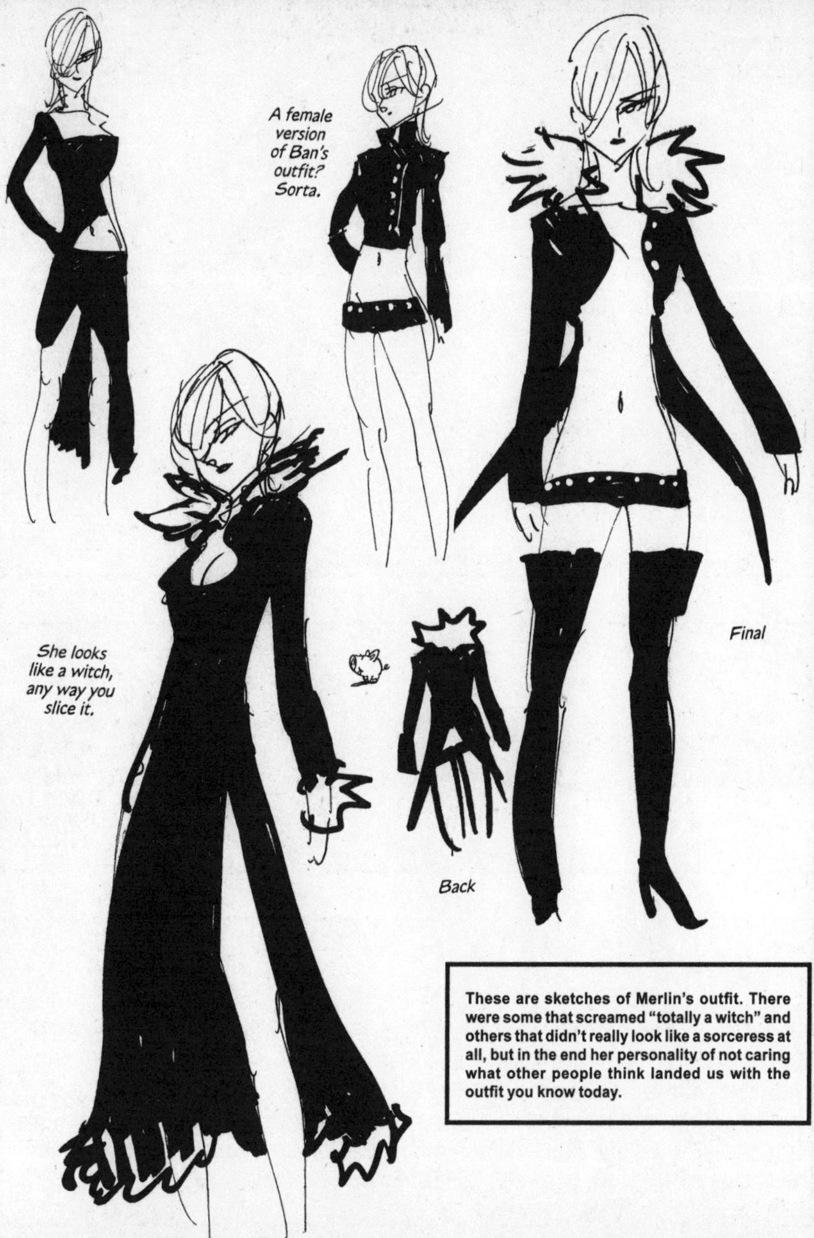
A female version of Ban's outfit? Sorta.
Final
She looks like a witch, any way you slice it.
Back

These are sketches of Merlin's outfit. There were some that screamed "totally a witch" and others that didn't really look like a sorceress at all, but in the end her personality of not caring what other people think landed us with the outfit you know today.

SWAPPED WITH A KISS?!

Class troublemaker Ryu Yamada is already having a bad day when he stumbles down a staircase along with star student Urara Shiraishi. When he wakes up, he realizes they have switched bodies—and that Ryu has the power to trade places with anyone just by kissing them! Ryu and Urara take full advantage of the situation to improve their lives, but with such an oddly amazing power, just how long will they be able to keep their secret under wraps?

Available now in print and digitally!

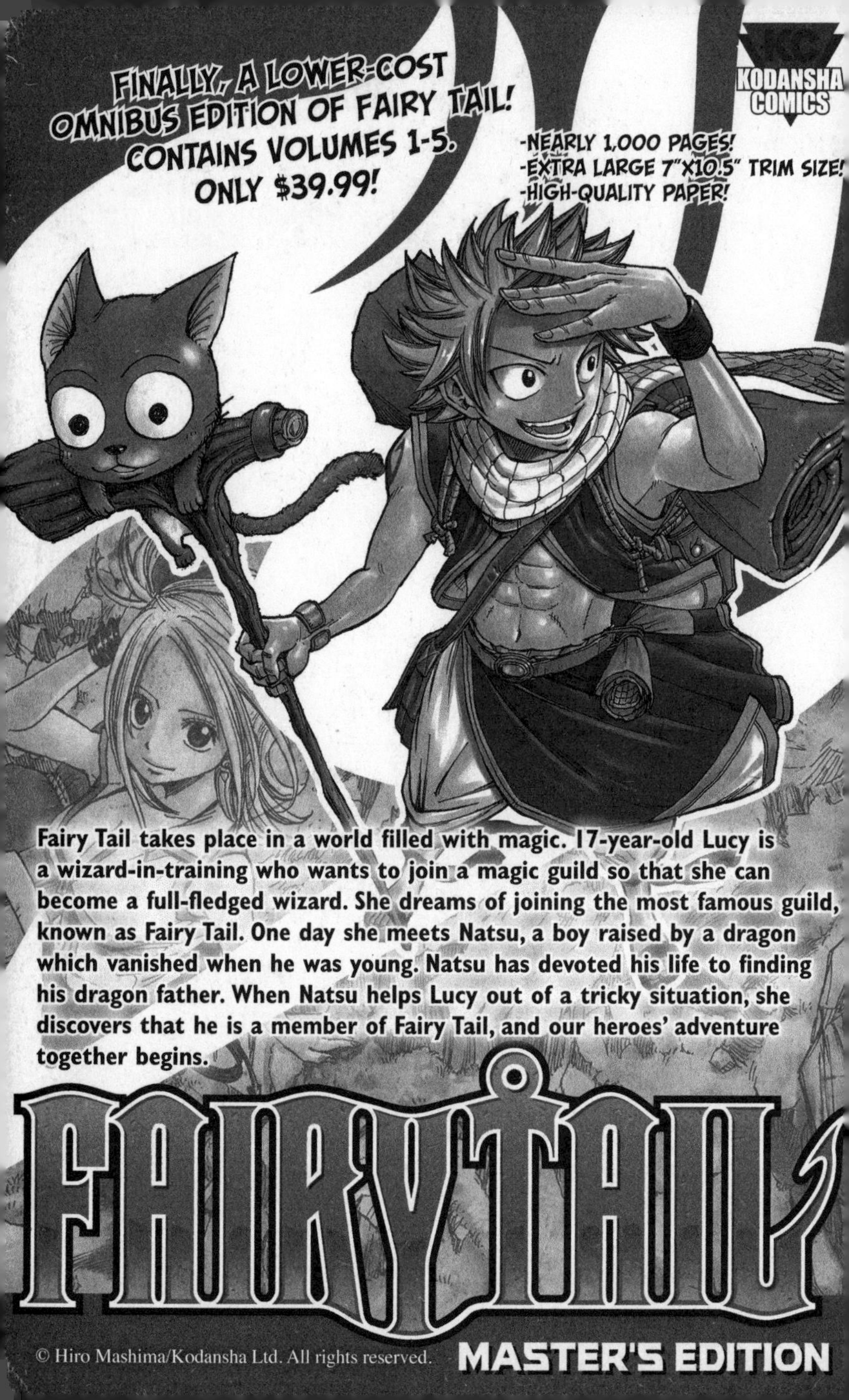
KODANSHA COMICS
FINALLY, A LOWER-COST OMNIBUS EDITION OF FAIRY TAIL! CONTAINS VOLUMES 1-5. ONLY $39.99!
-NEARLY 1,000 PAGES!
-EXTRA LARGE 7"X10.5" TRIM SIZE!
-HIGH-QUALITY PAPER!
Fairy Tail takes place in a world filled with magic. 17-year-old Lucy is a wizard-in-training who wants to join a magic guild so that she can become a full-fledged wizard. She dreams of joining the most famous guild, known as Fairy Tail. One day she meets Natsu, a boy raised by a dragon which vanished when he was young. Natsu has devoted his life to finding his dragon father. When Natsu helps Lucy out of a tricky situation, she discovers that he is a member of Fairy Tail, and our heroes' adventure together begins.
FAIRY TAIL
© Hiro Mashima/Kodansha Ltd. All rights reserved.
MASTER'S EDITION

The Seven Deadly Sins volume 12 is a work of fiction. Names, characters, places, and incidents are the products of the author's imagination or are used fictitiously. Any resemblance to actual events, locales, or persons, living or dead, is entirely coincidental.

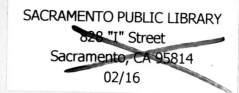

A Kodansha Comics Trade Paperback Original.

Published in the United States by Kodansha Comics, an imprint of Kodansha USA Publishing, LLC, New York.

Publication rights for this English edition arranged through Kodansha Ltd., Tokyo.

First published in Japan in 2015 by Kodansha Ltd., Tokyo.

ISBN 978-1-63236-129-5

Printed in the United States of America.

www.kodanshacomics.com

9 8 7 6 5 4 3 2 1

Translator: Christine Dashiell
Lettering: James Dashiell
Editor: Lauren Scanlan